Salish and Kootenai Indian Chiefs Speak for Their People and Land, 1865-1909

Salish and Kootenai Indian Chiefs Speak for Their People and Land, 1865-1909

edited by
Robert Bigart
and
Joseph McDonald

published by
Salish Kootenai College Press
Pablo, Montana

distributed by
University of Nebraska Press
Lincoln, Nebraska

Cover design: Corky Clairmont, artist/graphic designer, Pablo, Montana.

Cover illustrations: Top: Chief Victor, drawing by Gustavus Sohon, National Anthropological Archives, Smithsonian Institution, Washington, D.C. (negative number 08502300). Bottom: Chief Ambrose, drawing by Gustavus Sohon, National Anthropological Archives, Smithsonian Institution, Washington, D.C. (negative number 08502000).

Library of Congress, Cataloging-in-Publication:
Names: Bigart, Robert, editor. | McDonald, Joseph, 1933- editor.
Title: Salish and Kootenai Indian chiefs speak for their people and land, 1865-1909 / edited by Robert Bigart and Joseph McDonald.
Description: Pablo, Montana : Salish Kootenai College Press, [2023]. | Includes bibliographical references and index.
Identifiers: LCCN 2023000500 | ISBN 9781934594346 (paperback)
Subjecs: LCSH: Salish Indians--History--19th century--Sources. | Salish Indians--History--20th century--Sources. | Kootenai Indians--History--19th century--Sources. | Kootenai Indians--History--20th century--Sources. | Indians of North America--Government relations--1869-1934--Sources. | Flathead Indian Reservation (Mont.)--History--19th century--Sources. | Flathead Indian Reservation (Mont.)--History--20th century--Sources.
Classification: LCC E 99.S2 S24 2023 | DDC 978.6004/979435--dc23/eng/20230126
LC record available at https://lccn.loc.gov/2023000500

Published by Salish Kootenai College Press, PO Box 70, Pablo, MT 59855.

Distributed by University of Nebraska Press, 1111 Lincoln Mall, Lincoln, NE 68588-0630, order 1-800-755-1105, www.nebraskapress.unl.edu.

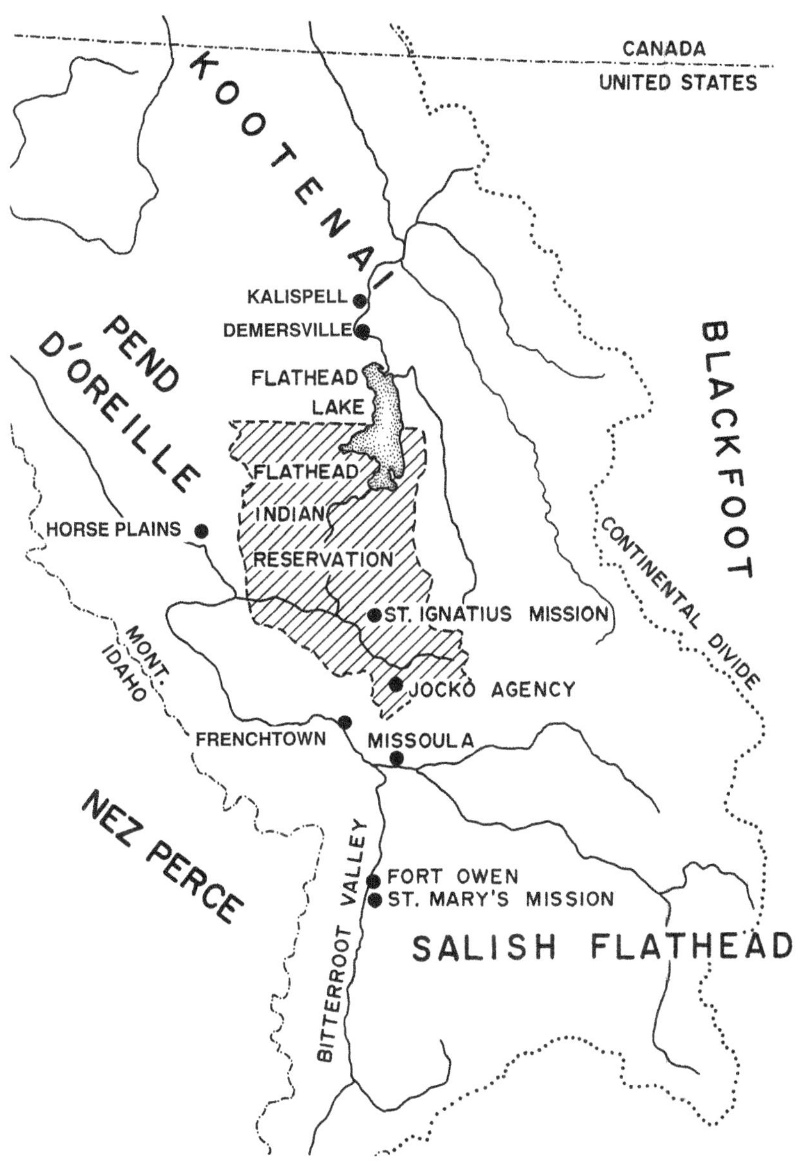

Flathead Indian Reservation
Showing Tribal Territories
and Surrounding Towns

Table of Contents

Introduction

The nineteenth century was a challenging time for the Salish, Pend d'Oreille, and Kootenai Indian people of western Montana. Buffeted by war and disease during the first half of the century, the tribes were locked in a battle for survival against enemy tribes that were much larger and often better armed. During the second half of the century, they had to struggle with a strange new tribe of white people who wanted Indian land and resources. Fortunately, the tribes found capable chiefs and leaders who made it possible for the Indian people to navigate the challenges and survive.

Smallpox and other diseases killed many tribal members in the late eighteenth and early nineteenth centuries. At the same time, the Blackfeet and other Plains tribes were expanding their hunting territories at the expense of the Salish and Kootenai tribes. The Salish and Kootenai fought bravely. The tribes allied with other tribes from west of the Continental Divide such as the Nez Perce, Colville, and Spokanes. By 1855, Governor Isaac Stevens found that

> The Flatheads [Salish] number about sixty lodges, but many of them are only inhabited by old women and their daughters. The tribe has been almost exterminated by the Blackfeet, and the mass of the nation consist of Pend d'Oreilles, Spokanes, Nez Perces, and Iroquois. I estimated their number at 350.[1]

The Salish and Kootenai also allied with white trappers and finally missionaries. The new teachings of the missionaries gave the Salish people valuable spiritual powers in their fight against the Plains tribes. According to Father Pierre De Smet, S.J., in 1840 sixty Salish warriors prayed before a battle against eight hundred Blackfeet: "Confident of success they [the Salish] rose from their knees in the presence of their enemies, and engaged the overwhelming odds against them. The battle lasted five days. The Black-Feet were defeated, leaving eighty warriors dead upon the field; while the Flat-Heads and Pends-d'Oreilles sustained a loss of only one man."[2]

The Salish and Kootenai appreciated the assistance the white men provided in their conflict with the Plains tribes. For example, in late 1862 a white prospector named John D. Brown was traveling with a Salish party on the plains led by Chief Moiese. When the camp was threatened by Crow Indian horse thieves, Moiese asked Brown if the whites would join the Salish in defending their horse herd. Brown readily agreed and prepared to fight. Later in Christmas eve 1862, Brown was Moiese's guest at a special Christmas feast on the Plains.[3]

In July 1855, a group of white soldiers led by Isaac I. Stevens met the Salish, Pend d'Oreille, and Kootenai chiefs at the mouth of the Bitterroot River in western Montana. Stevens and the whites had been talking about negotiating peace with the Blackfeet which the Salish and Kootenai approved. Salish Chief Victor commented: "The Blackfeet have troubled us very much."[4] But Stevens began talking about selling tribal land and starting farms.

The treaty presented new and challenging questions for the tribal leaders. Big Canoe, a Pend d'Oreille chief, asked, "Talk about treaty, where did I kill you? when did you kill me? What is the reason we are talking about treaties; that is what I said, we are friends, you are not my enemy." But Stevens insisted on talking about reservations and selling Indian land. The chiefs would not agree to settle on one reservation in the Flathead Valley. Salish Chief Victor wanted to remain in the Bitterroot Valley. Stevens was condescending and impatient: "We must finish the council today, we have other work to do." Exchanges got heated and Victor complained, "I was talking to you and I told you no." Victor walked out of the council. The chiefs finally signed the treaty, but confusion reigned over some of the provisions.[5]

The Hellgate Treaty negotiations were not only an example of confused negotiations. Isaac Stevens and the white negotiators had a long tradition of treating land as a commodity that could be owned, traded, and sold. The Salish and Kootenai did not have similar concepts. The Indians recognized certain lands as their home territory, but they traditionally shared use of that land and its products with friendly tribes. They defended themselves against hostile war parties, but did not consider land as an investment that could be sold.

In addition to the different cultural concepts, the treaty negotiations suffered from translation problems. The negotiations were only recorded in English, not Salish or Kootenai. According to Father Adrian Hoecken, S.J., a missionary priest present at the treaty negotiations: "Not a tenth of it [the council] was actually understood by either party, for Ben Kyser [the interpreter] speaks Flathead very badly and is no better at translating into English."[6]

Some of the later interpreters of speeches included in this collection, such as Francois Saxa and Michel Revais, had better Salish language skills. But readers should read the English transcriptions with a critical eye. Additional problems could also have been introduced by mistakes made by the clerks recording the English translations on paper. Many of the written copies of the speeches may have accurately reflected the chiefs' main viewpoints, but specific details are always in question. These documents are evidence, but they also look through a smoky glass darkly.

The Salish, Pend d'Oreille, and Kootenai chiefs were competent and capable and deeply committed to protecting the interests of the tribes. The written historical record from 1865 through 1909 documents the continuing efforts of the chiefs to complain when the government did not fulfill its promises and later when government representatives tried to pressure the tribes to give up more land.

The speeches in this collection give only fragments of the historical events buffeting the Salish, Pend d'Oreille, and Kootenai Indians in the second half of the nineteenth and early twentieth century. The glimpses of tribal leaders were obscured by the fact they were recorded in English rather than Salish or Kootenai. But even given these limitations, the historical sources show the competence of the Indian leaders and their determination to protect tribal interests. In the early twentieth century the chiefs were finally unable to prevent the allotment and opening of the Flathead Indian Reservation, but they never stopped fighting. That battle to protect the tribes continues now in the twenty-first century under new and capable tribal leaders.

Notes

I. Isaac I. Sevens, "Report of Explorations for a Route for the Pacific Railroad," in *Reports of Explorations and Surveys, to Ascertain the Most Practicable and Economical Route for a Railroad from the Mississippi River to the Pacific Ocean, 1853-4* (Washington, D.C.: Beverly Tucker, Printer, 1855), vol. 1, p. 150.

2. Robert Bigart and Joseph McDonald, eds., *"Sometimes My People Get Mad When the Blackfeet Kill Us": A Documentary History of the Salish and Pend d'Oreille Indians, 1845–1874* (Pablo, Mont.: Salish Kootenai College Press, 2019), p. 31.

3. Ibid, pp. 228-230.

4. Robert Bigart and Clarence Woodcock, eds., *In the Name of the Salish & Kootenai Nation: The 1855 Hell Gate Treaty and the Origin of the Flathead Indian Reservation* (Pablo, Mont.: Salish Kootenai College Press, 1996), pp. 19-65, quote from p. 22.

5. Ibid, pp. 18, 22, 33, 47-55.

6. Ibid, p. 142.

Document 1

Bitterroot Salish Chiefs Petition Montana Governor April 25, 1865

Source: Victor, et. al., to Chief of the Whites, Virginia, M. T., Apr. 25, 1865, Sidney Edgerton Family Papers, MC 26, Montana Historical Society Archives, Helena, box 1, folder 8.

Editors' note: This letter from Victor and the other Bitterroot Salish chiefs to the Montana Governor complained about white men moving into the Bitterroot Valley despite the Indian interpretation of the 1855 Hellgate Treaty. The chiefs complained about horses stolen by the Snake Indians. They had exhorted the young Salish men to not go to war, but asked the whites to refrain from feeding Salish warriors who were on war parties. Their final plea was for the white authorities to stop the sale of whiskey to young tribal members. It is not known who actually wrote the letter, but presumably the writer was expressing the concerns of the Salish chiefs who signed it.

The chief of the flatheads to the Chief of the whites, Virginia, Montana Ty.

Four horses have been Stolen by some of our young men, but I cannot find them in the camp. Therefore I, Victor the chief, Send you four horses of our own to pay for; and I the Chief Send to you the Chief of the whites a horse of mine, which I present you with for yourself.

I Send back also five oxen found, not stolen by our men, far below the Marias. You will see to whom do they belong.

Last Summer we had been requested of four horses stolen. I, Victor, found them out and delivered them to Mr Thomas Harris, a white Settler of this our valley, to be Kept for the right owner, who can recover them addressing themselves to him. One of the horses died.

Now I address myself to you the Great Chief of the whites of this country. Some of the big men among the white Settlers in this our land spoke to send us away from our country. This thing vexed a great deal me, and all the other Chiefs, and all my children. I, Victor, therefore do Send you the horse above mentioned to pray you to take pity on us, and to put an end to Such talkings, and to Stop the whites from building themselves houses in our own land guaranteed to us by treaty. We are almost given to despondency seeing every

Chief Victor
Source: Drawing by Gustavus Sohon, National Anthropological Archives, Smithsonian Institution, Washington, D.C. (negative number 08502300)

day new houses started up, and farms taken by whites in our land. We got this spring Some ploughs from Government, and we are all busy, and in great earnest to make ourselves fields; but after a little while there will be no more room for us in our own country, if you do not Stop the whites.

Tell the Snake indians to come no more to steal our horses. We have always been good friends to them, and we are glad that they come to see us, but not to steal horses.

I, Victor, Spoke already to my children not to go to war. But you must tell your white children to give nothing to eat to these warriors or horse stealers both Snakes, or Flatheads, but to let them Starve. Though our boys go not much to war, but other indians of other tribes go, and say to the whites that they are Flatheads, because we are good friends of the whites.

The last favor that I and all my fellow-Chiefs beg from you, is, that you would give order to the whites Settled in our valley to Sell no Wisky to our boys, who go to buy it against our will. I, Victor, an old man already, I could not Sleep all the winter, because the whites and indians, both drunk, were always fighting in the camp. My heart was broken Seeing the whites compelling by force our boys and girls, young men and women to drink, you Know for what purpose.

I. Victor, I think I fall not short of my duty towards the Whites; Therefore I hope you will take into consideration my words, I have done.

From the Flathead camp in Bitterroot Valley, Apr. the 25th 1865th

+Victor the Chief of the Flatheads.
+ Ambroise a chief
+ Moys a chief
+ Adolphe a chief
+ Fidel a chief
+ Harry a chief

Document 2

Salish Chiefs Ambrose and Adolph Complain About Hellgate Treaty Failures August 22, 1868

Source: W. J. Cullen, Special Indian Agent, Montana Territory, Helena, Mont., to Hon. N. G. Taylor, Commissioner of Indian Affairs, Washington, D.C., Aug. 22, 1868, *Annual Report of the Commissioner of Indian Affairs* (1868), pages 676-681; "Minutes of the remarks of 'Ambrose'. . .," U.S. Office of Indian Affairs, "Letters Received by the Office of Indian Affairs, 1824-1880," National Archives Microfilm Publication M234, reel 489, fr. 306-309.

Editors' note: Cullen's report included a transcript of the remarks of Salish Chiefs Ambrose and Adolph at an August 1868 council at Fort Owen. The chiefs' remarks capture their complaints about the failure of the government to carry out its obligations under the 1855 Hellgate Treaty. They especially note that many of the annuity goods were not received and those that were received were not the farming implements and tools that they needed to develop their farms. The Cullen report corraborates and details the failure of the government to fulfill the terms of the Hellgate Treaty.

Helena, Montana Territory,
August 22, 1868.

Sir:

I have the honor to report, that in pursuance of my instructions from the department of the 30th April, 1868, I have visited the Flatheads, Pend d'Oreilles, and Kootenays. On account of the many complaints which I have heard from this quarter, I induced the Hon. James Tufts, acting governor and *ex officio* superintendent of Indian affairs, to accompany me on a tour of observation.

We arrived at the Flathead agency on the 10th of the present month. We found the agency situated near the head of the Jocko valley, in a very beautiful and attractive spot. The valley is about ten miles long by five or six miles wide, and is surrounded by a chain of towering snowcapped mountains. It has a good soil, well adapted to the productions of all the cereals and vegetables which can be grown in this latitude. The valley is skirted by heavy bodies of timber, affording some of as fine lumber as I have ever seen. The Jocko, a beautiful, clear mountain stream, abounding in trout, and large enough to afford a good mill privilege at all seasons of the year, meanders through the valley, affording plenty of water for all purposes.

We found the Flathead agency in charge of Special Agent A. J. McCormick [i.e., W. J. McCormick], and, I regret to say, in very bad condition. Everything looks dilapidated and seems fast going to ruin. The agency building, now occupied by the farmer, is a small frame house with only two rooms, inconvenient in every particular, and very much dilapidated. The mess-house, or boarding-house for the men, is an old log building, which was erected several years ago by Major [John] Owen, and was never designed for anything more than a mere temporary concern. The roof of this building has fallen into such a state of decay as to afford but little shelter from either rain or snow. The barn, if the venerable pile of logs which compose it may be so termed, is without roof, save a few boards very badly warped up by the sun, laid at irregular intervals. The blacksmith and carpenter shops are pretty good buildings, but the former is entirely without iron, and the latter without nails. These indispensable articles were very scarce, there not being a pound of either to be found at the agency. The grist and saw mills are good buildings, and in very fair condition of repair, but both are lying idle on account of the mill-dam having been swept away. The dam was carried away some time last summer, and has not since been rebuilt. The farm cultivated for the employés, contains something over 100 acres. They are growing this year wheat, oats, and barley, besides a variety of vegetables. Everything looks very well, but how they have managed to grow such fine crops, with the stock and the farm implements at their command, is something of a mystery. Upon taking a careful inventory of farm property we found it to consist of two yokes of work-oxen, two old worn-out horses worth about $10 each, two milch cows borrowed from the mission of St. Ignatius, 45 head of hogs and pigs, three old wagons torn apart, four old broken ploughs, together with a few antiquated hoes, picks, shovels, &c.

The agency is very much in debt, and there are loud complaints among the employés on account of the non-payment of their wages. I could find no record, letter, report, or data of any kind at the agency, by which I could determine the amount in which it is involved, but as near as I could approximate to it I should judge the total indebtedness to be something over $30,000. Most of it is in the shape of vouchers issued by the agents. Over $25,000 of this sum has been issued by Agent McCormick, who claims that he has never received any money, and that it has cost him this sum to keep up the expenses of the agency.

On account of the very unsatisfactory condition of affairs at his agency Major McCormick asked to be relieved from duty at the Flathead agency, which was promptly done by Governor Tufts, and the property turned over to

Mr. L. L. Blake, the farmer, with instructions to save the harvest immediately and then employ his men in repairing the mill-dam.

While at the agency I had my attention called to the condition of the Flathead annuity goods for the present year. These goods, consisting of 15 bales of blankets, were shipped by Major George B. Wright, agent for the Blackfeet, from Fort Benton, Montana Territory, where they were received by him. The cost of transportation from Fort Benton to the Flathead agency should not be over eight or ten cents per pound, but Major Wright, in a spirit of extended liberality, contracted these at 20 cents per pound. These goods had but recently arrived, and a very casual observation convinced us that some of the bales had been opened, as they had been sewed up with a different kind of thread from that use in putting up the packages originally. Governor Tufts and myself, in the presence of Agent McCormick, Mr. L. L. Blake, and others, proceeded to open the bales which appeared to have been meddled with, five in number, and counted the blankets. We found that the inside wrappers of these bales were missing, and that the five bales were 113 pair of blankets short of the number they should have contained. Mr. Blake testified that the goods had not been opened or disturbed in any manner since they had been received, and from his and other affidavits which we took relative to the matter I am of opinion that the blankets must have been abstracted before they reached this agency. These peculations and frauds upon the Indians should be closely looked into, and the perpetrators of them dealt with summarily. They give rise to much dissatisfaction and complaint among the Indians, many of whom know very well what amount of annuities they should receive. Besides, rumor, with her thousand tongues, is sure to spread anything of this kind far and wide, and magnify it a thousand fold. There were a number of charges of fraud in the disposition of Indian goods, property, &c., which came to my ears during my stay at the agency, but the proof not being in my possession I shall refrain from mentioning them in detail at present.

With regard to this agency I may say further, before leaving this part of my report, that there never has been any hospital built or agricultural school established, as provided by the treaty. There is no physician residing at the agency, but there is one at Missoula Mills, 25 miles away, under pay as Indian physician.

Pend d'Oreilles and Kootenays.

On the 12th instant, in company with Rev. Fathers [Lawrence] Palladino and Van Zaio [James Vanzina?], of the St. Ignatius mission, who kindly came to accompany me, I started on a visit to their mission and to the Pend d'Oreilles and Kootenays, who are located there. The mission is situated in the St. Ignatius valley, about 15 miles from the Flathead agency. It was founded in 1844 by Father P. J. DeSmet, the veteran missionary of the Rocky mountains, and has been instrumental in doing much good among the Indians. At present the mission is in charge of Fathers Palladino and Van Zaio, who are assisted in their labors by four sisters of charity and several lay brethren. The mission consists of a large fame church, a large log school-house, dwelling-houses for the clergy, a grist and saw mill, shops for the mechanics, &c., surrounded by a great number of Indian houses. These latter are built of logs, and seem to be well tenanted. The Pend d'Oreilles who reside here number 895 souls, and the Kootenays number 300 more. Some of these Indians are in destitute circumstances, but others are comparatively comfortable and well off. They have raised this year about 80 fields of wheat, besides other grains and vegetables, all of which are in splendid condition. Most of these Indians have embraced the Catholic religion, and are in some degree civilized. During my stay I attended church twice, once in the morning and once in the evening. There were present each time about 500 persons, men, women, and children, and seldom have I seen a more orderly or devout congregation. The Indians all joined in the services, which were held in their own tongue.

The Sisters have here an orphan school, and many of their pupils are full-blooded Indian girls. These little Indian girls showed great proficiency in the branches taught, particularly as all instruction is in the English language. The mission is very poor, and the school-room is in an unfinished condition. In view of this and of the great good they seem to be accomplishing among the Indians, I sent each of the little girls a new dress, and the Sisters five kegs of nails to complete their school-room, besides some other needful articles of smaller importance.

The lay brethren employed oversee, instruct, and assist the Indians in all their mechanical and agricultural pursuits, and under their instructions the Indians have made good progress in farming as well as the more necessary trades. The grist-mill and the saw-mill have been run entirely for the benefit of the Indian, and indeed everything that has been done here seems to have but that one common object. It would be hard to speak in terms of too high praise of the efforts for the civilization and improvement of the Indians which have been made by the devoted men having this mission in charge.

The Flatheads.

Upon the 14th instant I returned to the Flathead agency, where I rejoined Governor Tufts, who had busied himself in the mean time in taking an inventory of the farm property, and in preparing affidavits relative to the missing blankets. We then repaired to Fort Owen, in the Bitter Root valley, where the Flathead nation resides, and 53 miles from the Flathead agency. This tribe numbers about 550, and though in destitute circumstances, they are remarkably peaceable and well disposed. We made them a feast, and invited the chiefs and headmen of their tribe to a council inside the fort. The Indians complained, and we thought with good cause, that the provisions of the treaty made with them by Governor [Isaac] Stevens, July 16, 1855, had not been faithfully observed on the part of the United States; that they had received annuities but five years since the treaty, and then, they believed, in deficient quantities; that there had been no hospital or school-house built for them as provided for in the treaty; that the mills in the Jocko valley were inaccessible to them; that no houses had been built for their chiefs, land broken, &c. They also seemed very desirous of having a part of their annuities in farm implements, as they have scarcely anything to cultivate their farms with. One old man, showing his hands, said: "Look at these; they are my tools; I scratch the ground with my nails." Upon inquiry, we learned that the old man had planted a considerable crop this year, literally scratching it in with his nails. But I append to this minutes of the speeches of one or two of their principal men, taken at the time by Governor Tufts, which will serve to show the nature of their demands.

The removal of these Indians from the Bitter Root valley, where they have heretofore lived, to their reservation in the Jocko, is a question of deep interest to the Indians as well as to the white settlers of the valley, and is one by no means easy of solution. The Bitter Root valley is about 100 miles long by from 7 to 10 miles wide. It has a very fertile soil, a mild and genial climate, is well watered and timbered, and is one of the best, if not the very best, agricultural districts in Montana. In this inviting region have settled a large number of whites, many of whom have opened and cultivated large farms, and made valuable improvements thereon. These settlers, very naturally, are anxious that the Indians should be removed, so that they may retain their homesteads, and ultimately secure title from the government to the same. The Flatheads, too, who were the original owners of the soil, with all their strong Indian attachment for a locality which has long been their homes, and which contains the graves of their ancestors, are very desirous of being permitted to remain where they are. They would like to have a survey made, as contemplated by the 11th article of the treaty above referred to, and a reservation set off to them above the Loo-Loo-Fork. They say a reservation can be made there large enough to accommodate both themselves and the Pend d'Oreilles and Kootenays, and that they will then cede their interest in the Jocko, as well as all of the Bitter Root valley not embraced within their reservation. They think that a small deputation of their chiefs and headmen should be permitted to go to Washington, with a view of settling these difficulties. Unless it is settled soon, it will undoubtedly breed disturbances and cause bloodshed between the whites and Indians.

The matter may be settled satisfactorily to both the whites and Indians, I think, in either of two ways.

1st. If the provisions of the Stevens treaty were faithfully carried out, and particularly those contained in the 5th article, I have little doubt that the Indians could be induced to remove to their reservation in the Jocko valley. The improvements for their chiefs and headmen should be first made, land broken, houses built, &c. Then it would be well to make a treaty with them, by which they should receive a liberal compensation for the improvements made by them in the Bitter Root valley. Whatever may be given them on this account should be judiciously expended in the purchase of stock, farming tools, &c., to enable them to carry on farming upon a large scale on their reservation. The Flatheads have about 50 farms under cultivation where they are, and have made considerable progress in the art of farming. The miller at Fort Owen, where they have their flouring done, told me that the wheat raised by the Indians was of better quality and better cleaned than that grown by their white neighbors. Now, if these people could have $35,000 or $40,000 expended in the purchase of stock, farm implements, seeds, &c., with perhaps $5,000 or $10,000 per annum for ten years for incidentals, I think that they could be brought to see that they would be infinitely better off upon their reservation than where they are.

2d. If deemed most expedient, a suitable reservation for the accommodation of the three tribes might be made in the Bitter Root valley, as desired by the Flatheads. Four townships of six miles square each would probably be sufficient for all. This would necessitate the removal of a considerable number of white settlers, and in my opinion would not be so good for the Indians, as it would leave them on a main thoroughfare of travel, and liable to be outraged at all times by evil-disposed persons.

In conclusion, allow me most earnestly to recommend that something be done at once looking to the permanent settlement of these Indians upon a reservation. By reason of the encroachments of the white settlers upon them, these Indians are liable to cause serious trouble at any day. They are very peaceably and friendly disposed, and, as they claimed in council, have never killed but one white man; but they are nevertheless a very brave and warlike people, whose enmity is not to be scorned. Besides, until they are permanently settled no expenditure of money made by the government in their behalf can be of any appreciable benefit to them.

I would also recommend that the expenditures of money appropriated under the treaty here referred to be closely examined into, to the end that if

Top: Chief Ambrose
Source: Drawing by Gustavus Sohon, National Anthropological Archives, Smithsonian Institution, Washington, D.C. (negative number 08502000)
Botton: Chief Adolph
Source: Drawing by Gustavus Sohon, National Athropological Archives, Smithsonian Institution, Washington, D.C. (negative number 08502500)

any frauds have been committed the perpetrators of them may be brought to justice. The Flatheads have always conducted themselves with utmost good faith towards us. In all my experience with Indians I have never seen a nation whom I thought more deserving in every respect than the Flatheads, and I may add that I have never seen a tribe whom I thought had more just grounds of complaint.

With every consideration of respect, I have the honor to be your obedient servant,

W. J. Cullen,
Special Indian Agent, Montana Territory.

Hon. N. G. Taylor,
Commissioner of Indian Affairs, Washington, D.C.

* * * * * *

Minutes of the remarks of "Ambrose" one of the headmen of the Flatheads, at a Council held at Fort Owen M.T. Aug [blank space] 1868 —

"The provissions [sic] of the Treaty which we made with Govr Stevens long ago have never been complied with. Not one half of what was promised us has ever been received by us.

"We hear that a great road for the whites is to be built through the Jocko, if so it would be no place for us. The Bitter Root is our old home, here are the graves of our Fathers, our own and our childrens birth place and here we wish to die and be burried. We would be glad to have the Pen d Oreills and Kootenais come and live with us but we do not want to leave the Bitter Root.

"We wish our Great Father would send us a list of the goods which he gives us so that we may Know if it all comes. We are afraid that we do not get all the goods which are sent to us. We do not think that our Great Father will promise anything and not do it. He could not do wrong and will do justice.

"We want some farming tools, ploughs, axes, hoes &c. We hope our Great Father will send them."

"Adolphe another head man of the Flatheads spoke about as follows

"I am glad to welcome our friends here, who come with word from the Great Father. This fine day I call them our friends though I have never seen them before, because they talk and look like honest men. I know they are our friends and we can talk to them. The treaty which we made with Govr Stevens has not been Kept. We have received annuities only five years since our treaty. Gov Stevens promised us that we should live all alone and not be molested by the whites. He told us that our trail to our hunting grounds and camas roots should be Kept open. He promised us a hospital for our sick, a Doctor and a Blacksmith, and to build a school for our children. He also promised to build fences and houses for us all of which has never been done. The Grist mill and saw mill are far away we never see them. The young men are sometimes bad and we are afraid to live among the whites lest we have trouble with them. We want to Know if our Great Father allows the whites to settle upon our lands. Some of them threaten to shoot us. Old chief wants to stick to the word which he has promised the Great Father. The treaty promised us annuities twenty years, but the annuities do not come. We send for things which we want but do not get them. Our Great Father lives so far off we think he does not get our word. If we could go and see him we could tell him. The Agents have told us we could select such goods as we wanted. We want farming tools. My hands! Look at them!! They are my tools. I scratch the ground with my nails. The Great Father wants us to make farms. He ought to send us tools.

"Gov Stevens promised us a choice of of [sic] reservations. We want to stay in the Bitter Root Valley as long as we live.

"We are nearly naked. We want good clothes. This year again our Annuities have not all come. What is the reason? Our hands are not stained with white blood. We never Killed but one white man and he was a thief and a murderer. We had to Kill him or get Killed ourselves.

"Our Great Father I think at last takes pity on our old chief and on us, and that is the reason you have come to see us. You will tell him all that is wrong and he will make everything right."

Document 3

Salish Chief Victor Complains About Treatment by the Government May 3, 1869

Source: Victor, Hd Chief Flathead Nation, Fort Owen, M.T., to Our Great Am. Father, May 3, 1869, U.S. Office of Indian Affairs, "Letters Received by the Office of Indian Affairs, 1824-1880," National Archives Microfilm Publication M234, reel 489, fr. 454-456.

Editors' note: In 1869 the Bitterroot Salish were still trying to get the government help promised in 1855. They were not willing to move from the Bitterroot Valley, but were anxious to develop farms to supplement their hunting and gathering. Victor outlined the history of the Bitterroot Salish contact with the white men beginning with the Lewis and Clark Expedition. Captain William Clark fathered a child named Sintusensin while with the Salish. Victor complained about white men who sold whiskey to young Salish men and asked the President to help the Salish. The letter is written in John Owen's handwriting, but presumably expresses Victor's ideas.

Fort owen Bitter root valley
Montana Territory
May 3rd 1869

To our
Great Am. Father,

Victor Head Chief of the Flathead Nation wants to Speak his heart. Some 65 Snows ago My people saw the first Pale faced Men. I was then a boy. They gave My fathers people the first Tobacco & Blkts they Ever saw. Then we saw the first guns. & Many things the pale faced Men had were wonders to us. The pale faced Chiefs (Lewis & Clarke) told My father & his people that they were the Great Fathers Children & that he would be Kind to us if we would listen to what he told us. One of the "white" Chiefs (Capt Clarke [William Clark]) had an Indian wife. She had a son now among us. Who we call "Sintusensin" (Clarke) the son of the first pale faced chief we ever saw. He is a good Man. The pale faced Men looked Strange to us. They said they came from towards the rising Sun & were going to the great waters where the Sun set. Their horses were tired. We gave them fresh good horses in exchange. Which Made their hearts feel good. We have always loved the pale face Man. We have Never wet our hands with his blood. The Blkfeet our Enemies have Killed Many White Men. Still our Great Father seems Kind to them. He gives them Guns, Powder & Ball, Blankets & provisions, &c. Why is this!

Our friend IntuKiaKin (Gov. [Isaac] Stevens) Made a treaty with us & our Enemies the Blkfeet some 14 Snows ago. We have Kept it. Our friend Simolsin (Mr [John] Owen) has lived With us some 20 Snows. He built a fort & Mill here. Was our trader. Married among us. He never had but one tongue. We love him for his Kindness. When our Meat is gone he gives us flour & Tobacco too. We are never hungry when he is with us. We shall Never forget him. My people love this valley. Their fathers & Children are buried here. & We hope you our Great Father won't drive us from here. Gov Stevens said he would speak a Kind word to our Great Father for us. But he is dead Now So who will be our friend but Mr. Owen. Last Summer two more White Chiefs Visited us (Gov [James] Tufts & Maj. [W. J.] Cullen). We had a long talk with them in Simolsin's house. We told them that we did not want to leave this valley. That we would give the Great Father the Jocko valley if he would give us this. The big road of the White Man runs through the Jocko valley. & the Whites are hauling thru all the Year round. Our Young Men get Whiskey from bad White Men & then they do Mischief, Abuse their Woman & Children. We Can't do any thing with our Young Men when their [hearts?] are on fire. I want this stopd. It will be better for us all. Then we can live on good terms with our White friends. My people are poor. We have No one to help us plow & farm as Gov Stevens promised us. Our white Chief (Ind Agt [Michael M.] McCaulay) lives Sixty Miles from here. It is a long way for us to go to get a plow, gun, or Kettle fixd. IntuKiaKins promises are fresh in my Mind. I dont forget what our White friends tell us. When the Indian, although friendly with us, have Strung their bows & filled their Quiver with arrows to Make War on the White Man We have Never joined them. Some Eleven (11) Snows ago when Kamiakin the great Chief, with the bands of our friends Made war upon the Whites in the Spokan Country we would not join him, although he offered My people Many horses if we would. But I said No. My word to Intukiakin & Simolsin was not a dry stick to be broken. Our word came from our hearts & We Must Keep it. And we have to this day & hope we always will. We Know the good Equilux (Revd Father [Pierre] De Smet) he is our friend & the friend of all good Indians. His heart is big & good. In council he talks Many good things to us. After all this talk we hope our Great Father Wont drive us from this Valley of our poor Fathers who sleep here. We have some fields & potatoes and if we had some one here to help us we could raise all the wheat we would want. The country being filld up with White Men have driven the Buffalo off. They are not close & plenty as they were before the White Man Came among us to hunt for Gold, Which they seem to love so Much. We Must farm now or Starve. May My words react from heart. Simolsin tells us You are a great Soldier. That Makes our hearts feel good. Please hear us & help us.

Victor Hd Chief
Flathead Nation
His Mark +
Witness
L. L. Blake

Document 4

Petition for the President to Honor the Hellgate Treaty May 7, 1871

Source: Charlos, et. al., to Ulysses S. Grant, President, May 7, 1871, U.S. Office of Indian Affairs, "Letters Received by the Office of Indian Affairs, 1824-1880," National Archives Microfilm Publication M234, reel 491, fr. 351-353.

Editors' note: Sixteen years after 1855 Charlo had become chief of the Bitterroot Salish and the tribe was still waiting for the survey of the Bitterroot Valley promised in the treaty. The expanding population of white settlers in the valley was making the Salish anxious about the status of the Bitterroot as their reservation home. Father Jerome D'Aste of St. Mary's Mission witnessed the marks, but the letter was not in his handwriting.

Flathead Nation,
Bitter Root Valley,
Stevensville P. O.
Montana Terry.
May 7th 1871.

To His Excellency,
Ulysses S. Grant,
President of the United States.

The undersigned, Chiefs and Headmen of the Flathead Nation of Indians, beg leave respectfully to represent to you the importance and necessity of some final and definite action in regard to our future continuance and residence in the Bitter Root Valley.

By the 11th article of the Treaty made by us with the United States at Hell Gate, in this Territory, during the year 1855, our right here was guaranteed until His Excellency the President should have ordered a survey of this Valley with a view to determine whether we should always remain here, or else remove to the regular Reservation set apart for this and other Confederated tribes on the Jocko River. Connected with this was an express provision that no part of this valley above the Loo Loo Fork should be open to settlement or occupancy by the Whites, until the survey and decision by the President under the Treaty as before stated.

Notwithstanding these solemn guarantees, no survey of the valley has as yet been made, although eleven years have elapsed since the U.S. Government ratified the Treaty; and still worse and what we most complain of is that almost our entire valley is occupied and overrun by white settlers, who impose on us in many ways, subjecting us to annoyance, inconvenience and injustice, which seem to call aloud for redress at your hands, and to you, therefore, we respectfully appeal.

We are, in violation of Treaty obligations, as we conceive, encompassed on all sides by white settlers, even to the extent of villages in the midst of our settlement, and the results of the contact and association are, the drunkenness of our young men, to whom the whites will sell whiskey, as well as the demoralization of our women, which it seems impossible, with the greatest watchfulness on our part, to prevent.

In view of these and other details of trouble with which we will not burden you, we ask and urge that a delegation of our tribe be allowed to visit you at Washington for the purpose of arranging and finally settling the difficulties under which we suffer, superinduced mainly as we humbly suggest, by the failure of the United States to perform its duties under the Treaty made with us. We prefer to settle these difficulties at Washington, because we believe justice will best be secured to us there; or at any rate, it will be far more satisfactory to use [us?], as we have many grievances which we want the great Father to hear. None of our tribe, living or dead, have ever been to see you, although we hear of Chiefs of other tribes, who are always making war on you, being allowed that privilege, while we have always been the friends of the whites.

We do not desire to come for amusement, but for really pressing, important, and, to us, vital business, affecting the present happiness and continued existence of our people.

We ask this our Great Father, and will be thankful for such a favor.

Witness Rev. J. D'Aste SJ Missionary Priest — Charlos his + mark.
Witness Rev. J. D'Aste SJ Miss. Priest — Henry his + mark.
Witness Rev. J. D'Aste SJ Miss. Priest — Adolph his + mark.
Witness Rev. J. D'Aste SJ Miss. Priest — Francis, his + mark.
Witness Rev. J. D'Aste SJ Miss. Priest — Laurence, his + mark.
Witness Rev. J. D'Aste SJ Miss. Priest — Henry, his + mark.
Witness Rev. J. D'Aste SJ Miss. Priest — Joseph Ngantà, his + mark.

Document 5

1872 Contract for Tribal Attorney

July 1, 1872

Source: Charlos, et. al., [Attorney contract with James Fullerton], July 1, 1872, "Treaty with United States" file, MONAC Papers, MS 184, box 124, Eastern Washington State Historical Society, Spokane, Wash.

Editors' note: By this contract the Salish, Pend d'Oreille, and Kootenai tribes hired attorney James Fullerton of Washington, D.C., to pressure the United States government to fulfill the promises of the 1855 Hellgate Treaty. A copy of this contract was found in a collection at the Eastern Washington State Historical Society which originally came from the Oregon Province Archives of the Society of Jesus in Spokane, Washington. No reference to the contract has been found in the Commissioner of Indian Affairs Papers at the National Archives or any other source. James Fullerton was a Washington, D.C., attorney in the late nineteenth century, but no record has been found of any suits or actions coming out of this contract. Presumably this was the first tribal attorney contract for the Flathead Reservation tribes.

Copy of the official copy.

Flathead Indian Agency
near Missoula, Montana Territory
July 1st 1872.

Know all men by these presents that we the chiefs and headmen of the Confederate Flathead Nation of Indians, have constituted, made and appointed, and by these presents do constitute, make and appoint James Fullerton Esqr. of Washington City, District of Columbia to be our true and lawful attorney for us, and in our name and stead, and to our use to ask, demand and recover from the United States of America, all such sum and sums of money, debts, dues, accounts and other demands whatsoever, growing out of or in reference to annuities from or treaties with the United States; or relating to lands as connected with or growing out of such treaties, which are or shall become due, owing, payable or belonging to us, or detained from us in any manner of ways or means whatsoever by the United States giving and granting unto our said attorney by these presents our full and whole power, strength and authority in and about the premises, to have use and take all lawful ways and means, in our name for the recovery thereof; and generally all and every other act and acts, thing and things, device and devices in the law whatsoever needful and necessary to be done in and about the premises for us and in our name to do, execute and perform as largely and amply to all intents and purposes as we might or would do if personally present or the matter required more special authority than is herein given: And attorneys, one or more under him for the purpose aforesaid to make and constitute and again at pleasure to revoke, satisfying, demand and recover from the United States of America, all such sum and sums of money, debts, dues, accounts and other demands whatsoever, growing out of or in reference to annuities from or treaties with the United States; or relating to lands as connected with or growing out of such treaties, which are or shall become due, owing, payable or belonging to us, or detained from us in any manner of ways or means whatsoever by the United States giving and granting unto our said attorney by these presents our full and whole power, strength and authority in and about the premises, to have use and take all lawful ways and means, in our name for the recovery thereof; and generally all and every other act and acts, thing and things, device and devices in the law whatsoever needful and necessary to be done in and about premises for us and in our name to do, execute and perform as largely and amply to all intents and purposes as we might or would do if personally present or the matter required more special authority than is herein given: And attorneys, one or more under him for the purpose aforesaid to make and constitute and again at pleasure to revoke, satisfying, allowing and holding for firm and effectual all and whatever our said Attorney shall lawfully do in and about the premises by virtue hereof.

In testimony whereof we have hereunto affixed our signatures and seals, on this First day of July A.D. One Thousand Eight Hundred and Seventy Two.

S. (L.S.) Charlos His x mark, Head Chief of Flatheads
S. (L.S.) Michelle His x mark, Head Chief of Pend d'Oreilles
S. (L.S.) Eneas His x mark, Head Chief of Kootenays
S. (L.S.) Arlee His x mark, Flathead Chief
S. (L.S.) Adolfe His x mark, Flathead Chief
S. (L.S.) Big Canoe His x mark, Pend d'Oreilles Chief
S. (L.S.) Andrè His x mark, Pend d'Oreilles Chief
S. (L.S.) Paul His x mark, Cootenay Chief
S. (L.S.) Kinlacko His x mark, Cootenay Chief
S. (L.S.) Lickoss His x mark, Cootenay Chief

S. Baptiste His x mark Marengo, Interpreter
S. Lorette Hix x mark Pablo, Interpreter.

Signed, sealed and delivered in presence of Chas Schafft (S) John W. Ragan (S) James House (S) Wm. W. Jones.

Certified to be a true copy from the Original. C. S. Jones U.S. Indian Agent.

I certify, on honor, that the above recited power of Attorney, was duly acknowledged and signed by the subscribers in my presence on this the first day of July A. D. One Thousand Eight Hundred and Seventy Two, and that before taking such acknowledgment I satisfied myself by personal investigation that is [sic] was fairly and duly obtained, and that I fully explained the contents and purports thereof to the parties acknowledging the execution of the same; and in accordance with letter of instruction from the department of the interior dated January 21st 1871.

(S) C. S. Jones
U.S. Ind. Agent.

Document 6

First Negotiations with General James Garfield in the Bitterroot Valley August 22 and 23, 1872

Source: "Indian Council," *The Pioneer* (Missoula, Mont.), Aug. 31, 1872, page 2, col. 2-4.

Editors' note: These negotiations between the Bitterroot Salish chiefs and James A. Garfield were held near St. Mary's Mission. The President had already decided the Salish should move from the Bitterroot Valley to the Flathead Valley, without the benefit of the survey provided for in the Hellgate Treaty. Garfield promised the Salish assistance in starting farms in the Jocko Valley if they moved. But Stevens had promised the same help in 1855, and the government had failed to deliver. Chief Arlee complained, "We dont get our money, we don't know what to think about what you say." Garfield lamely responded, "If the President can get men honest enough to give you this money you shall have it." These talks brought together the desire of the Salish to have a reservation in the Bitterroot Valley and the intention of the white government negotiators to pressure them to remove to the Jocko Valley. Confusion over the final agreement reached with Garfield was to lead to years of hard feelings on the part of the Salish. Note Chief Adolph's complaints about his problems planting crops without proper farm equipment: "I have ploughed with my hands, they are worn out."

Indian Council.

Gen'l James A. Garfield, Commissioner on the part of the United States for the removal of the Flathead Indians from the Bitter Root valley to the Jocko reservation accompanied by Major Swaim, of the U.S. Army, Gov. B. F. Potts, Hon. W. H. Clagget, Col. J. A. Viall, superintendent of Indians affairs, and Col. W. F. Sanders, of Helena, met the Chiefs and head men of the Flathead tribe, in council about 1 o'clock on Thursday the 22d near the St. Mary's mission in the Bitter Root valley. Baptiste Maringo and Francois, two half-breeds were selected as Interpreters. As the day was intensely hot, three of the largest Indian tents made of dressed Buffalo and Elk skins had been constructed into one large tent or pavilion in which the council was held. The Chiefs, Victor [i.e., Charlo], Adolph and Arley came forward and took seats immediately in front of Gen'l Garfield and through the interpreters signified their readiness to hear what the General had to say to them. Addressing the Chiefs, the General said: I have been sent by the President from Washington to see the Flatheads in regard to their affairs in the Bitter Root valley. The President thinks very highly of the Flatheads. Since the time of Lewis and Clark, they have been friendly to the whites. He told me that the Flatheads were learning and doing well. Before we talk about the matter of business, I want to inquire whether the Chiefs understand the Stevens treaty in reference to the Bitter Root valley made 17 years ago with Victor. Do you understand under that treaty the Flatheads were to go to the Jocko, if the President should think best?

Chiefs. We understand the treaty.

Gen'l G. Do you know that the President last fall decided not to set the Bitter Root valley apart as a reservation for the Flathead tribe.

Chiefs. We understand that he did.

Gen'l G. Now the President has sent me here to find out what would be the most agreeable way for you to go to the Jocko. The President has heard that some of the Flatheads want to stay here on their farms, and leave the tribe, and that any such may remain, Congress has made a law allowiing [sic] such to remain and leave the tribe. Congress will give those who are farming and desire to remain from 40 to 160 acres of land. Congress thought that some bad white men might get these farms from you, so they provided that the Indians should not sell them.

The other Indians that have not been farming, the President and Congress will provide farming tools to help them start farms on the Jocko. They will have their annuities until the Stevens treaty runs out but the President knows for several years that some of the agents have cheated the Flatheads and he want[s] to make up for it. So the money for which there [sic] lands are sold shall be given to the Flatheads. The law which Congress made, provides that $5,000 shall be given each year for ten years to the Indians that go to the Jocko. Now the President will pay that $5,000 in any kind of goods, farming tools, or cattle that he thinks is best for them. He wants me to ask the Chiefs what they want this money in. Besides the $50,000 the President has given me $5,000 to be used in moving the Indians to the Jocko. I want you to tell me how you want that money expended. Those Indians that stay here and take farms will become citizens, and will not have any of the annuities, or any part of the $50,000. The Pen d Oreilles and Kootenais will get no part of the $50,000, it belongs to the Flatheads. The President thinks it will be better for the Flatheads to go to the Jocko where white men can't settle, and where they can have cattle then to remain here where white men and the railroad will come. The President and Congress are keeping all the treaties and paying all the money, that belong to them, and they know there are rascals that cheat them, but that is no fault of theirs. I am now ready to hear what you have to say to me, and will answer as best I can.

Charlois, the Chief rose, shook hands with the Gen'l and then spoke as follows: When the Flatheads made the treaty with [Isaac] Stevens it was understood they were to stay here. The great Father does not come here and see the Bitter Root valley, nor the land on the Jocko, where he wants us to go. Gov. Stevens gave us blankets and told us we could stay here. I have no more to say. Charlois presents to Gen'l G. copy of the Stevens treaty, and commission from Gov Stevens to Victor the old chief of the Flatheads, and invited Major [John] Owen to a seat in the council as their friend. Arley, a sub-chief was the next speaker he said. Here is Major Owen, he has been here 22 years with us, he is our friend, he knows our wants, he can tell you all about us. We keep the treaty in our hands we know what it is. You may think that Steven and Victor are dead, but we don't take it so. We hold the treaty all the time. The President sent Gov. Stevens to make a treaty with us, we listened to him and heard his words. There are four things we have not got that was promised us, a Schoolmaster, a Blacksmith, a Carpenter and a Doctor.

They promised that the Flatheads should be taught for twenty years, how to read and write, and then they would be like white men, know how to do everything, but nothing has been done.

Gen'l G. Did you understand that you were to have these things here.

Arley. We understood that we were to have these things when our lands were given us. There is a man (pointing to Col. Viall) about my shape, with a big belly on, who told the Flatheads to put their names down. We don't understand anything, we are like the brutes of the valley. I felt very sorry when I put my name down. I think I have more right on this land than anybody. You white men belong to another tribe. I can't do things as you do. I have another way. You whites have different laws from the Flatheads. The whites have strong laws so have the Indians. The Indians are following their own laws, we don't want to be white men and live under their laws.

Now if I was to ask you to be an Indian and do like Indians would you do it?

If I was to find your people in another country as the white men found us here, and tell them to go away, that I wanted to put my people there would you like it? That is the reason I want to stay here, because we were here first. The Flatheads have always been here, they have lived and died here, the bones of our fathers and mothers are mixed with the dirt of this valley. There is not one of my people that thinks of going to the Jocko.

Gen'l G. The great father did not understand that he was to go and hunt other lands for the Flatheads, he understood that he was to have this valley and Jocko examined by his officers. He thinks that if there should be a railroad through this valley then it would not be a good place for the Flatheads. The Stevens treaty allows railroads to be built through the Indians land, and when we build railroads, the whites will come and settle for forty miles on each side of the road. By the order of the President which he made last fall this valley has been given to the whites, and he thinks it will not be good for the Flatheads to stay here. He has seen white men from this country and has received a great many letters and in that way he thinks it would not be good for the Indians to stay here.

Arlee. If this land is no account we don't see what the whites want to come here so thick for.

Gen'l G. We have to build railroads through low passes in the mountains.

Arlee. We dont get our money, we don't know what to think about what you say.

Gen'l G. If the President can get men honest enough to give you this money you shall have it. We dont want you to become white men. We want you to be by yourselves.

Arlee. God has given you a manner and he has given us a manner, and when we are dead we will know who was right and who was wrong.

Gen'l. I wan't [sic] you Chiefs to go with me to the Jocko, and show me where you want to settle and what kind of houses you want so I can tell the President.

Arlee. White men came among the Indians poor, the Indians took their part and took care of them. Now the white men are rich and the Indians are poor, why does the great father take the part of the white men now? We used to take pity on the whites when they were poor. Our chiefs told us to take care of the white men, our people obeyed their chiefs. We did not think that the white people would disobey their chiefs and steal our property. The Flatheads never drew the white man's blood.

Adolph. When Gov. Stevens made the treaty he told Victor that the Flatheads should never leave this land. Gov. Stevens put flour on his head, said he was a white man. I don't understand the line across the Lo Lo Fork. When Gov. Stevens held up his hands after making the treaty what did he mean? My hands are dry. I don't tell lies. I think you are a friend.

When the Flatheads made the treaty with Gov. Stevens, we took our bows and arrows and threw them away, made peace with everybody. Did God tell you to come and drive the poor Indians away from this land? You see morning and night they don't move, they are the same so are the Flatheads. God put the

Flatheads here and when they are moved he will move them, in no other way will they be moved. I have showed you my hands my head and my heart, they are good.

Gov. Stevens promised us two horses and two cows each where are they, he promised us plows, where are they? I have ploughed with my hands, they are worn out.

Gov. Stevens asked us to do right and said the great father would do right, we have done right. The Sioux are whipping you. You ought to put them in the timber in bad places, and not the Flatheads. I don't want to spill my blood.

Gen'l. The Flatheads were in the Crow country when their 17 young men were killed and not on their reservation.

Adoph. We feel good when you are here. When you are gone white men will ask us to do wrong. We ought to be good and laugh all the time.

Gen'l. Do I understand the Chiefs to say, that their people will not leave the Bitter Root valley.

Charlois. We will not go, we will not accept the terms. I speak for my tribe.

General Garfield here explained to the chiefs at length the advantages to the Indians in removing to the Jocko. The order of the President directing their removal, the trouble that would come upon them eventually from contact with the whites, the building of the R. R. followed by the Bitter Root valley settling up with whites, that in seven years more their annuities would run out, that if they would go to the Jocko, they should have $5,000 each year for ten years, besides their annuities closing with the question, "are the chiefs willing to go with me to the Jocko and select their farms."

Charlois. We know the Jocko, we have been there many times, only wheat and potatoes can be raised there.

Gen'l. The $50,000 given under the law of Congress goes to the Flatheads alone. The Pen d O'reilles and Kootenais will get none of it. But you cannot have this $50,000 unless you go to the Jocko. I want you to tell me before I go if you want me to say to the great father when I go back that his children the Flatheads will not leave the Bitter Root valley, and will not obey his order. You can give me your answer in the morning.

Council adjournment until 9 o'clock in the morning.

Friday morning, Aug. 23. — On the reassembling of the council Charlois said I don't want you to go back and tell the great father that his children the Flatheads will not obey his order. The Chiefs will go with you to the Jocko as you desire, and will then tell you what you may say to the great father for his children.

Document 7

Partial Agreement on the Bitterroot and Tragic Consequences August 25, 1872

Source: "Conference of Hon. James A. Garfield, Special Commissioner, with the Indians of the Bitter Root Valley, Montana," U.S. Board of Indian Commissioners, *Annual Report of the Board of Indian Commissioners* (Washington, D.C.: U.S. Government Printing Office, 1872), pages 171-174.

Editors' note: The final talks between Garfield and the Bitterroot Salish chiefs were held at the Jocko Agency in the Jocko Valley. The chiefs feared the government would not keep its promise to protect the Indians on the reservation. Garfield claimed, "This land belongs to the three tribes, and the Great Father will never take it away nor allow any one else to take it away, unless they want to part with it." Chief Arlee replied, "Some are afraid this land [the Jocko Reservation] will go as the Bitterroot has." Chiefs Arlee and Adolph signed Garfield's agreement, but Charlo refused.

These negotiations had some strange and tragic consequences. Despite recording the clear statement by Charlo that "I won't sign it," when Garfield's final report was published an x was entered next to Charlo's name suggesting that he had signed. Many Montana whites seized on this to say Charlo had broken his word and had promised Garfield he would move to Jocko. Charlo was bitter about this charge and many historians have criticized this "forgery." The editors have never found a place where Garfield claimed that Charlo had signed the agreement, and there is no x on the original copy of the 1872 agreement in the Office of Indian Affairs file. General Garfield swore that the government would never take the Jocko Reservation away from the Indians or allow the land to be sold without their consent. This promise was violated by Congressman Joseph Dixon in 1904.

Conference of Hon. James A. Garfield, Special Commissioner, with the Indians of the Bitter Root Valley, Montana.

General Garfield met the chiefs at the Flathead agency pursuant to the appointments. We report the following as having occurred at the interview:

General Garfield. The Great Father understands that the three tribes own this reservation and that the Flathead is the leading tribe, and he thinks it would be better for them to be here, near the agency farm and mill, where their goods are distributed, so that they can see to their own interests; and he made this order for their removal on their account and for their good. Would you like to know what this Great Father will do for you if you come over here?

Charlois. Will what I say be taken in good part?

General Garfield. Yes.

Charlois. We will not talk mean against the Great Chief. We do not like to come here, nor do we like to become citizens and remain on the Bitter Root. How could I be a white man? My skin is red. This is my land as well as the Bitter Root. I do not see why he wants to put me here borrowing this land. I want you to tell me how it is going to be about this land.

General Garfield. This land belongs to the three tribes, and the Great Father will never take it away nor allow any one else to take it away, unless they want to part with it. In the Stevens treat[y] you agreed to let a railroad be built through it; but the Great Father will not allow the land to be sold without your consent. He does not know that he will want to build a railroad through here; but you gave the right to do so and no more. The Great Father has built a mill here to saw lumber and grind grain for Indians without expense to them, and here they have a farmer, blacksmith, and carpenter to teach them. Here you can learn to farm. The Great Father will have men here. He wants you to have horses and land and learn to work. Then you can go and hunt, but have homes to come to. The Great Father does not expect Charlois to be a white man, but wants him to learn some of their ways and have a home here. The Great Father is glad to know Charlois does not allow the Flatheads to drink, but punishes them for so doing; but he fears, if the Flatheads remain in the Bitter Root among the whites, that he cannot keep them from becoming drunkards. I want to know how many families you have among the Flatheads, and the Great Father will build them houses. We know you have been badly treated; your money and goods have not come as they should; but the Great Father does not intend this shall happen any more. He does not want you to come over here without homes, and has given me money to build houses, so that you can have places to live in when you come. He wants you to select the places where you want these houses built, and he will have them placed there.

Adoph. Only one thing, Charlois and I do not believe all we hear. Since I got sense enough to know I fear the Great Chief. You are a great chief. I am afraid of you. You are like Charlois; when we want a talk nobody comes to talk with us. I told you once before I do not mean any harm.

General Garfield. The Great Father told me to tell you just how he feels and what I promise you will be done. I want to know how many houses you want and I want you to see the crops, mill, and shops, and know what he has done to help the Indians. Lumber, shingles, flour, carpenter and blacksmith work will call you here. There are ten or twelve acres of wheat up here, and if you come over I shall give that to you. I shall plow you some ground and you shall have plows, harrows, hoes, shovels, and tools you need. I shall have the agent and superintendent go to work now and fix up places. If you do as he desires, the Great Father will take care of you.

Charlois's brother. Charlois says he will not come over here and live. Victor liked the Bitter Root, and took the land there, and as long as he lived he liked it, and when he died he dropped it to Charlois, who is in his place and feels just so and won't let it go. I want to know if the Great Father sent you to remove us over here?

Arley. Have what I say well written down. I shall talk to you and Charlois, both chiefs. I studied what I say; if you think it is so, it will be so. I have a place in the Bitter Root, — three houses, and fields, and good crops, like white man. I get money for it. Now over here when we get to talking about it, I have two hearts, one to come and one to stay. I have been there nine years; I go nowhere. Now you know what I think. You were to give us money for ten years; why is this? This land will only last ten years; it will wear out. The money does not go far enough. There is no end to the Bitter Root; there is to your money. My land is worth considerable; if I live long enough, I shall have considerable property. The man who is fat like me told us the Great Father would give us money as long as we lived about the houses. Perhaps your $5,000 would only last to build ten houses. I do not think $5,000 enough to start on. Some are afraid this land will go as the Bitter Root has. They told us we should always have that, but in a few years they take it away. I wish it could be always for Indians. This is the way my heart is for this place. The Flatheads feel as if they were getting lost for white men. I wish this place was always for the Flatheads; Victor would come again and should be a great chief once more over all our people. If the Flatheads should come here and be white men, then the Flatheads would be chief of all. If white men come we want troops to drive them out. I do not know how you feel, or how Charlois feels, but if you will give more money we will go with you; if not, we will go to the Bitter Root.

General Garfield. I see you occupy middle ground; you stand between us. I hope we shall all meet on Arley's own ground. If the superintendent said you were always to have $5,000 he was mistaken; it is for ten years — no longer. After that I can not promise, for I do not know as I could perform it. Colonel [Jasper] Viall does not mean that, I guess. I will build fifty or sixty houses if you need so many. I know $5,000 will not do it, but the Great Father has men, and all will be put in, so it will be as good as ten thousand. I know Arley loves the Bitter Root and has a nice farm, but fear his children will not love it. You must

Chief Charlo
Source: Photograph by John K. Hillers, Bureau of American Ethnology, Washington, D.C., Montana Historical Society Archives, Helena, Mont. (detail from negative number 954-526)

think of your children, and not yourselves. If you come here the Great Father will not let whites in here. Victor consented to whites going into Bitter Root at first. That was because they were not crowded by whites. Here it must be different. In this treaty I see Victor was chief of Flatheads, Pend d'Oreilles, and Kootenais. When Lewis and Clarke stopped at Lo-lo Fork, Victor was a little boy, but his tribe was a great nation. But now they have dwindled down. If they come up here I trust their tribes will increase and Charlois, Arley, and Adolph will be chiefs of the whole Flathead nation, because *they* do not drink nor fight.

Arley. Will you give more?

General Garfield. I cannot promise more; it is all I have. I will say to the Great Father he ought to give more to the Flatheads. The annuities are divided among the three tribes, but the $5,000 I have, and the $5,000 for ten years is for the Flatheads alone. Besides this, I am authorized to bring some presents for the chiefs and Victor's wife. You who have improvements in the Bitter Root can sell them to the whites. The fathers sold their houses twenty years ago for $250 to John Owen. So Indians can sell out. Do you think I am telling you the truth? If not you need not listen longer. I want to put it in writing, that the Great Father will build houses and fences, and pay this money, and that you will come here. (Here the chiefs requested that the agent, Mr. [C. S.] Jones, to examine General Garfield's credentials, and they were subject to a searching scrutiny and explained as being formal and genuine.)

General Garfield. I am in favor of whites being wholly excluded from this place.

Charlois. Is the land in the Bitter Root the Great Father's or ours? We want money one year, wagons next, teams next, tools next, not blankets all the time. (To Agent Jones.) Are you going to the Great Father?

Jones. I hope to.

Charlois. I want you to set us right before the Great Father, and tell him what I say and what white men are doing against us. I won't go to the Jocko. The young men of the Kootenais or Pend d'Oreilles will do something foolish, and then there may be a fight right there. When Stevens made the treaty, Lo-Lo Fork was made the line, and I never forget it and I stay there. If I go I shall go another way, but not to Jocko. Here they will steal. If Major Jones says the Great Father wants me to go, I will go the other way. If only my people where here, I would come, but there are bad people here. If you want me to starve, I tell you I am a chief too; I will go toward the buffalo country. Major Jones, you tell the Great Father what I say. The Flatheads about all feel as I feel.

A Young Brave. I feel as Charlois; where he goes I will go.

(General Garfield here resolved to reduce his proposition to writing, and a recess of an hour was taken, at the close of which there was a farther conference, in which the paper was interpreted to them and duplicates prepared.)

General Garfield, (to Charlois.) Have you a paper making Victor chief of three tribes?

Charlois. Yes.

General Garfield. I think you should be chief of all three tribes. Have you received a paper?

Charlois. No.

General Garfield. I am willing to ask the Great Father to give you such a paper. Do you want it?

Charlois. No.

General Garfield. We have had a long talk, and now I must go back to the Great Father. You have been very kind to me, and I must tell him all about our talk. I will carry this paper to the Great Father, and if you sign it, it is a contract between us. If you do not sign it, it will show the Great Father what I propose and what you are not willing to do. You have heard it read and know what it is. I want you each to answer, so that I can tell the Great Father whether the Flatheads will obey his order or no.

Charlois. I won't sign it.

Arley. I will sign it. When shall I come over? I do not want to leave until spring, until my cattle are wintered in the Bitter Root.

General Garfield. That will do; but you want to be here, so that you and your people can put in crops. How many will you bring; all your family?

Adolph. I know what you want, but I am not talking. I think may be it is so, may be not so. I have two hearts. Is it true that Charlois is to be head of three tribes?

General Garfield. It can be so I think, and I will ask the Great Father to make Charlois chief of three tribes.

Adolph. Will you move us from here if we come?

General Garfield. We should be everlastingly cursed if we do without your consent.

Adolph. Will the Great Father keep whites away?

General Garfield. Yes, I will ask him to take means to do so.

Adolph. (Showing hands blistered by hard work.) Will my hands get well if I come? The whites up in Bitter Root say you will drive us off in three days if we come.

General Garfield. There are some bad men who tell you these things. They told me you had got the Nez Percés there to fight the whites and pretended you were going to be bad Indians; but before I saw you I wrote back to the

Great Father that it was not true, and now I want you here away from those bad whites, and I want Charlois to come and be chief of the three tribes and maintain the glory of Victor. He is young and we want him to live as chief of these tribes many years. Now I shall order the men to go to work and build houses for the Indians, and three houses for the chiefs, and Charlois's house will be very lonesome until he comes over to the Jocko. I will take this paper to the Great Father and tell him Charlois will not sign it; that Arley will; that Adolph won't say whether he will or no.

Charlois. Young men like this (selecting one) will go with me.

Adolph. I don't know what to say. If my chief was alive, I would answer. I don't know what the Great Father will say.

General Garfield. The Bitter Root will soon be settled up; the Great Father has so ordered, and he will not take that order back.

Charlois. I have told you once what I am going to do. When Major Jones goes east I will go the other way. My father felt so, and so do I. I would not like to be head chief over the three tribes.

General Garfield. I must say another word. The promises here are for those who come over. They will do all promised in this paper.

(Here Arley and Adolph signed the paper.)

(Charlois, to General Garfield.) I am not mad, but I must see what is done here and see my people.

Colonel Viall. When you (chiefs) come to Helena, call and see me at the Indian office.

Charlois. (laughing.) Do you want to whip me?

Colonel Viall. No, I want to give you some tobacco.

Charlois. You ought to whip me, I think.

This closed the negotiation. The three chiefs went out in the afternoon, and Arley and Adolph selected their farms and places of residence, and houses will be constructed at once.

Accompanying the chiefs to Missoula, General Garfield made them each some valuable presents and departed to go east, while they went to the Bitter Root.

Document 8

Arlee Asks for More Money from the Government October 18, 1873

Source: "From Jocko Agency," *The New North-West* (Deer Lodge, Mont.), Nov. 1, 1873, page 3, col. 6.

Editors' note: This letter was written by Charles Schafft, the longtime Flathead Agency clerk in the 1870s. Arlee asked for an extension of the support payments under the 1872 agreement with Congressman James Garfield.

From Jocko Agency.
"Arley Makes a Speech."

Editor New North-West. —

The following address was made by Arley, second chief of the Flatheads, to Agent [Daniel] Shanahan, Oct. 18, 1873, and is placed on the official records. Arley and sixteen families of the Flatheads have elected to reside on the reservation, and the address will show Arley's feelings on the removal question.

Arley's Address:

"I left my place (in the Bitter Root valley) to come here, and stop here. I shook hands with you, and think you are glad to see me here. I do not know if the President likes it that [I] came here to stop on the Reservation. All the white people have a chief, and when he talks to them they are glad. I listened to the President, and came here to stop. It is for that I ask if he is glad. I am going to talk to the President. Last year I came here to have a talk with General [James] Garfield. He told me, 'You will get pay for your land ten years, then it will stop.' I said it was too short a time, and he told me, 'I can't tell you now, but when I go to Washington I will tell the President what you said, and I think he will give you more, perhaps for twenty years.' Since that I have not heard news.

"I am here to stop and now I speak. I ask to have five more years in addition to the ten promised: you all know what I said last year; it is on paper. I did not want the railroad to pass here. In the spring you will commence to give me my money promised last year. As the Flatheads come here I want the President to help me for three years — because the people are poor and have nothing to eat. I want him to listen to me, and what I say, and I will be glad. If this letter goes to the President he will be glad that I have come to stop here. I want you to tell the President to write a letter to my people, and I will give it to the Priest and he will tell them to come here, because many white men are in the Bitter Root Valley who told my people not to go to the Reservation, that we would be poor there and starve. I think they will believe the Priest, and he will tell the truth. If the letter comes to this office, I will take it to the Priest in the Bitter Root valley."

Yours truly,
K.

Flathead Agency, Oct. 28, '73.

Document 9

Theft and Murder by the Crow Indians

December 29, 1873

Source: Charles Schafft to Daniel Shanahan, Dec. 29, 1873, U.S. Office of Indian Affairs, "Letters Received by the Office of Indian Affairs, 1824-1880," National Archives Microfilm Publication M234, reel 500, fr. 268-272.

Editors' note: In December 1873 Flathead Agent Shanahan was in Washington, D.C. and Dr. James Wright was the Montana Superintendent of Indian Affairs in Helena. The statements from Chiefs Michelle and Arlee illustrate just how complicated and dangerous intertribal war was on the plains in the early 1870s. Schafft was the Flathead Agency clerk. The punctuation in the original letter was hard to read, but is rendered here as accurately as possible.

Flathead Indian Agency
December 29, 1873

Major Daniel Shanahan
Dear Sir:

The enclosed letter from the Commissioner was received here on the 27th minus the enclosure from James Wright Esqr mentioned therein. I immediately mentioned the subject to the Chiefs and gave till to-day for an answer. Accordingly Arlee and Michelle came here at the appointed time and also were present Baptiste Robwain, Frank Robwain and Dandy Jim Louis as Interpreters. Having again read the Commissioner's letter to them, Michelle expressed himself as follows:

"We will not give up any horses to the Crows — the Crows are sorry because we steal their horses and we are sorry that they kill our people — they killed four of our people last summer — among them a chief named Cow-ackan my father-in-law — Last Spring they killed two of my people and wounded three women and a boy — one of the women is now lying before your door and will die" (Penama the woman who was shot through the hip) "Last fall a year ago the Crows stole 31 horses and a Jack-ass from my people while hunting on the little Blackfoot. We made peace with the Snakes once and the Crows came and stole 80 horses from us, that was 10 years ago — the Crows told us it was the Snakes and we made war on them but we found that the Crows were the thieves and they have been our enemies since that time and we made peace again with the Snakes and are at peace with them now. What our people have stolen from the Crows since last winter we will Keep — but after to-day when my people steal horses from the Crows or other I will have them returned and I want the Crows to do the same. When we go to the Crow country we always go in peace but the Crows always attack us first. I don't Know of any white man's horses but if you will get a description I will look around and see if they are here. That is all I have to say."

Arlee then said: (after having read enclosed description sent here by Dr Wright last fall and the only description of stolen stock from the Crow Country on file here) (as far as Dr Wright is concerned):

"I know about those white men's horses you have described they are with my people of the Bitter Root Valley.

"Kul-Kul-tui has the stallion.

"Charl Quall-che-nee has the brown mare and colt.

"Francois has the blue horse and the other brown mare was left behind on the way given out — the blue horse is now in the Bitter Root Valley and I will go and get it when the weather is more warm." (He is suffering with a bad cold just now) "The other two are with the people on the buffalo hunt but when they return with them I will get them also and deliver them to you — there is not a horse belonging to the Crows in the Flathead village — If my people stole any horses from them we have them no longer and cannot return them but if my people steal from them after to-day I will have them returned. I mean what I say. We have tried to be friendly with the Crows for a long time but whenever we make peace they are the first to break it.

"The first Flathead they Killed was an old man named 'One Night' while peaceably trapping near Heart mountain.

"Then they killed 2 of our people last spring — they went to the Crow village to eat and smoke. the Crows shook hands with them and then they killed them. one of them was the brother of 'Nine Pipes' and the other was Pascal the son of a chief. After these two were Killed we still were friendly to the Crows and we hunted together. When we were together we missed some of our horses and thought the Crows had stolen them but we found them in the Pend d'Oreille camp. Then we all camped at the Crow Agency and were happy. Then we moved camp and stopped about 8 miles from the Crow Agency. Here we saw some Blackfoot tracks in the snow and we sent a messenger to the Agency to warn the Crows to tie up their horses. The messenger went to the chiefs lodge but was told the Chief was with the Agent and he went to the house of the Interpreter and there they Killed him and threw his body into a well right at the Agency — that was last Spring and the messenger's name was Chawl-paw-paw-tcheel. A young man who had accompanied the messenger" (Baptiste Marengo's Cousin) "saved his life by the fastness of his horse but he was shot in many places. The Crows said that the Flatheads had stolen their horses the night previous, which we denied but the Crows said they had found a hat belonging to a Flathead — but those horses were stolen by the Blackfeet and they Killed this man for nothing. One of the white men working at the Agency pulled his body out of the well.

"When I was over here my people stole those white men's horses while I was gone. When I returned they were going to war and said they would Kill the Crows wherever they would meet them. I said of course your hearts are sorry because they killed our people.

"Now I will say something to the great chief:

"The Crows and Blackfeet have the best of us because the government gives them good guns and plenty ammunition. I don't know what to make of it. Is it because we have never spilled the blood of a white man that we do not get guns from the great father also. The other Indians kill our people and they Kill the whites and they get guns and ammunition and plenty of everything. I can't understand it."

I asked him if he would consent to meet the Crow chiefs and try to make some peaceable arrangements but he said, "No we have tried that too often. The Crows will always break the peace."

I send you the remarks of the chiefs in full. what they said is true as you know well yourself — and you have already done all you could do while you were here and for reference I enclose you also copy of a letter you wrote Dr Wright on the subject in October. I am satisfied that I can get back any white man's horses now among them if I had a description of them but the Commissioner did not enclose Dr Wright's letter referred to and I will have to write the latter for information. When Arlee gets ready to go to Bitter Root I will send an employ with him for that Blue horse according to his request. And when here will notify Dr Wright of the fact. Whatever other horses there may be I think are in the buffalo country.

Very Respectfully
Chas Schafft

Please call the Hon Commissioner's special attention to the matter and have justice done to *our* Indians. it seems to be altogether a one sided question with Dr. Wright.

The Flatheads who have located here will not go to the buffalo country anymore — if promises made them are kept and if the government would furnish them with a few good arms they would be to the Agency the same as soldiers — these are certainly under the control of their chief Arlee — who is worth half a dozen Charlots, and his salary as Head chief will be earned. Michelle should also have a few good carbines for his local police.

Document 10

Complaints from Pend d'Oreille Chief Michel

May 2, 1874

Source: "Statement of Michel one of the chief the Flat Head nation," May 2, 1874, enclosure in T. J. De Mers, Frenchtown, to M. Maginnis, May 2, 1874, Martin Maginnis Papers, MC 50, box 1, folder 22, Montana Historical Society Archives, Helena.

Editors' note: The signatures to this statement were witnessed by a local Justice of the Peace, but the handwriting is that of T. J. DeMers, a Frenchtown merchant who was married to a Pend d'Oreille woman. DeMers also operated stores on the reservation. Agent Daniel Shanahan was involved in a conflict at this time with the priests at the mission over the treaty funding for a school on the reservation. Some of the complaints in the statement were probably from DeMers as well as Michel. Note especially the third recommendation that "the choice of an agent be left to the Indians" with the approval of the priests at St. Ignatius Mission.

Statement of Michel one of the chief the Flat Head nation

On This 2nd day of May A.D. 1874 Michel one of the Chief of the Flat Head Nation, personally appeared before me, Al Pichette, a Justice of the Peace for Missoula County, Montana Territory, — and under oath made the following declaration. —

That him and his Tribe has been ill used by the United States Indian agent Major Daniel Shanahan present agent at the Flat Head agency on the Jocko Valley in Montana Territory. That the said Major D. Shanahan is trying to create a disturbance among his people by trying to have a part of the Indians on the reservation work against the other part. — so as to create disatisfaction — and that the said Major D. Shanahan is not giving them all of their annuity goods, — but Robbing them of a good part of their annuities. — and that he can prove that said Major D. Shanahan has already sold goods that was sent by government for the Indians, as annuities. —

And that by the Treaty made with the United States in the year 1855 that any white man who wishes to live among the Indians on the reservation, can do so providing the chief and the agent are willing to let them stay on said

Chief Michelle
Source: Drawing by Gustavus Sohon, National Anthropological Archives, Smithsonian Institution, Washington, D.C. (negative number 08501400)

reservation. — And that according to that part of the Treaty. — he the said Michel one of the Chief of said Flat Head nation, and with the consent of the U.S. agent he has given permission to Five (5) white men who are married to Idian [sic] woman and have famillies of Half breed children. — to locate and settle on the reservation and that they them white men have taken up farm and made improvements on the lands which are expensive, and never have been troubled by any body to leave the reservation. — and now this present United States agent has ordered them to leave the reservation, and has given them only 30 days. —

Now the said Michel, one of the Chief of the Flat Heads, and also his tribe do not want these white men removed, — that they have given them permission to settle and locate there and that they consider that they have a perfect right to allow a few white men if they Think it is to their interest to have them there to obtain knowledge of Civivilization. Said Michel says that him and his tribe do not wish to have any difficulty with the White men but wishes to remain friendly with them, — but that he said Michel feels it his duty to inform the government that unless there is a change in the present way of conducting affairs at this Flat Head Agency, — he really believes that there will be trouble before long and that he wishes to avoid it. — And that he does propose to the government the following changes to secure permanent peace and satisfaction among the Indians. —

1st. That an Inspector be sent immediately by the U.S. government to inquire into the management of affairs. —

2nd. the Removal of Major D. Shanahan.

3rd. That the choice of an agent for them be left to the Indians themselves and that they by Election or otherwise with the approval of the reverend fathers of the mission — shall name who shall be agent for them. —

Said Michel wishes further to state that Said Major D. Shanahan is trying to create disturbance between his people of the Reverend Fathers of the mission, — and that said Shanahan has stopt the pay of the Sisters for teaching schools to their orphans — and that at present they have no schools, no black smith, no tin smith, no gun smith, no hospital, no Farmers. — only one miller, and that according to treaty they are entitled to all these things. And said Chief Michel wishes the Peace commissioners or whoever are the proper authorities to take immidiate steps to settle the present state of affairs. and that he would be thankful if there was an answer send to him immidiately. — to know whether there will be anything done for them soon.

Address. — the answer, at French Town as he does not wish to trust the Postal department at the Agency —

Michel Michel his x mark, one of the Chief of Flathead nation
Indian Chief of the Flat Head. —
French Town
Missoula Co
Montana

Subscribed & sworn before me this 2nd day of May A.D. 1874 — Al. Pichette
Witness to the above, Louis Brown
Ignace his x mark (Indians), witness of Ignace mark, T. J. De Mers
Thimothy his x mark (Indian).

Document 11

Chief Arlee Complains About Not Receiving the Garfield Agreement Payments November 1, 1874

Source: Alley Quill-quill-squa, Flathead Chief, to U. S. Grant, President of the U.S., Nov. 1, 1874, U.S. Office of Indian Affairs, "Letters Received by the Office of Indian Affairs, 1824-1880," National Archives Microfilm Publication M234, reel 500, fr.191-195.

Editors' note: This letter of complaint from Salish Chief Arlee was written by Duncan McDonald. McDonald was a mixed blood trader and businessman on the reservation, and there is no way to tell how much of the letter reflects his complaints rather than Chief Arlee's. Chief Arlee opposed the priests at St. Ignatius Mission and the new agent, Peter Whaley, who supported the mission. The new agent had dismissed Fred Decker, a white man married to a tribal member, and hired his teenage son, David Whaley. Some periods have been added to the transcript to separate sentences.

Flathead Indian Agency
Nobr 1st 1874

U.S. Grant
President of the U.S.
Washington D.C.
Sir

I write you to let you know how this Department has been carrying on & how they are treating us. I want to Know where is the money that is coming to us in the treaty of 1872 with General [James] Garfield this is $5000.00 five thousand dollars that we ought to get yearly since Agt 27th 1872. we did not get a cent yet & we must have it. Further more Peter Whaley our new Agent is not fit to hold this office. he is lead by the Jesuite priests by the nose. Such Agent that is governed by priests we do not wish to have him around here whatever. The Priests has taken enough money say to the amount of $22000.00 twenty two thousand dollars for schooling from this agency. And where is our Students. we have not got one that can read or write. is it possible that we could not get one of our natives that could not read or write after the government spending $22000.00 twenty two thousand dollars. It is a shame for the priests & most of the Agent except Maj. [Daniel] Shanahan to use us in This manner after getting so much money from us. We could send 5 Indian boys to West point or other colleges five or six years ago & spend as much as the above amount. we could be have those boys by this time fit for the Senators but we have not one fit for any thing.

About Peter Whaley did you send him here as a prize fighter or for the Interests of the Indians. He wanted to whip one of my chiefs on account of our threashing machain. Whaley he wanted some of our employees to take the meachian to the Mission & threash for the priests & Michael one of my chiefs would not allow it. he wanted his Indians wheat threashed first. Now you can see that the Agent is working for priests & not for us. The priests & agent are a band of speculators.

We believe in the Holy Catholic Church but not in this firm that are around here.

I'll will State you another affair. we had a good man here that was honest & true man by the name of FK Daker an Engineer. he was discharged by Whaley because he was honest & hired a man that can cheat us & harm us & Steal. we would like to have your answer in this question if we the six Chiefs select a good man that we Know is honest if you will appoint as Agent. Then if he does not suit you you may turn him off. if your answer is yes we will send you his name. There is a boy 12 or 14 years old hired as a laborer getting $60.00 dollars pr month doing nothing only eating. his name is David Whaley son of the agent. 4 or more driving cattle for the agent & drawing governments money. those men ought to be working for us. What Kind of a government is this. No Doctor Interpreter No Miller no Wagon maker &c. I could post you more but it is to long a complaint if I was to tell you all. I wish to get the money for the Flatheads due for last two years.

This letter is written by a half blood. he is one of my own tribe a native of this Reservation.

I remain
Your Affct Svt
Alley x Quill-Quill-squa
Flathead Chief

pr Duncan McDonald

Address
Alley Quill-quill-squa
Care of Frank Daker
Flat Head Indian Agency
Montana Territory.

Document 12

Chief Arlee and Father Philip Rappagliosi

April 14, 1875

Source: Father Philip Rappagliosi, *Letters from the Rocky Mountain Indian Missions,* ed. Robert Bigart, by permission of the University of Nebraska Press, Lincoln, copyright 2003 by the Board of Regents of the University of Nebraska, pages 55-58.

Editors' note: In the spring of 1875, Father Rappagliosi was stationed at St. Ignatius Mission on the Flathead Indian Reservation. The chief he wrote about in this letter was Chief Arlee, who lived in the Jocko Valley and was chief of the Bitterroot Salish Indians on the reservation. Rappagliosi was visiting the church at the Jocko Agency. This letter gives a detailed description of Rappagliosi's dealings with Chief Arlee, but no record has been found to give Chief Arlee's version of the interactions. According to Rappagliosi, his skillful management of Arlee's vanity "placated his [Arlee's] ego quite well." Rappagliosi concluded, "I had won him back completely." Arlee's version of the events would probably have been quite different. Some footnotes have been omitted. This letter from Father Rappagliosi was originally published in a German Catholic mission publication, *Katholischen Missionen*, in 1876.

Dealings with an Indian Chief

[Another letter of Philip Rappagliosi from April 14, 1875, makes us familiar with the difficulty which missionaries among the Indians must face frequently, namely the moodiness, touchiness, and small-minded vanity of the chiefs. The ability of the Father to appease and to win over the offended chief and the picture of Indian ways of life that is presented to us at this occasion leads us to submit this letter to our readers. — 1876 editor of *Katholischen Missionen*.]

Since I wrote my last letter, I spent two weeks in another Indian camp to teach those who were making their first communion. The chief of that camp had been angry at us for some time. He is a very eloquent (in Indian terms) and extremely proud man; some Whites and Protestants or Catholics (in name only) used this to change his mind about us. As a result of recent contracts between the government of the United States and his tribe, he received much money since part of the Indian land was ceded. This caused him to become conceited so that he became demanding and unmalleable. Therefore my trip had two purposes: I wanted to teach the children about the Catechism, and to win back the heart of that stubborn Indian and his people. When I arrived at the camp he was not there; but I knew that he would have to return the day after and this was exactly what happened. Our first talk was rather cold, especially in the beginning. When I got off my horse in front of his cabin, he was by coincidence standing by the door and looked at me as if he did not know me. I went over, shook his hand, and welcomed him back. He turned his head away and gave no answer. Pretending not to have realized, I continued: "I am coming to visit you." Then he waved me over into his house and said: "Come in!" I entered and saw two women who offered me a big wooden chair. I believed that this was the throne of the ruler of the Indians, who was still standing angrily outside. Therefore, I only took a seat on a little bench. After some minutes the chief came in too and immediately sat down on the big armchair. I was very happy that I had left it free. Then I told him that I had come to teach those who were making their first Communion, and that I was going to stay in the camp for a couple of days. He did not pay attention to this and started right away to express his anger about something that had happened to him with one of the Blackrobes. I already knew about the whole story and had expected this eruption. That's why I patiently let him speak and, when I realized that he was about to get to the end of his expressions of anger, I calmly said: "I appreciate your opening your heart to me; but maybe we should talk about it another time. I will come back. Today I just wanted to come for a short while and now I will head back to the one who offered shelter to me for tonight." And, putting my hand on his shoulder, I whispered into his ear as if he were my best friend: "I want to stay and eat with you too a couple of times for as you know I do not have a residence here." He answered calmly, "Oh!" which meant good. This "Oh" was not unimportant to me, but being content with my first visit, I climbed up on my horse with the hope that the "Oh" would be followed by what still needed to be said.

Two days later I was back and the reception was much friendlier. He shook my hand, had me sit down on his chair, and passed me the pipe — the strongest sign of friendship among the Indians. Then he said to me: "Philip, I love you," and added a flattering compliment about my knowledge and pronunciation of the Indian language. I used this moment of good humor to tell him that I had not eaten since the early morning. At once he had a good meal prepared for me. In order to honor me he wanted me to eat by myself, but I realized that he would rather eat with me. Then he took a seat next to me and called for three or four others of the best educated to join us. After the meal we sat down around the fireplace again. Quietly and ceremoniously we lit the pipe and

Chief Arlee

Source: Peter Ronan, *Historical Sketch of the Flathead Indians from the Year 1813 to 1890* (Helena, Mont.: Journal Publishing Co., 1890), p. 78

passed it around in the circle. As soon as the first clouds of smoke had begun dancing in the air the chief interrupted the silence and spoke: "Blackrobe, when the Indian has finished a meal with his friends he smokes, and when he smokes he talks about what he wants." I saw what this whole introduction was aiming at. I answered: "Oh!" and he repeated the whole of his angry speech from two days before. The thing was like this: At Christmas a Mission had been completed for the Indians which ended at Epiphany or Three Kings Day. Because the Indians were still on the hunt it was impossible to gather them earlier. On Christmas Eve, as usual, a long ceremonious service took place with many Indian participants. The Father who held Mass, however, recommended they postpone Communion until the end of the Mission, although he allowed people to take Communion during this Holy Night if they wished. My chief arrived just the night before Christmas and went to the Father in order to confess and take Communion. The Father gave him the Sacraments but then he made the comment that all the other chiefs had preferred to wait until the end of the Mission to prepare themselves more fully, and that he would have done better to wait as well. Haughtily he went away swearing about everything.

When he started complaining to me, he asked why Christmas had not been celebrated with the tribe of Saint Ignatius this year. I replied to him and said that it had been celebrated and that I had gathered the people at midnight, decorated and lit up the church, and that there had been a Christ Child on the altar, etc. Hypocritically he threw in that Christmas had not been celebrated because there had not been any Communion. I responded: "Everybody who wanted to could take Communion." He answered: "But the Father refused to give it to me." "The Father did not refuse," I said, "but he told you what he told everybody else as well, namely, to wait until the end of the Mission to become more fully prepared." He did not know what to say now and seemed to be satisfied. Then he started to ask me other random questions which were not his own ideas but had been taught to him in an evil manner by the Whites. I slowly answered all of them, and when he had nothing else to say anymore I spoke to all the bystanders and reminded them to keep the faith. When I had finished they said all together: "We agree." Since it was already nighttime we prayed and everybody went to sleep. Early in the morning I went away to hold Mass in the cabin of a sick man as I had promised. I, nevertheless, informed the chief of the fact that I would celebrate Mass at his place next Sunday and that's where the Indians should be gathered. That placated his ego quite well, and I took the chance to offer him the Sacrament of Confession. During the week I continued teaching Catechism. On Saturday I returned to the chief; he received me in a friendly fashion and confessed as did several others after him. The conversation during the evening went on very amicably and no angry word was said. On Sunday morning the Indians gathered and the chief and the others took Communion. When I said goodbye the chief shook my hand, affirmed his contendedness to me, and promised to come to the mission church at Easter — a promise that cheered me up and gave evidence of the fact that I had won him back completely. He kept his word and visited the other Fathers also. All the ones whom I had prepared for their first Communion came with him. They all received their first Communion at the biggest feast of the ecclesiastical year.

Document 13

Chief Charlo's Anger Over Taxes

April 26, 1876

Source: Chief Charlo, "Indian Taxation," *The Weekly Missoulian*, April 26, 1876, page 3, col. 3-4.

Editors' note: In this angry speech, Charlo laid out the injustice of taxing the Bitterroot Salish Indians. The Missoula County government wanted the tax money to avoid bankruptcy, but also hoped the taxes would force the Salish to leave the Bitterroot Valley. Charlo included several examples of white men refusing to treat the Salish with the friendship the Salish had shown to the whites. Charlo concluded, "Other tribes kill and ravish his women and stake his children, and eat his steers, and he gives them blankets and sugar for it. We the poor Flatheads, who never troubled him, he wants now to distress and make poorer." Charlo's anger was obvious, but the reader must be careful, because the *Missoulian* editor probably colored the transcript. The speech has been reprinted and quoted many times over the years.

Indian Taxation.
Recent Speech of a Flathead Chief, Presenting the Question from an Indian Standpoint.

Yes, my people, the white man wants us to pay him. He comes in his intent, and says we must pay him — pay him for our own — for the things we have from our God and our forefathers; for things he never owned and never gave us. What law or right is that? What shame or what charity? The Indian says that a woman is more shameless than a man; but the white man has less shame than our women. Since our forefathers first beheld him, more than seven times ten winters have snowed and melted. Most of them like those snows have dissolved away. Their spirits went whither they came; his, they say, go there too. Do they meet and see us here. Can he blush before his Maker, or is he forever dead. Is his prayer his promise — a trust of the wind? Is it a sound without sense? Is it a thing whose life is a foul thing? And is he not foul? He has filled graves with our bones. His horses, his cattle, his sheep, his men, his women have a rot. Does not his breath, his gums, stink? His jaws lose their teeth, and he stamps them with false ones; yet he is not ashamed. No, no; his course is destruction; he spoils what the Spirit who gave us this country made beautiful and clean. But that is not enough; he wants us to pay him besides his enslaving our country. Yes, and our people, besides, that degredation of a tribe who never were his enemies. What is he? Who sent him here? We were happy when he first came; since then we often saw him, always heard him, and of him. We first thought he came from the light; but he comes like the dusk of the evening now, not like the dawn of the morning. He comes like a day that has passed, and night enters our future with him.

To take and to lie should be burnt on his forehead, as he burns the sides of my stolen horses with his own name. Had Heaven's Chief burnt him with some mark to refuse him, we might have refused him. No; we did not refuse him in his weakness; in his poverty we fed, we cherished him — yes, befriended him, and showed the fords and defiles of our lands. Yet we did think his face was concealed with hair, and that he often smiled like a rabbit in his own beard. A long-tailed, skulking thing, fond of flat lands and soft grass and woods.

Did he not feast us with our own cattle, on our own land, yes, on our own plain by the cold spring? Did he not invite our hands to his papers; did he not promise before the sun, and before the eye that put fire in it, and in the name of both, and in the name of his own Chief, promise us what he promised — to give us what he has not given; to do what he knew he would never do. Now, because he lied, and because he yet lies, without friendship, manhood, justice, or charity, he wants us to give him money — pay him more. When shall he be satisfied? A roving skulk, first; a natural liar, next; and, withal, a murderer, a tyrant.

To confirm his purpose; to make the trees and stones and his own people hear him, he whispers soldiers, lock houses and iron chains. My people, we are poor; we are fatherless. The white man fathers this doom — yes, this curse on us and on the few that may yet see a few days more. He, the cause of our ruin, is his own snake, which he says stole on his mother in her own country to lie to her. He says his story is that man was rejected and cast off. Why did we not reject him forever? He says one of his virgins had a son nailed to death on two cross sticks to save him. Were all of them dead then when that young man died, we would be all safe now and our country our own.

But he lives to persist; yes, the rascal is also an unsatisfied beggar, and his hangman and swine follow his walk. Pay him money! Did he inquire, how? No, no; his meanness ropes his charity, his avarice wives his envy, his race breeds to extort. Did he speak at all like a friend? He saw a few horses and some cows, and so many tens of rails, with the few of us that own them. His envy thereon baited to the quick. Why thus? Because he himself says says [sic] he is in a big debt, and wants us to help him pay it. His avarice put him in debt, and he wants us to pay him for it and be his fools. Did he ask how many a helpless widow, how many a fatherless child, how many a blind and naked thing fare a little of that little we have. Did he — in a destroying night when the mountains and the firmaments put their faces together to freeze us — did he inquire if we had a spare rag of a blanket to save his lost and perishing steps to our fires? No, no; cold he is, you know, and merciless. Four times in one shivering night I last winter knew the old one-eyed Indian, Keneth, that gray man of full seven tens of winters, was refused shelter in four of the white man's houses on his way in that bad night; yet the aged, blnded [blind] man was turned out to his fate. No, no; he is cold and merciless, haughty and overbearing. Look at him, and he looks at you — how? His fishy eye scans you as the why-oops do the shelled blue cock. He is cold, and stealth and envy are with him, and fit him as do his hands and feet. We owe him nothing; he owes us more than he will pay, yet he says there is a God.

I know another aged Indian, with his only daughter and wife alone in their lodge. He had a few beaver skins and four or five poor horses — all he had. The night was bad, and held every stream in thick ice; the earth was white; the stars burned nearer us as if to pity us, but the more they burned the more stood the hair of the deer on end with cold, nor heeded they the frost-bursting barks of the willows. Two of the white man's people came to the lodge, lost and freezing pitifully. They fared well inside that lodge. The old wife and only daughter unbound and cut off their frozen shoes; gave them new ones, and crushed sage-bark rind to put therein to keep their feet smooth and warm. She gave then warm soup; boiled deer meat, and boiled beaver. They were saved; their safety returned to make them live. After a while they would not stop; they would go. They went away. Mind you; remember well: at midnight they returned, murdered the old father, and his daughter and her mother asleep, took the beaver skins and horses, and left. Next day, the first and only Indian they met, a fine young man, they killed, put his body under the ice and rode away on his horse.

Yet, they say we are not good. Will he tell his own crimes? No, no; his crimes to us are left untold. But the Desolator bawls and cries the dangers of the country from us, the few left of us. Other tribes kill and ravish his women and stake his children, and eat his steers, and he gives them blankets and sugar for it. We the poor Flatheads, who never troubled him, he wants now to distress and make poorer.

I have more to say, my people; but this much I have said, and close to hear your minds about this payment. We never begot laws or rights to ask it. His laws never gave us a blade nor a tree, nor a duck; nor a grouse, nor a trout. No;

like the wolverine that steals your *cache*, how often does he come? You know he comes as long as he lives, and takes more and more, and dirties what he leaves.

Document 14

Tribal Law Enforcement on the Reservation

March-April 1878

Source: "Why Indians Abandon the Reservation," *The Weekly Missoulian*, March 29, 1878, page 3, col. 3-4; "The Indian Side of the Question," *The Weekly Missoulian*, April 12, 1878, page 3, col. 3-4; Omar G. V. Gregg, "An Open Letter," *The New North-West* (Deer Lodge, Mont.), April 26, 1878, page 3, col. 6; *The Weekly Missoulian*, May 3, 1878, page 3, col. 2.

Editors' note: Local whites and the United States government tried to impose white concepts of justice on tribal leaders on the Flathead Indian Reservation. Omar G. V. Gregg was a Confederate Civil War veteran who was employed in the late 1870s by the St. Ignatius Mission print shop publishing Indian language books. See Robert Bigart and Joseph McDonald, *Duncan McDonald: Flathead Indian Reservation Leader and Cultural Broker, 1849-1937* (Pablo, Mont.: Salish Kootenai College Press, 2016), p. 32. Andra was the chief of the Indian police at the St. ignatius Mission. Andra argued that his punishments for adultery were reasonable and humane.

Why Indians Abandon the Reservation.

O. G. V. Gregg, writing from Flathead Agency, upon a subject of which he has had abundant opportunities to become well informed, sends a lengthy communication upon this subject, from which the following extracts are taken:

"Much has been said of late regarding the continuous camping of Indians belonging to the reservation in and around Missoula. To any one versed in Indian nature this does not seem strange, as it is the height of an Indian's nature to make a living for himself and his family as easily as possible. Were it not for the inducements that they receive from the different villages throughout the Territory, doubtless they would have to devote more time to hunting and fishing. The treaty framed between the U.S. Government and themselves grants them the privilege of hunting and fishing throughout the Territory; that is, as long as they observe the treaty.

"One small party, belonging to the confederated tribes, seldom, if ever, comes on to the reservation, for fear of being punished in a most brutal manner. Flogging, carried into effect by one of their petty chiefs, has caused many to abandon their homes and seek refuge from the hands of tyrants in other localities. A little over one year ago, the U.S. Grand Jury, then convened at Deer Lodge, ordered flogging abolished, since which time it has been practiced in the dead hours of night.

"It may be necessary here to state that there are only two crimes that are punishable — fornication or adultery. The punishment that now awaits the perpetrators of the above crimes is to be confined in a small log cabin, dark as a dungeon, to be placed in a lying position, tied hands and feet, to subsist upon a scanty allowance of bread and water for weeks at a time, whilst those that have committed theft, and those who have murdered their wives and daughters, are permitted to roam at large.

"That the Indian would be better off if he were to remain upon his reservation, and that there should be some mode of punishment inflicted upon all that are guilty of crime, all will admit, but, whatever the punishment is, let it be accordance with the customs of civilized nations."

The communication in regard to the punishment of offences among Indians may be construed as an intimation of censure upon the authorities at the Agency. It cannot be properly so regarded. It is merely the opening up of one of the great questions where the Indian policy is radically at fault, and discloses the fact that, under that policy, Indians are amenable to no law. An Indian can commit murder or steal anywhere in the Territory, and the probabilities are that, if his punishment is attempted by the civil authorities, he will be demanded by the government. The government pursues a manifestly vicious policy in allowing Indians to deal with their own offenders in their own way. The whole theory of Indian jurisprudence is a compelling of recompense to the party injured. We ought to be persuaded that it is dangerous to allow a people who have but faint ideas of what is necessary for the welfare of society to administer laws for the good of society. We ought to be persuaded that barbarians, who are allowed to continue the practices of barbarians, will forever remain barbarians. They should be taught better things, and be taught them by the strong arm of the law. If an Indian is convinced that he will be punished for wrong doing, he will not be long in finding out the expediency of doing right. They should not be allowed to make and execute their own laws, but should have them framed and executed by a people of superior civilization. Republican institutions among savages are not wholesome. The only punishment, according to our correspondent, is that designed to enforce a conviction of the sanctity of the marriage relation among Indians. Their ideas are loose upon this question. The original Indian idea made a wife a purchasable article, value computed in ponies, and to be put away at will. The eradication of this idea cannot be accomplished in one generation, and the teachers who have been among the

Indians are entitled to much credit for the advanced state of the inculcation of this idea of our religion. The opinion that the Indians possess superior traits of character in many respects has frequently been expressed in these columns. Take the same number of the white race, and let them become vagabonds in the country, spending their time in idleness, and deriving their subsistence as they can, and they would speedily degenerate into outlaws and fall to cutting each other's throats. But it does seem possible that Indians can be made better, and one important step in this direction is to encourage them to quit their nomadic habits and adopt the habits of civilization, in their domestic relations and in their methods of subsistence, as speedily as possible.

— *The Weekly Missoulian*

* * * * * * * * *

The Indian Side of the Question.

The question of Indian cruelty assumed a tangible shape two weeks ago. An old Indian woman was circulating disparaging reports, and appealed to the citizens to interfere in behalf of humanity. In no spirit of officiousness, but as friends of the Agent, and well-wishers for a correct administration of affairs upon the reservation, two citizens of this place joined in a letter to the agent. Here is the letter, and the proceedings thereon:

Missoula, Montana, April 2, 1878.

Maj. Ronan:

Dear Sir — This old woman says her daughter has been in the Indian jail twenty-one days; that her wrists have been tied with cords until her hands are fearfully swollen. For the credit of the Agency, it seems a case requiring your investigation, and, if the case is as reported, you out to stretch your authority to see that she has better treatment.

\- - - - - - - - -

Gentleman:

Your letter of April 2d reached me by messenger on the same date, and on the 3d I repaired to the Mission, taking with me the bearer of the letter and my official interpreter. I was much pleased that the opportunity arose, through your letter, to set the good people of Missoula and elsewhere right upon the matter referred to, as interested parties, as my investigation proves, have foully and wilfully [sic] misrepresented the conduct of Indian laws and discipline upon this reservation.

Andra, one of the head men and chief of Indian police, immediately upon my arrival, called his policemen together in council, and I told my interpreter to carefully interpret your letter, as I read it, word for word, to them, and ask if it contained the truth.

Andra made the following reply to it:

"I am now sixty-eight years of age — I never committed a cruel act in my life. The daughter of this woman, who brought that letter to you, is in jail under sentence of 26 days; her time will expire on Sunday morning, when she will be let out, and her lawful husband will be here to take her to his lodge. Her husband is an older man than I am, a chief in our tribe; his name is 'Big Lance.' She deserted him, and ran off with a young Indian of the Spokane tribe. I heard of it, and sent out my police and overhauled them at Horse Plains, and brought them back. The Spokane Indian I will keep in jail for 30 days, and then send him back to his people, who will again punish him — perhaps not so much, but he will be punished. The woman, on next Sunday, I will give to her husband, who will be here to take her to his lodge. Is there anything wrong in this?"

Agent — "The letter says the woman's wrists are tied and lacerated."

Andra — "Your government built the jail; no separate rooms are made. I keep a guard about the jail nearly all the time. When we have a pair of adulterers in jail, we must keep them separate. When my guard goes away, they are tied to keep them apart, but never to hurt them."

Agent — "The letter says the woman is starved to a skeleton."

Andra — "The letter lies. Three times a day the prisoners are fed everything that my people and family have to eat themselves; and three times a day they are taken out to walk in the air and sun — all day Sunday they are allowed out under a guard."

Agent — (to the woman) — "Have you seen your daughter, and are you satisfied with her treatment?"

Woman — "I have seen her, and she is sorry for what she has done; she is not badly treated."

Agent — "Why did you bring me such a letter?"

Woman — "A young Indian told me a lie at Missoula."

Agent — "Are you satisfied with what Andra says?"

Woman — "Yes; Andra told me to live and eat with his family until Sunday, when he will let my daughter go back to her husband's lodge, and I will stay and visit her, and try to make it up between them."

Agent — "Then you are satisfied."

Woman — "Yes."

Agent — "It has been written to Missoula, and printed in the paper, that you whip prisoners in the dead hour of night."

Andra — "Indians are not cowards; if we had any whipping to do, we would do it in the day-time."

Agent — "Then you do not whip prisoners."

Andra — "For over a year that law is changed, and no one is whipped; nor has any one been whipped for any offense. I try to keep my Indians good. The most of them are good; but it takes force to keep some in the straight road."

Agent — "What crimes are punishable?"

Andra — "Every wrong that is done: stealing from each other, gambling, adultery, drunkenness, or anything else that is wrong. You white men have a law to send your people to jail for many months for giving whisky to Indians. Now, I can send any one of my young men to Missoula, and give him something to trade, and he will come back with all the whisky I want; but I do not let them trade for whisky; they go to jail if they do — it is our law. In Missoula, they can get drunk and get whisky. You have a law against it, why is it not enforced. Why do not the white people drive our bad Indians away from their town. They hide bad people when I send for them. White men would not like to have me hide their bad people here. You said it was printed in the paper that my prisoners were whipped in the dead of night. Who is my enemy that told such a lie?"

Agent — "It will do you no good to know."

* * * * * * * * *

An Open Letter.
How the Flathead Police Administer Punishment.

To the Editor New North-West:

The question of Indian brutality as published a short time since in the *Missoulian*, led to a partial investigation on the 9th instant. It is not necessary to repeat the full proceedings of the council held, only suffice it to say that it has not changed public opinion in the least. It could reasonably be expected by all persons of intelligence that it would be denied by Chief Andra and his police force. Had the investigation alluded to been held with those who have shared in this punishment, or even with spectators, things might have borne a different aspect. But it stands today just where it has for years, unmolested. Over one year ago the U.S. Court, then convened in Deer Lodge, ordered flogging abolished; but it seems that afterwards it was kept up for a short space of time. Determined to not get foiled in their fiendish mode of punishment Chief Andra and his advisers adopted another method more brutal because of its long duration, viz.: The prisoners to be confined in a small log cabin and to be tied with cords for weeks at a time. Often is it the case that for weeks after the prisoners are given their liberty the prints of these cords are quite noticeable. Andra's report as published in the *Missoulian* regarding the kind treatment prisoners receive at his hands is a manufactured falsehood, gotten up in order to exhonorate [sic] himself and shield from further comment his tyranical advisers undoubtedly premeditated several days prior to having this interview. He gives for an excuse, that tying is his only method of keeping separated two adulterers. Has he forgot that the log building referred to contains five separate apartments, or does he think for a moment that no one outside of an *Indian* has knowledge of the fact? His statement, contradictory to flogging, may or may not be true, as my informant may have testified falsely, but positive evidence can be produced that he did flog after receiving orders to stop it. As before stated, women have been arrested at midnight in the town of Missoula for prostitution and taken to the Reservation and punished severely, whilst murderers and thieves are allowed to run at large, thus bidding defiance to both Territorial and Indian law. One thing quite noticeable regarding the crime they utterly detest is that certain parties even bid defiance to their law, living in adultery for years at a time under their observation, and simply because Andra and his police force know quite well they would resist being arrested, do not make an effort to meddle with them. Whence this change from brutal to kind treatment? Will some one rise and explain? When was this jail building altered so as to contain only one room? Dark as a dungeon, with scarcely ventilation enough to sustain life, the prisoner there remains to serve out the sentence pronounced upon him by his tyranical judge. Have not their cries been heard the whole night long? Whether it is better for the people of Missoula to tolerate the continual camping of these Indians around their town, or to see that they be allowed to return to their reservation unmolested; or, if punishment is necessary to check that crime, to see that it is done according to the laws and customs of the United States, time alone will prove.

Omar G. V. Gregg.

Flathead Agency, April 18, 1878.

* * * * * * * * *

Omar G. V. Gregg, well known in this county, and who has secured the title of "Jocko Missionary," from his connection with the Flathead Mission, as printer for the Fathers, was ordered off the reservation by Agent [Peter] Ronan on Tuesday — a few minutes after the receipt of the last *North-west* at the Agency.

Document 15

Flathead Reservation Chiefs Complain About Ammunition Ban May 1, 1878

Source: "Tales of the Times," *The Anaconda Standard*, April 30, 1893, page 9, col. 1-2.

Editors' note: The three principal chiefs of the Flathead Reservation tribes complained in 1878 about the unfairness of withholding ammunition and guns from peaceful tribes. The Indians needed guns and ammunition to feed themselves and protect them from enemy tribes on the Great Plains. Applying the ammunition sales ban to the Flathead Reservation tribes was especially outrageous after they had refused to join the Nez Perce Indians in fighting the white men in 1877. The Bitterroot Salish under Chief Charlo had even protected the lives of the Bitterroot whites when the hostile Nez Perce Indians passed through the valley.

Tales of the Times.

True Stories and Fanciful Yarns Illustrative of Modern Life and Character.

Written for the Standard.

The following letter was dictated nearly 15 years ago by Arlee, chief of the Flatheads, Michel, chief of the Pend d'Oreilles, and Eneas, chief of the Kootenais. The two latter chieftains are living still, but Arlee has gone to the happy hunting grounds. The station near the Flathead Agency was called Arlee in honor of this Flathead chief, and his burial place is in the Indian burying ground, near the church at the agency:

Flathead Agency, Mont., May 1, '78.

E. A. Hoyt, Commissioner of Indian Affairs, Washington, D.C.

Honored Sir:

We cannot read words but from those we hear spoken from our agent, and others we feel that you have a good heart for the Indian, and whenever it is in your power, you will try to do him justice and smooth his rough road. For over 30 years we have had Catholic missionaries among us, who teach us the gospel, and try to point out the trail which will lead to the white man's road. Some of us have houses to live in — have good farms fenced — have crops now planted — have families growing up around us; and our laws forbid that we have more than one wife. We never have had war or trouble with your people, and during all our lives, until last summer we could go to traders and buy guns and ammunition. While the Nez Perces were on the warpath we did not care to buy ammunition or guns as it might look bad to the whites, as that tribe of Indians has always been our friends and allies in our wars against the Blackfeet, the Sioux and other enemies. War is over now and our young men after laboring in the fields and gathering in their crops, thought it hard when the agent told them they could not buy ammunition with which to hunt. We know his advice is good to stay at home and cultivate the land and take care of one's crops, as in the near future the disappearance of game, as the whites advance upon our hunting grounds, will compel us to rely upon the earth to produce food from our toil to support our children. But our crops are planted, and the buffalo are only a short distance from us across the mountains on the east side, over a trail that leads through no white settlements. They are plentiful and our young men desire to hunt them and procure meat while the old people stay at home and take care of the crops until they ripen, when all will return from the hunt and help to gather them; but our agent tells us we cannot buy ammunition except powder, ball and caps. Such ammunition is of no use to us as we have no muzzle loading guns, nor could we buy them if we had the money, as they are not now for sale that we know of. We cannot throw our good guns away — they cost us very much money. We have forgotten the use of the bow and arrow. We are told it is your wish that we stay at home; this is good advice; we are doing our best to bring our children up to work, but when the crops are planted and nothing to do, we feel that it would be a great wrong to force our young men to stay at home when they so much love to hunt the buffalo, and return the time work commences, cheerful and happy and well supplied with meat and furs to gladden the hears of the old people. We who address you are the head chiefs of the tribes — the time is fast coming when we will be in our graves, for we are three old men; we love our people, and we hope you will not refuse us the only source of great pleasure we have in our lives, the opportunity to have guns and ammunition with which to kill game. The Great Spirit knows we do not want them for war, for when the white people were few in our country we always treated them as friends. The great war chief of the soldiers. General [John] Gibbon, was here lately, and he knew us and most of our old men. He was willing that we should have metallic ammunition, good to hunt with, but our agent says that he must obey the orders of a greater peace chief, who gave the order that fixed ammunition must not be sold to Indians. Now we will await anxiously to hear your written words, and hope our prayer will be granted.

Arlee, (his X)
Head Chief Flatheads.
Michel, (his X)
Head Chief Pend d'Oreilles.
Eneas, (his X)
Head Chief Kootenais.

Interpreter, Michel Revais.
Witness to marks, N. A. Lambert.

Hardly 75 years have passed since the foregoing letter was dictated by the Indians chiefs of the Flathead reservation, and for several years past not a vestige of those magnificent wild animals are to be found upon the former hunting ground, or in fact anywhere in the boundaries of the United States. A herd of nearly 100 head are now owned by two half-breed dwellers on the Flathead reservation. This herd came from the natural increase of one yearling bull and two heifers driven by an Indian from the vicinity of Fort Shaw, or Sun river, across the Rocky mountains and over the Cadot pass about 11 years ago to the Flathead reservation. The increase of this herd has averaged about the same as a herd of cattle. Several of the males have been slaughtered, and their meat disposed of in the Missoula butcher shops, while the heads and skins have brought fancy prices. This slaughter of male buffalo was necessary in order to decrease their number in conformity with the number of cows running in the herd. It is understood that the herd will be placed on exhibition at the world's fair, as a resident of Butte has been negotiating with the owners to give bonds for the safe return of the buffalo on the range on the Flathead reservation or a stipulated value of any animal that may not be returned. Twenty thousand dollars was the amount stipulated to be paid to Charles Allard and Michael Pabolo, the mixed blood owners of the herd, for their use for exhibition at the world's fair for six months, the full bond to be put up, is said to be in the neighborhood of $400,000. It will be a great disappointment if anything should occur to prevent the exhibition of this magnificent herd of Montana buffalo at Chicago.

Document 16

Chief Michelle Wants Peace with the Whites

July 14, 1878

Source: Peter Ronan, "Indian Matters," *The Helena Independent* (daily), July 21, 1878, page 3, col. 3.

Editors' note: According to Agent Ronan, Pend d'Oreille Chief Michelle refused to join the Sioux in fighting the whites, despite threats from Sitting Bull. Michelle also refused support for Nez Perce refugees traveling home through western Montana.

Indian Matters.
Agent Ronan Interviews Chief Michel.
Sitting Bull Wants the Pen d'Oreilles to Join Him.

Flathead Agency, M.T.,
July 14th, 1879 [i.e., 1878]

B. F. Potts, Governor Montana Territory,
Helena, M. T.:
Sir —

I have to report the following council held with Michel, head chief of the Pen d'Oreilles, Sunday, July 14th, for your information, and any action you may suggest:

Having narrated to Chief Michel the particulars of the murders committed by a band of Nez Perces, who came from the North by way of the north fork of Sun river, murdering as they came along two men at the Dearborn, in Lewis and Clark county; two men at Deep creek, Bear gulch, Deer Lodge county, and four or five miners at the head of Rock creek, in Missoula county; all of which murders were committed in the direct Nez Perces trail from the North to Idaho Territory, known as the Elk city trail. In reply the chief said:

"A few days ago a messenger came to me from Sitting Bull's camp with word from that chief, that if I valued the lives and welfare of my people to gather them together and leave the reservation. If I did not feel like joining him and making war upon the whites — that after he had done his work among the settlers myself and people would come back again and occupy our land without fear of obtrusion."

Agent — "What reply did you send back?"

Michel — "I told the runner to tell his chief that the Pen d'Oreilles were friends of the whites; that years ago, when I was young, the Pen d'Oreilles and the Sioux had met in battle and were enemies. We are now quietly settled down, supporting our families by raising stock and planting crops. Our homes we love. Our lands are beautiful. The crops are ripening, and we will soon be gathering them in. We are not well armed, and have nearly forgotten the modes of war; but a mouse, though small, if trodden upon will turn and bite. Tell your chief if he comes we will give him battle, and die by our homes. This is my answer."

Agent — "What do you think of the murders just committed?"

Michel — "I think that perhaps White Bird — the Nez Perces chief, whose voice is for war — has arranged with Sitting Bull and has sent out small murdering parties to come through Montana to the Lapwai reserve in Idaho, to murder as they go through this country and commit all sorts of crimes in Idaho, and incite the reservation Nez Perces to war, with a promise that Sitting Bull with his warriors will come and help them. This is only my opinion. Perhaps this band of marauders has broken away from White Bird without his consent."

Agent — "Do you not think it best, in order to be prepared, to send scouts on the two trails leading from the North through this reservation?"

Michel — "It is the only way to protect the country. Indians can scout on the trails north of here, and can give you and me information in time to head them off?"

Agent — "Will you send out scouts?"

Michel — "Yes; if they can have arms, ammunition, blankets and provisions and some hope of reward."

Agent — "Providing I can get you these things will you be willing to have white men go with them!"

Michel — "Yes; provided you choose the white men and half-breeds, and that the scouts will be under your and my own control and report to you, when you can easily report to the soldiers when signs are seen. Three lodges of my people are camped on the trail leading in by the Jocko, I will send them word to look out for Nez Perces and bring in news of what route they take. These people are fishing at the lake and are not well armed; they cannot fight, but they can bring us news. If regular scouts go they should be armed, because they cannot otherwise protect themselves if they get into a fight, which they would be apt to do, as the Nez Perces do not feel friendly because we would not join their cause last summer."

Very respectfully,
Peter Ronan,
U.S. Indian Agent.

Document 17

Tribal Chiefs Bargain for Railroad Right of Way Land August 31 – September 2, 1882

Source: U.S. President, "Message from the President of the United States, Transmitting a Letter from the Secretary of the Interior Respecting the Ratification of an Agreement with the Confederated Tribes of Flathead, Kootenay, and Upper Pend d'Oreilles Indians, for the Sale of a Portion of Their Reservation in Montana Territory," Senate Executive Document No. 44 (1883), 47th Congress, 2d Session, serial 2076, pages 8-18.

Editors' note: The transcript of the 1882 negotiations for the Northern Pacific Railroad right of way through the Flathead Reservation was a remarkable document of the astute and capable tribal leadership in the late nineteenth century. The tribal leaders held discussions before the actual council, so they could decide on strategy and present a united front to Joseph McCammon, the government negotiator. Their first preference was to have the railroad avoid the reservation entirely. When this object proved unattainable, they asked McCammon to extend the reservation north to the Canadian line. They pointed out that many of the government promises in the 1855 Hellgate Treaty had not been fulfilled and most of the annuities had not been received. McCammon's condescension was palpable, but he did agree to support the tribes' appeal for a northern extension of the reservation. This question became moot in 1883 when Senator G. G. Vest visited the reservation, because tribal leaders feared that the whites would manipulate any changes in the reservation boundaries against the interests of the Indians and withdrew the request. Chief Arlee asked for a million dollars for the right of way as a bargaining tactic. McCammon refused to consider that much money, but did agree to raise the payment to $16,000. Two hundred nineteen tribal members signed the agreement in 1882. At the negotiations, McCammon argued that the railroad was only getting the use of the land, not full ownership, however the agreement stated the tribes were selling all their interest in the right of way land. McCammon promised free rides for Indians on the railroad, but there was no mention of this in the agreement. The written agreement was vague, but the government did finally pay for the land in a cash per capita payment rather than annuities.

Council held by Hon. Joseph K. McCammon, Assistant Attorney-General, appointed by the Secretary of the Interior to negotiate an agreement with the Indians on the Flathead Reservation for right of way for the Northern Pacific Railroad through the reservation.

August 31, 1882 — 3 p.m.

Present: Arlee, Adolphe, Eneas, and Michelle, with headmen and Indians of the Flathead, Pend d'Oreilles, and Kootenais tribes.

Agent [Peter] Ronan said: Mr. McCammon is here from Washington, representing the United States Government, to meet the Indians in council; and it is desired to have them listen attentively. He is here with the voice of the Great Father, and brings his words to the Indians. I have no further words of introduction.

Commissioner McCammon. My friends of the Flathead, Pend d'Oreilles, Kootenais, and other tribes living on the Jocko Reservation: I have been sent by the Great Father at Washington a great many miles to see you and talk with you. He knows how well you have treated the white people these many years; that you have been peaceful and happy, and have taken care of yourselves; that you have always been his friends and the friends of his people. Knowing these things he does not wish to take from you your lands. He knows, however, that a railroad is to be built on the borders of your reservation. Twenty-seven years ago you and your fathers made a treaty with the whites. That treaty which you and the others made provided for a country here in which you and your fathers should live. In that treaty you and your fathers agreed "if necessary for the public convenience roads may be run through the said reservation." By another treaty, made the same year at the treaty grounds, near the mouth of the Judith River, in Nebraska, which treaty was signed by the Flathead Nation and other Indians, it was provided that "for the purpose of establishing traveling thoroughfares through the country, and better to enable the President to execute the provisions of this treaty, the aforesaid nations and tribes do hereby consent and agree that the United States may, within the countries respectively occupied and claimed by them, construct roads of every description, establish lines of telegraph," &c. The Great Father and the Great council in 1864 gave the Northern Pacific Railroad Company the right to build a railroad through this country. The railroad company now say to the Great Father, "We want to build a railroad through the Jocko Reservation a few miles." The Great Father says, "The Indians on the Jocko Reservation gave me consent, years ago, to have roads of every description built through their land." He understands that a wagon road has been built and used for some time. That is one kind of road. Another kind of road is a railroad. It is a better and quicker way of traveling. It is a kind of road that other Indians all over the country have allowed to be built. But the Great Father says that he thinks the Indians should be paid for the little land that will be used by the railroad. He says he thinks the railroad will be good for the Indians as well as for the whites. The building of the road may bring white men on the reservation in order to grade the road, lay ties, &c., but when the road is built, no white men will remain except at stations and there only so many as are necessary. I will now show you a map of your reservation (shows map). The railroad is to come up here from the Missoula, entering the reservation by the Jocko River, and then going along the Jocko and Pend d'Oreille Rivers to the west line of the reservation. Now, as all the lands on the reservation belong to the Indians the United States wants to pay, and thinks it right to pay, for 100 feet of road on each side of the track, for a distance of 53.26 miles on this narrow line; and also for five squares of ground alongside, to be used as stations, being about 130 acres in addition, fully described on the map. These stations are where cars will stop to take on passengers, Indians and others, and Indian wheat and grain, if you want it carried off to sell; and where goods will be sent or received. This will cover a very small part of the reservation — like a spider web or fly track across the reservation (illustrating). Your reservation contains about 3,000,000 acres; the railroad will occupy 1,500 acres, just about as much as an ordinary wagon road. Now the Great Father asks me to inquire of these Indians what will be a fair price for this small tract. He says you ought to be paid a fair, reasonable price, just as much as he would pay a white man, no more and no less. Where the railroad runs through the farms of Indians, those Indians will be paid for their fences, farms, houses, and crops, if interfered with, the money to be paid to each Indian, or to the agent to be used for them. I am appointed to find out how much this will damage each Indian farm. This refers only to houses, fences, crops, &c., that belong to individual Indians.

Michelle. You don't know how much individual Indians will get, do you?

Commissioner. No; that we will determine hereafter. I went last year to Fort Hall Reservation. The Indians there allowed a road to be built, and no white men have come on the reservation because of the road. That is on the same plan as this. Hundreds of miles of road are built through the Indian Territory, and yet white men are kept out, except the agents of the railroads. The Northern Pacific Railroad has stopped at the line of your reservation, and wishing well to the Indians, does not want to interfere with them, except by some arrangement so that the Indians may be paid. So the Great Father sends me to ask you what you want to be paid for this land which the railroad company needs. I want you to consider this matter and ask questions. I don't want any one to misunderstand. I want to be just to the Indians. I want to protect their rights. I want them to talk. I am ready to hear from Arlee, Michelle, Adolphe, Eneas, or the headmen who know what they want to say.

Eneas. I presume you will not ask us to answer now. There are some men here who have wild ideas, and we want to adjourn and talk the matter over.

Michelle. We don't want to detain you for a lot of humbug. Of course you and the Great Father claim that we ought to be paid for the land taken; we are not to be cheated; we are to be treated just the same as whites.

Commissioner. The Crows last year sold land to this company just the same as you are asked to do. Whatever time you wish will be granted.

Arlee. I am going to talk not about what you are talking about. The Great Chief don't pity me. I am crowded on both sides. White men go up and down the reservation with cattle. I lose cattle in plenty. I want you to get the whites off the land at the head of Flathead Lake. I am old. I will soon die. There are a lot of young ones. I would like to have them live happy. But they will always be in trouble with the white men if they remain so near us. It may be true that the railroad would help the Indians, but I would like to get the whites off the Flathead Lake.

Commissioner. Cattle are driven through the reservation because the treaty provided for it. White men who steal are bad men. There are bad white men and bad Indians. White men punish bad white men when they can find them. Fewer cattle will go through the reservation after the building of the railroad, for then many cattle will go through on cars. I will report your wishes to the Great Father. The Great Father did not know them.

Arlee. The country we gave to the government is very valuable. Lots of white men have made independent fortunes in my country. Since twenty-seven years ago, when my forefathers made the treaty and gave you the country east and south of this, you have been digging gold there; that country is very valuable. You must not think there are so few here. Lots of others think of coming over here and living on this reservation. Be sure to tell the Great Father my wishes.

Michelle. I and Eneas think as does Arlee.

Commissioner. Tell him I (not the Great Father) think if they want that country up north they should have it. I will tell the Great Father. They got the price they asked for their land; they sold it to the white man. Gold was not yet discovered there. They yet have fine lands, noble rivers, and majestic mountains.

Ronan. In my talks I feel as if I knew what Arlee wished to say. On the north side of the Flathead reservation there is a narrow tract of United States land. Arlee fears that strip will be settled by whites, and Arlee feels if the Great Father will let the Indians have that then they will not be surrounded by whites.

September 1, 1882 — 1.40 p.m.

Commissioner McCammon. My friends, I am glad to see you to-day, and hope your hearts are good towards the Great Father. I will be pleased to hear what the chiefs have to say. If there is anything they don't understand in the talk of yesterday I will try to make it clear. I am ready to hear from them now.

Eneas. I am the chief and you see me now. I have not [sic] doubt you are sent to see us by the Great Father. I am the chief and this is my country. I am not joking in telling you I would like to get the Flathead Lake country back. There are things that the government promised me in that treaty that I have never seen. The government promised me everything we needed. The government told me it would send a blacksmith, and build school-houses, and furnish teachers at the agencies to instruct Indians, and a head farmer, and build houses for us. The government wished us to be like white men, and these were to instruct us. It promised me a tinner, a wagon-maker, a plow-maker, a hospital, and a doctor to look after the sick; and that is the reason we signed the treaty. I was glad to think we were to have these things. We had a big country, and under those conditions we signed the treaty. Seven years after that we learned that the line of the reservation ran across the middle of Flathead Lake. We didn't know that when we signed the treaty. That is the reason we want that country back. Besides, we did not get one-half of the annuities that belonged to us. It was divided among yourselves. You told us that after a while we would be intelligent and rich and like white men. We are poor now. We try to have whites to assist us, and they won't because we are Indians. That is the reason we want to have the whites kept out of that Flathead Lake country.

Commissioner. I am glad to hear Eneas. I know what a good man he is. Major Ronan has told me what wrong has been done years ago; he can now trust Major Ronan; what he gets he gives the Indians. One reason why the Great Father forgot the Flatheads is that they have been so far from Washington; but now when the railroad is built they will be within four or five days from Washington; and the Great Father and his people will see and pity the Indians. That is one thing the Great Father means when he says the Indians will be benefited by the railroad. I will tell the Great Father about Eneas's desires, and do all I can to carry out his wishes.

Arlee. What is the reason you are not able to treat with the Indians about that country? You have full power.

Commissioner. Arlee is mistaken; I have not power to treat about everything. As I said yesterday, the Great Father did not know what your wishes were about that strip of land. He only knew about the railroad, and he told me to agree to pay for the land to be used by the railroad. The land is not taken by the railroad, but is taken by the Great Father, who lets the railroad use it. Possibly you will understand my power by an example. You are a chief of your tribe; you send one of your young men to fish, but he goes off to visit his friends miles away; you are waiting for your fish all the time; the young man had no right to visit his friends until he got his fish. So I have no right to do more than the Great Father told me, but must return to him. Do you understand?

Arlee. I understand.

Commissioner. That is my position.

Arlee. Is it true the Great Father don't know of the men north of the Flathead Lake?

Commissioner. The country there belongs to the Great Father, so whites have a right to go there; but I will tell the Great Father all you say. It is all written down.

Arlee. We will now quit talking about the head of Flathead Lake.

Commissioner. Now, I will be glad to hear about the money to be paid for the use of the land for the railroad.

Eneas. You know what I said, that the government did not give half it agreed about annuities; and I think I don't wish the road to pass through this reservation. The Great Father is a good man, and when the Great Father tells me a thing I do it. I wish the Great Father to do me a favor and consult my wishes, and not let the road go through this reservation. There is a good way down the Missouri [i.e., Missoula] to Horse Prairie. You are a great people, and when you want to do a thing you can do it. What makes you think the railroad can't go down there? This reservation is a small country, and yet you want five depots upon it. These are the best spots on the reservation. What is the reason I should be encouraged when you take the best part of my country? My country was like a flower and I gave you its best part. What I gave I don't look for back, and I never have asked for it back. The Great Father gave it to us for three tribes, Flathead, Upper Pend d'Oreilles, and Kootenais. What are we going to do when you build the road? We have no place to go. That is why it is my wish that you should go down the Missoula River. I am not telling you that you are mean, but this is a small country, and we are hanging on to it like a child on to a piece of candy.

Commissioner. The line selected by the railroad company was selected ten years ago, because it was the best route, and because down the Missoula River would not be a good route. The men who selected it then and continued to prefer it are able men, and know the best route; and they say this is the only route that is good. The Great Father believes these men, and he sent me to represent him, not them, in this council. He thinks it is the best route, and the Indians won't be injured, the amount of land to be taken is so small. The Great

Father has respect for the wishes of the Indians, but he thinks he knows what is best for them, and feeling that way he wants to know what money they want for the land. The Great Father will take care that bad white men do not sell whisky to Indians. He thinks he can do that better with a railroad through your reservation than with one down the Missoula. He wants it here. He says, "You have told me I can build roads through your reservation"; but he also says you shall be paid, he having pity on you. The Indians should remember that they got no pay for the wagon road built through their reservation, but he thinks they should be paid for the land used by the railroad. The amount of land that will be taken by the government is very small. Only a few pieces of land owned and improved by Indians will be taken. There is plenty of good land in this and other valleys and reservations, and all that have to move will be paid; they will have the money to pay them for moving, or to do what they please with. I am now talking about improvements. The land belongs to all the Indians, but the improvements to individuals. All the Indians will be paid by the Great Council at Washington for all the land taken, when an appropriation is made, and this money will be used for the benefit of all the Indians; but the money for the fences, houses, and other improvements will be paid to the individual Indians whose improvements are taken. The Great Father has this matter much at heart.

Eneas. Who established the lines of this reservation? It was the Great Father that got these lines established. Why does he want to break the lines? If we had no lines I would say no word. Lines are just like a fence. He told us so. No white man is allowed to live and work on the reservation. You know it is so in the treaty. That is the reason I say you had better go the other way. Why do you wish us to go away? It is a small country; it is valuable to us; we support ourselves by it; there is no end to these lands supporting us; they will do it for generations. If you say you will give us money for our lands, I doubt if we get it, because we didn't before.

Commissioner. Eneas and the rest do not understand what I said yesterday. The two treaties signed by your chiefs provide for roads of all kinds through your reservation. The Great Father is not asking for leave to build roads through your reservation; that was given twenty-seven years ago. The Great Father is not treated with great respect when I am told you will not get the money. The matter will be submitted to the Great Council, and the Indians will get the money; and whatever has been done in the past about these matters, you can rely upon the good faith of those who now have control of the government. I do not understand why this opposition comes, when the Indians gave their faith years ago to the Great Father that this road might be built. I am sorry to hear what has been said. I come here as an honest man to talk to honest men, and I want you to consider well the words of the Great Father.

(An Indian in the audience says, "Railroads are not mentioned.")

The commissioner read from the treaties of July and October, 1855, about roads, and continued: You can read it in the paper Arlee has. As I have told you, railroads run through nearly all the reservations in the country. There are a few they do not run through; but where they go Indians see less of whites than they did before, because the whites traveled by railroads. This very railroad runs through the Crow Reservation on the Yellowstone. A railroad runs through the country of the Shoshones in Idaho, and this same railroad through the Umatilla Reservation. None of these Indians object to it. They are wise Indians; they have received their money. The Crows and the Bannocks and the Shoshones have received theirs. The Great Father expends the money for the benefit of those Indians. The Great Father will be sorry when he hears that Indians do not believe in his good faith. Shall I go back and say to the Great Father that these Indians do not believe he is treating them right? He has but one object, and that is your good; and if I go back without your having named a price for the lands, he will say they are not the good Indians and faithful friends I thought.

Michelle. I am going to speak to Indians and no word to white men. I told the agent it was useless for us to oppose giving the white men this strip of land. We don't know the plans of the white man; there is no use of us thinking. Just now he has something to compel. You spoke yesterday of the land at the head of Flathead Lake. I agree with you. That is my wish. You were here yesterday. No word he mentioned was bad. I think it was all good. When you get a gentle horse if you beat him he is bound to get mean; and you are to blame when you beat a dumb brute. He spoke to us gentlemanly; he used no hard words; and we ought to be glad. We are all Americans. The British line is north, and beyond that are the British Indians. If the President thinks it best for a railroad to run through this land, I am quite willing. It is true this country has been reserved for us. When [James] Garfield came here he told us this was our country; our agent and another big chief from Washington told us the same. Our agent is acting friendly with us. I do not think this gentleman has said a wrong word to us yesterday or to-day. He only wants a little strip of land; he might take it without asking, but he is going to ask us first, and then leave it to the chiefs. It is a thing that is bound to go through anyhow; and so you must not blame your chiefs.

Commissioner. The whole country is not taken from you; just a little narrow strip is used for railroads; you can use it, except the narrow strip for a track and depot grounds. I remember last year, the Great Father, General Garfield, sent me to the Bannocks and Shoshones on this business. You all knew that great and good man, and he knew you and loved the Indians. I have heard that he thought much of you. What he said to me last year about the Shoshones and Bannocks, the Great Father said of you this year. Consider well his words and be men. I want to ask Arlee and Michelle if the wagon road has taken the country from them? If not, then a railroad will not. It is only a road with rail ties and locomotives to go through.

Arlee. We don't think anything bad, but we don't want the railroad to go through the reservation here, because these white men are bad people. At Camas Prairie they sell whisky; they go there and get whisky, and our boys bother us about whisky. This is why we don't want the railroad to go through our reservation, because when the white men come in to work there will be trouble; that is all.

Commissioner. About the man who sold liquor, we had him arrested and taken to jail. The same thing will be done by your agent; when he finds white men selling liquor he will arrest them. While the road is being built white men will have to come and build it; but after it is built there will be no white men to sell liquor. On the Crow and Shoshone reservations no liquor was sold to Indians while the road was being built. It won't be as bad as Arlee thinks; I hope not bad at all for the Indians. No liquor will be sold on the reservation at the depots.

Arlee. It was our old people that were good; we had good chiefs; I don't know how many years it is since the white people came, and we have never had fights between us and the whites; nor have we ever killed you at all; and that is why I want to remain in my country quiet and undisturbed. I hear every few days that other tribes of Indians are fighting with the whites; then you win their country. You did not win my country from me at all; the big chief made our lines and told us to stay here all the time, and a few years ago Garfield sent me here to stay. But you don't mind what he said at all. Garfield said, "Take it easy, don't be uneasy." It was nine years ago that Garfield said "Don't think we will thrust you from that country; that land belongs to you." Last winter I was at home lying down, when they told me men were surveying the place. Some said it did not amount to anything, but I said it would cut our reservation in two; and now to-day I see you here trying to get our land from us for the railroad. But I do not want any railroad here, for this is my country.

Commissioner. This is your country; there is no doubt about that. The Great Father did not send me to ask for your country; he sent me to say he was going to build a railroad across your country, and he wanted to pay you for it. All this country is still yours and will remain yours. He wants you to feel good and remember his kindness. There is no intention to take the country away from you. A railroad is like the wagon road. The wagon road did not take your country from you and the railroad won't. How long has the wagon road been here? Your fathers were good men; they knew the treaty allowed a wagon road, and the same treaty will allow a railroad. The railroad will help you more than the wagon road. It will keep white people out of your reservation. You can ship grain and all other goods by it. I want you to let me go to Washington and tell the Great Father you believe in his word. I will tell him what faithful children you are, how kind, and full of peace and happiness you are. I will tell him of the great sight I saw yesterday; how well you treated me because he sent me. My heart was glad, and I said the Indians will listen to what the Great Father has to say and obey his words. I will again ask you if you can name what money you want for this right of way. If you cannot, I will name a sum for you. When the railroad is built, the Great Father will probably come out himself to see his country and you. It is too far from the railroad now.

Adolphe. It is true that you only want a small strip of my country; it is true that there will be no white men in our country. All will be glad if you only take a small strip of our country. Look at my hand (uplifted); this is what they do in Washington. I lift my hand; the President does the same thing. It is true that what you say is in the treaty in regards to roads. In the treaty at Hell Gate in 1855 the Indians said the white men could have railroads through here. Governor [Isaac] Stevens said to Victor, "You are the head chief of three tribes here, and of the whites here too"; and they said we will talk about this land here by and by; and we are having that talk now. Some time ago I did not know about talking, nor what it was to sign my name; now I know. If the whites are good I am good. When there is blood on my hands, they are not wet with white people's blood. If what you have told me to-day is true, I will be glad. In this country you see no blood; other countries are stained with blood. The line of my country extends from earth up to heaven.

Commissioner. I want to talk again about this road going through your reservation. I want to explain to you that the Great Father sells land near and adjoining your reservation for $2.50 per acre. The railroad sells its land for $2.50 per acre near your reservation. It has land down towards the Missoula. I wish to be liberal. The Great Father told me to propose a fair price, and I think that $10 per acre is a fair price for the 1,500 acres. That is four times as much as the Great Father gets for his land. This would make altogether for the land $15,000. The Crows got only about five thousand, and the Shoshones seven thousand, or nearly eight. In addition, each Indians will be paid for his fences and barns where this railroad interferes with him. The $15,000 will be for the benefit of the whole tribe.

Arlee. I object to depots.

Commissioner. Arlee never having seen railroads, don't know the amount of land required. Here is a glass with a few drops of water in it (illustrating). The whole tumbler represents the reservation, the water the amount of land wanted for the rail- railroad [sic]. The railroad wanted six stations; the Great Father said five would be enough. They wanted these for water for the engines. The railroad wanted a strip 400 feet wide; the Great Father said, "No 200"; the railroad wanted larger and more stations; the Great Father said, "No, five stations, and these must be small ones." The Great Father was thinking of the wishes and the interest of the Indians. . . . .The railroad down below is not done. The Indian don't know, but the Great Father knows and the engineers know how much is required. The railroad don't want the Indian lands, nor does the Great Father, but he cares for your interests.

(After a delay.)

Commissioner. Have you anything to say?

Arlee. I want to know about the depots; what are they?

Commissioner. Every railroad in this country has stations once in 10 miles for water, at the side of the track. If the railroad at Spokane has not stations every 10 miles it is because it is not yet finished. I have here the law of the great council, and it says the right of way through the lands of the United States is given for 100 feet each side, and station for depots, &c., every 10 miles of its road. Let any young Indian read it if you want to hear it.

Arlee. It is so.

Commissioner. These stations are to accommodate you. We are not trifling with you. Arlee ought to be satisfied.

Arlee. I want $1,000,000 for it.

Commissioner. The whole reservation would not be worth that.

Arlee. I thought you were here to help us.

Commissioner. I am. I represent the Great Father, as well as the Indians. I offer for the land four times what the government sells its land near here for — $2.50 per acre. And $10 would be eight times what the government usually sells its land for. Michelle, Eneas, and Arlee, are you ready to come to agreement with the government.

Eneas. There is one thing I don't understand. How big are these stations?

Commissioner. Eight hundred yards long and ninety yards wide, for small ones; and all others about four times as large, right along the road (shows a sketch and also a map). I hope Eneas' mind is happy and that he understands.

Eneas. I understand it now.

Commissioner. I will read to Michelle the agreement drawn by direction of the Great Father.

Michelle. When, I heard you the first time I was glad; but now when I hear what you offer, I do not feel so well, because now you say that all the reservation is not worth $1,000,000. Now I do not agree with you.

Commissioner. I am sorry if Michelle misunderstands me. I do not mean that the land is not worth $1,000,000 to the Indians, but that the same kind of land would bring no more among the whites. I only referred to that, as they all refused four times what was the selling price of such land among the whites.

Michelle. When a railroad runs through the railroad company will get the money back in one day. They will run through my ranch and take my timber to build it with. I would not take $15,000. I do not mean we will make trouble; I only say we will not take $15,000. If you want to go through, go; but we won't take $15,000. I don't speak now, any more, because you offer only $15,000.

Commissioner. Michelle should understand that what I offer is four times as much as the government sells the same kind of land for to white men. Don't let him say that $1,000,000 is a fair price; I say I offer what is reasonable. I do not represent the railroad, nor have I anything to do with the railroad; I represent the Great Father.

Arlee. We have said.

Commissioner. We will not talk any more about the million dollars; the Great Father will not allow us to talk of that.

Arlee. All right; then go by the Missoula. If the railroad don't want to give the money, let it go by Frenchtown.

Commissioner. The Great Father says the railroad is to go here. The railroad, according to the agreement, does not pay the money to the Indians, the United States pays it.

Arlee. Why do you want to pass here? You have to make a big bend to come here; why not go by the Missoula? The treaty only talked about a trail, not about a railroad.

Commissioner. Why, Governor Stevens was here to survey this country for a line of railroad. There is no attempt to take the country from you. You know that we are not proposing to take the country from you at all, and yet you speak as if we were.

Arlee. Governor Stevens said in twenty years another treaty would end this.

Commissioner. Arlee is mistaken. Of course this treaty is in force. Governor Stevens may have said that he or others would come back in twenty years, but not that the treaty would expire in that time. Do you want me to return to the Great Father and tell him that the good Indians, whom he always thought his friends, refused to sell a little land for ten dollars per acre, when not even the bad Indians of the country have asked that for their lands?

Michelle. How would it be if you had a good horse and I offered you a price that you did not think was right; if I took the horse wouldn't you complain? When we made the treaty we did not say railroads could pass through our country, only common roads.

Commissioner. They said roads of every description. Suppose I were to give Michelle a loaf of bread every day, and then were to ask him to return me a very small slice, would he not be a very bad Indian if he did not give me the slice when I needed it? Especially if I had paid him the money for it? So the Great Father says, "You can have this country, but I want a small slice or strip for a road," and afterwards offers to pay for it.

Michelle. If you wanted a small piece of bread, I would say, "Here is a piece." If you say it is too small, I would say, "Take what you want."

Commissioner. Michelle does not understand; he never saw a million dollars; he don't know what it is. It is nearly seventy times $15,000. The Great Father could not afford to pay $10 an acre for the Indian lands in the United States. He could not afford to pay the price now offered you, and would not have offered this if these Indians had not always been friends and good. We are not trying to make a hard bargain; we want to be liberal to the Indians. That is all. Do you want me to go home and tell the Great Father, or do you want me stay till to-morrow?

Michelle. Do as you wish.

Commissioner. What do you wish?

Michelle. I do not understand. You know it is not done; the agreement is not made.

Commissioner. Then I will stay. Ask them to meet me earlier to-morrow.

September 2 — 1.30 p.m.

Commissioner McCammon. My friends, I am glad to see you; I hope you did not think I had unkind thoughts yesterday. I had none but kind thoughts in my mind. I desire to hear from you or to answer any questions you wish to ask. I talked long yesterday, but I wanted to make everything as plain as possible. I did not want any one to misunderstand what I said. I am sincerely your friend. I have had much to do with Indians, and I believe they all consider me their friend. The Great Father wishes to make a present to good Indians, and although the Indians had agreed, in the treaties of 1855, to let roads be built through this reservation without pay, he thought none the less they should be paid. The Great Father had the right to build the road without pay, but he thinks you should be paid; he thought you ought to receive some money from him as a present. I would like to hear from any of the chiefs what is in your minds this morning.

Arlee. I don't wish to change our calculations. When we heard that you were coming we made up our minds what to say to you. Yes, we are all good Indians, and we have a nice country, and I don't wish the Great Father should bother us by a big railroad through the reservation. When we heard of your coming we made up our minds what to say to you, and I said it to you yesterday. You seem to like your money, and we like our country; it is like our parents. I have the same feeling I had yesterday, and I am not the only one. I told you about the money, what we ask; and you said it was an exorbitant price. We do not wish to change our ideas; we told you yesterday about our wishes.

Commissioner. In the treaty of 1855, made by Governor Stevens, the Indian tribes now represented here sold to the Great Father the country which was then claimed by them. That country was great; it extended from the British line to Big Hole River, and was very broad east and west. The Indians were then satisfied with the treaty, and have never been dissatisfied since. The money paid to your tribes was the sum of $120,000. That was only about one-ninth of what you now claim for a little strip of country through your reservation. You ask about nine times more for this little strip than what you received for all that vast amount of land. So you see you are mistaken as to the value of this little strip of country. I want you to think of this; that the $15,000 I offered yesterday is very much more per acre than the money you received under the treaty of 1855. As I have been fair and reasonable, I have a right to ask that you should be, and that you should trust me. I am afraid some bad white men have been misleading you about the price. No man is your friend who tells you that you should receive $1,000,000 from the government.

Arlee. We are not any way dissatisfied or hostile towards you or the government. We only want a fair bargain; fair play on both sides. My forefathers, our chiefs, the head chiefs of the tribe, were like men with veils over their heads; they could not see at all; they were like blind men; and when Governor Stevens arrived and he began talking about this part of the country, they had no idea of their country; they were stupid. They signed the treaty. This reservation was offered by the man who made the treaty, and we are holding on to it. Our forefathers are all dead, and we are the chiefs nowadays, and are hanging on it.

Commissioner. You are quite right in holding on to your reservation. As your friend, I say hold on to it; it is your land. I would be willing to give you the land you want up north; but the little line that the railroad wants won't interfere with your land; it will give the Great Father a better chance to protect you. There are many white men in the East who look after your interest more than you do yourselves; they would not allow a wrong to be done to you; they would, I know, approve of what I have told you. If I have not told you what the little strip is worth, I would not dare to go back among those people. You can ask any of your friends here and they will tell you that those white people know more about your wants than you do yourselves. Their hearts are always good towards you. These friends will watch me, and if I have not a good heart towards you they would blame me; but I know you think I have a good heart for you.

Arlee. Now won't you try to raise it a little more?

Commissioner. I will consider for a moment. (After a pause.) I will tell the Great Father I gave you $16,000. I will tell him that you are good Indians, as he knows, and I thought you were entitled to $16,000.

Adolphe. How many years will this $16,000 last? (They consult.)

Arlee. We want the money. The reason we did not get the money before was because we took it in annuities. We prefer the cash.

Commissioner. The Great Father knows more about you than they did years ago; and whatever wrong was done you then, will not be repeated now. This very railroad will bring the Great Father nearer to you. The money will be expended for the benefit of the Indians in the manner the Great Father thinks best. If he thinks, after hearing from you, that it is better to let you have the money, he will pay the money. You must depend on his judgment as to how the money will be paid. The Great Father will never forget you. He gives you money from year to year; he has many whites and many Indians to look after, and he gives you what he can. Something has been said about your timber; no timber will be cut from your lands, except on the right of way through. Your forests will remain, except as they cut trees out in building a road. They may have to cut so the trees won't fall on the road; that is all the trees that will be cut.

Arlee. Yes, that is so. The timber is my property, and we demand some money for my property. There is timber cut on the reservation. I am sure you don't know; it is off the road entirely; it is on the creek near Pig Pen. I went up there and saw it.

Commissioner. The white men had no right to cut it, and they will be very careful not to repeat it.

Arlee. Yes, this council don't amount to much, because cunning white men cut it on the sly.

Commissioner. But the railroad cannot afford to allow white men to cut timber on your land.

Arlee. I am sure I saw it with my own eyes.

Commissioner. It may have been a mistake. The railroad people have been very careful in not coming on the reservation.

Arlee. It is tie timber.

Commissioner. Arlee should remember that there may have been a mistake as to the line, and if within the reservation they did not cut the timber intentionally. We will have that line surveyed, and see if timber has been cut inside of the reservation.

Arlee. It came to my mind and I wanted it explained.

Commissioner. I introduced the matter of timber to you because I do not wish any misunderstanding about it.

Arlee. Yes, that is right.

Commissioner. Arlee and the rest are wise to protect their people.

Arlee. I am glad for one thing to-day. I am happy about that strip of country north. Do you think we will get it back?

Commissioner. I hope so.

Arlee. I am your friend. I hold your hand a long time.

Michelle. Now, my friend, I am glad about this strip of country north. We want that strip of country. I don't wish to be bothered by men on the other side. I want a road clear to the line where the other Kootenais are. If we get it we want to get the few settlers away who are there. We have lost many cattle in the reservation by men going up and down and driving them away; and these Indians are glad when when [sic] you said you would increase the land. The railroad line goes right through my land; I am not uneasy about it; I am glad I am going to get money for it.

Commissioner. I will report to the Great Father what you say about the strip of country north.

Michelle. It won't take long, and you have got a telegraph.

Commissioner. The Great Father; is not now in Washington, and it will take longer than you think. I shall have to go back and explain to him by word of mouth, the same as I do to you here.

Michelle. I had five head of horses on the road lately, and the whites stole them. I am afoot now. I am very happy to-day. At first you said you would increase our land, but now you say you will report to the Great Father. I don't quite understand.

Commissioner. I said I was willing, but it is the Great Father's land, and if he thinks best he will give it to you. As to the strip north, the Great Father did not know what was in your minds, but when he does he will do what is best for you.

Michele. The way we understood it in 1855 was that the land north belonged to us, but the man who ran the line got lazy and did not go north far enough.

Commissioner. I now ask the interpreter to read the agreement to the Indians.

Michelle. I don't consider this a *bona fide* bargain; it is borrowing this strip of land.

Commissioner. It is the use of it.

Michelle. I don't want you, after you get away, to let the white people suppose you have bought the reservation, and let the white people squat on it. That is the way I think. It is like the railroad borrowing the strip of land.

Commissioner. It is just buying the use of the strip of land.

Michelle. When I buy a horse I pay for it. You told us the country was ours. I considered the matter, and let you have it for public travel on the road. You have told me there won't be any white men on the reservation; that is the way I consider the matter.

Commissioner. Michelle is quite right; he understands it. The railroad will only use the little strip, just like the wagon road. Michelle and the rest understand it perfectly. I suppose this by their approving what Michelle says.

Michelle. If you fulfill your promise I will be enjoying the reservation. Now, I understand you to say that when we go visiting we can jump on the railroad wagons and ride without paying expenses. I don't wish to pay a cent when I visit your country. Tell that to the Great Father.

Commissioner: Michelle is right; the Indians always ride without paying whenever they want to visit their friends or the white people; but the white people will not be allowed to go on the reservation. I will come every year or two, as often as I can, to see him, so he will see that my promises have been kept.

Michelle. I wish that you would come once in a while, so that I can complain of not being treated right by the white men. You say you are our friend and will come. I will be glad to see you. I want you to know my heart. I despise liquor, cards, a liar, and a thief. I don't want to see such people here. Tell that to the Great Father. A lot of Indians of this tribe are below; if they want to come here they can do so; and if other tribes want to stop here we will let them stop if they behave.

Commissioner. I promise for the Great Father and myself to help put gamblers and liquor sellers off the reservation, and all other bad men; and also to let such Indians as you want come on here and live. You must let the Great Father know when you want these Indians to come here.

Michelle. And I trust that the commanding officer over at the camp at Cold Springs will fix the bad white men and Indians. I am taken care of by white men, and my own Indian agent tells me Major [Wm. H.] Jordan will get after the bad whites and Indians. Of course if any of my Indians should spill blood, you can do with them as you please; I have nothing to say about it. Also I have nothing to say if you put in jail my drunken Indians. You need not ask my permission. Do the best you can to keep peace and the white men from our country. Try and keep the white men from selling whisky to my Indians. We are uneasy about whisky matters, for fear of getting into hostilities and losing our lands. I am glad to hear that the man on Camas Prairie is arrested, and I hope you will punish him severely. You saw how it was the day you came here.

Commissioner. Major Jordan, your agent, and the United States marshal will see that men who sell liquor to Indians are punished. They hate whisky; that is, they hate to have it sold to Indians, and they will do all in their power to prevent your young men from getting into trouble. You see what your agent did the other day in having that man on Camas Prairie put in prison. It is bad for Indians to drink whisky, but worse to sell it to them.

Michelle. My agent told me when that big gang of men came here from below, "I will be the man to watch and keep them from selling whisky to the Indians." I wish white men to come no nearer than Horse Prairie with liquor. My agent says we will be bothered while the road is being built, and I understand what he tells me. I wish you would do the best you can to keep bad men from doing damage. I suppose we will be bothered while the new road is being built, and I want Major Jordan to be ready any day to take my part. I will let the agent know first, and he will say to Major Jordan — and this big chief is listening.

Commissioner. Michelle understands it perfectly, and the rest.

Arlee. I don't want white men to bring stock here any more. There will be lots of people here when the railroad is finished. The officers can clear off white men.

Commissioner. While the road is being built some stock will be used by the white men. When an agent wants the commanding officer at Fort Missoula, he sends for him. I want you to understand that while the road is being built much stock will be here. If your agent wants troops he will send for them to protect you.

Afternoon Session, 3 p.m.

Commissioner. My friends, I am about through with our talk. From my heart I say you have done well. When you see me another year I hope you will say you have done well. You will not regret one thing that has been done. You have done the best that could be done for yourselves and for the white man. I will go down the river and put a value on the individual improvements on the ranches used by the railroads. I want you to ask Arlee, Adolphe, Eneas, Big Sam, Pattie, and all the rest, to come and sign this paper to-day, or go to the agency, so that all of their names will be on this paper. Then this will be the last time I will see my good friends of these tribes. To-morrow I will leave, and will go and see the Great Father, and will tell him all your wishes, particularly about your wanting that strip of land to the north. The Great Father wants to do the best for all his people, and he will listen to me and do what he thinks best about that and all other things. I am through.

Michelle. You told us you were going to have a fair understanding. You told us that you would be glad to have the amount of land increased. I was glad when you mentioned that; I jumped up from my chair and shook hands with you, and then you said it was not in your power, but you would mention it to the Great Father. It was that that made me let go of the million dollars. I don't quite understand why you say now you have no authority to treat for that strip, but will mention it to the Great Father. I would like to have a copy of the treaty, and have men who can read explain it to me.

Commissioner. Michelle is right; the land is not to be sold to the railroad company. He shall have a copy of the agreement. Michelle is mistaken if he thought I told him I had authority to treat now for the strip of land at the head of the lake. I said all along, yesterday and to-day, that I could only report to the Great Father what they wished, and he will likely send some one out here to see them about this land. I don't want to have Michelle make a mistake.

Arlee. I don't consider we are mistaken; that is the reason we jumped up and shook hands.

Commissioner. I explained it to Arlee, as I had done before. You must trust the Great Father, and trust that I will tell him. Now, I would like to go with the agent and see the farms. I would like to have you ask the agent whether I said I would treat about that north land to-day. I didn't understand Michelle's remark to be that he would sign this agreement on account of that strip of land. I said I would give you $16,000. I said we would stop talking about the north land.

Arlee. You were talking about that to Michelle. That money is a small sum. Donald says so. So far as I am concerned I agree with you. You said that personally you would be glad to have them have the land.

Commissioner. I told them from the first I had no authority to treat regarding that north land. I illustrated it to him yesterday when I spoke about his sending a man for fish.

Michelle. If we could get the strip of country north, we would not ask anything for the right of way.

Commissioner. I repeat what I before said, that I have no right to give the strip of land north; but I said I would tell the Great Father. Suppose Michelle, Arlee, and Eneas wanted to sell the reservation, and came to me for that purpose, you would say, "They have not consulted our people and have no right to sell our reservation." Unless they consult their people they could not bind them. That is what I said. I could not bind the Great Father until I told him about it. Your chiefs can do nothing without consulting their people. I can do nothing except by the orders of the Great Father. He has given me no orders about this strip.

Arlee. I knew you would not give that million of dollars. My people don't want the railroad through here, and that's why I asked a million dollars.

Commissioner. All I said is written down, and you can have a copy of what I said. I have told you the Great Father said the road was to be built, not for the benefit of the white man only, but also for the Indian.

Arlee. I don't know how the road would benefit the Indians.

Commissioner. That is because Arlee never saw a railroad. The Indians will be nearer the Great Father, and he will be better able to protect you. I told you also that if you followed the Great Father's wishes in this matter, he would do what was best for you and might give it to you.

Arlee. Yes, the only benefit I see is if you give us that strip of land north, when I die it will benefit my children. The papers you have do not say that we have sold the country.

Michelle. A great many have clear ideas; others are stupid, and cannot understand it; so we want a copy.

Commissioner. The white men think I have been very kind to the Indians, and have tried to explain everything as plainly as possible. The agent and commanding officer will say so. Agent Ronan and I will have to leave now. I want the men to sign the agreement.

Michelle. I am not bothering my head about the railroad going through my field. I know that is right. If we can get back that country north we don't care about the railroad going through; it may go through free. Don't have hard feelings toward us for saying this. We are all one. My skin is dark. We are one nation. The international line is far north, but we are under one flag. You treat me as one of your people, and I want to do the same. The agent told me himself that he had instructions to see that the Indians get their rights.

Commissioner. I will promise to use my influence to get that strip of land for you, and I want you in return to get signatures for this agreement. I feel kind to all the chiefs and to the rest of you. We all belong to one nation. We were all born in the United States.

Michelle. This reservation is only large enough for three depots.

Commissioner. The depots will be as small as possible. You will see what the railroad does. If you find reason to complain, your objections must be made to the Great Father. Everything possible will be done to make the Indians contented and happy. There will be only five stations, and if the Indians are good and sober, the railroad will probably employ them.

Michelle. That is all I have to say.

Adolphe. I am one of the Flatheads. I am going to speak to you. This and Bitter Root is my country. You told us once we should respect the Great Father, and I think you should respect what I have said; for this reason I have great faith in the Great Father and you, and therefore talk of this strip of land. I guess we will be happy on this reservation. Look at the blood the white man has spilled. Where is the blood we have spilled? Just for this I respect and honor the Great Father and you, for I know he is a good-hearted man. Our God is a good kind God. Our chiefs have been directed from above to treat your people well.

The council then adjourned.

Document 18

Senator G. G. Vest Negotiates with Flathead Reservation Chiefs September 5, 1883

Source: G. G. Vest and Martin Maginnis, "Report of the Subcommittee of the Special Committee of the United States Senate, Appointed to Visit the Indian Tribes in Northern Montana," part of Senate Report No. 283 (1884), 48th Congress, 1st Session, serial 2174, pages xxv-xxvii.

Editors' note: The transcript of these negotiations was especially important because it showed tribal leaders met ahead of time to present a united front when dealing with representatives from Washington, D.C. The chiefs decided to keep the current reservation boundaries and not risk any negative changes. The chiefs stated that they did not want the reservation allotted and opened to white settlers. Pend d'Oreille Chief Michelle made plain his views of the cattle industry on the reservation: "If I had good and plenty of land and a few cattle and a little money I would be glad. The reverse would not please me, because my children are cultivating the land more and so get money." The chiefs were satisfied with the St. Ignatius schools as long as the students were learning. Problems with the survey of the northern boundary of the reservation caused particular problems for Chief Eneas and the Kootenais.

Flathead Agency, Montana, *September* 5, 1883.

The Commission, having first had submitted to it a copy of a letter from Agent [Peter] Ronan to the Hon. Commissioner of Indian Affairs (a copy of which is hereto attached), more especially referring to Flathead Indians still resident in Bitter Root Valley, but also touching upon the desire of the Indians of this reservation to have their northern border extended to the British line, the better to enable them to welcome an immigration of friendly Indians, who, having been crowded out of their own homes, are anxious to settle here, held a council with the confederated tribes of Pend d'Oreilles, Kootenais and Flatheads, during which the following remarks, questions and answers were made:

Senator [G. G.] Vest, addressing the Indians, said: I desire, in the first place, to have you understand that this Commission is not sent to make a bargain for your lands; that the great white council from which we came does not want to take your lands away, or to do anything else which you do not wish done. We are sent here to find out your condition, and to learn what you want. Something was said during Mr. [Joseph] McCammon's visits about extending your reservation farther north, and we now desire to have your views on this subject. Your agent sent a writing to Washington making such a statement, and we now want to know whether you wish to exchange some land here for some farther north, or wish to keep the reservation as it is. Again, we understand that you have been somewhat troubled as to the payment of the money promised you for the railroad right of way; that you have had some apprehension that the money would not be given you. The reason of its nonpayment up to this time is that before the matter was quite settled the great white council finished its business for the year; such matters require to be attended to by it, and before the money was paid it adjourned. Since then the payment has been made, and the money will be paid over as soon as the council meets again; so you need have no uneasiness on that point. We also wish to talk with you about the Indians in the Bitter Root Valley. Do you wish them to come here? We are going over there, but do not wish to talk there until we get your opinions here. These are some of the matters about which we came to speak to you, and if you wish to counsel concerning them among yourselves, we can get your views by and by.

Michelle, chief of the Pend d'Oreilles, replied: It will not require much time to give you the answers to your questions, as we Indians have held a council together for the last two days; we have arrived at mutual conclusions, and what I am going to say is in the hearts of all the Indians. We never expect to move the lines of our reservation. Our children have been born here, and we like our country. The Great Father promised that we should always have it, and we depend on that promise. As to the Flatheads now living at Bitter Root, they are our people and our friends, and we will be glad if they come to live with us. These are our opinions on these two questions, and all that is necessary to be said.

Senator Vest. The replies on these points are plain. I understand them. Now let me know if you are satisfied as to the payment of the railroad money?

Michelle. Yes, we are satisfied. Before we were not. We have been looking for it. We did not know when it would come, but now, you having told us, makes us content.

Senator Vest. There is one other subject of which we desire to talk, and we wish an answer when you have had time to think it over. It is as to your each taking up 160 acres of land. We don't propose to decide this question at present, but only ask to have your views upon it, so as to be able to report them to the great council.

Michelle. It is with this as with the other questions. We don't require time to consult. That we have already done. We don't want to take up 160 acres each and sell the rest of our land. We want to keep the whole reservation, for there are plenty of Indians who wish to come and live with us, and we have told them they will be welcome.

Senator Vest. Don't you think it would be better to have more money and cattle and less land?

Michelle. If I had good and plenty of land and a few cattle and a little money I would be glad. The reverse would not please me, because my children are cultivating the land more and more and so get money.

Senator Vest. How are the Indians satisfied with the schools?

Michelle. Well when the treaty was first made we were told we would have a school-house, and I thought it would here at the agency, but it was placed at the mission.

Senator Vest. Do Indians like to send their children there?

Michelle. I don't know exactly, but I think the desire is stronger on the part of the fathers to get the children than on the part of the Indians to send them. When Governor [Isaac] Stevens made the treaty he said that no money would be required on account of the school, but now some of the people require to pay some money.

Senator Vest. The great council gives money for the school. This year it gives $8,000.

Michelle. I have heard so. That's why the fathers want all the children they can get.

Senator Vest. How much does any Indian have to pay for tuition?

Michelle. The Indians don't pay money, but work for their children. When we made the first treaty we were promised a school-house — where, we were not told, but some of the Indians would like it at the agency.

Senator Vest. Is the school-house not situated at about a central point?

Michelle. Yes; right in the center.

Governor [Schuyler] Crosby. We understand the children are happy. Is that so?

Michelle. Yes; because their fathers send the children to learn, and therefore they will be happy if they are taught to read and write.

Governor Crosby. The question was, are the children happy and contented?

Michelle. I don't know personally, having no children young enough to be at school.

Senator Vest. Well, you must have heard how they feel?

Michelle. No; I don't know; I never want to find out; the parents are satisfied.

Senator Vest. We wish now to hear anything that any other Indian may wish to say. Is there any of them desirous of expressing their views?

Michelle. What I have spoken is the voice and heart of all my children.

Baptise Shtil-Tah (a sub-chief of Pend d'Oreilles). What Michelle has said is what we all say.

(This was followed by unanimous "ughs" of approval from the Indians.)

Michelle. I already mentioned that we have for two days held a council, and that I came here to tell you the views we all hold; but now you wish to be told of other matters, and I wish to tell you of something I don't like. Liquor comes on the reservation — how, we don't know, but seeing you here to-day, I ask you to help me to stop that; to tell white people not to give any liquor at all to my people. Besides this my people gamble; the whites sell cards, and with them my people gamble off goods and horses, and the women and children are often to be found crying about their horses which have thus been lost by their relatives.

Senator Vest. We have already made many laws to stop these things, but we cannot even stop them among ourselves. We occasionally catch and punish the guilty parties. We have done the best we can, but bad white men will sometimes manage to break the law and evade punishment.

Michelle. I think white people are strong enough and smart enough to do what they please. Why don't they stop it?

Senator Vest. White men were never strong enough or smart enough to put a stop to gambling and drinking.

Major [Martin] Maginnis. How would you like to sell your ponies and buy cattle?

Michelle. That is what we are always doing, and that is the reason so many Indians here have cattle.

Agent [Peter] Ronan. In the course of my official duties I was directed to locate the northern boundary of this reservation, and, on proceeding to make an examination in connection therewith, found certain monuments and posts placed and marked in order to designate such boundary by Surveyor Thomas, sent for that purpose from the surveyor-general's office at Helena, in this Territory. Now, the Territory claims the line as surveyed by Thomas to be the correct boundary, while the Indians claim a line some four or five miles farther north, running through Medicine Lodge. The strip of land in dispute is generally unfit for settlement, there being only a small portion of it, sufficient perhaps for one or two occupants, suitable for pasture. This quantity, may not be inadequate to cause trouble, as the Indians have already removed one settler therefrom, and I desire Eneas (the chief of the Kootenais), whose home is in that vicinity, to express his views on that subject to the Commission.

Eneas (chief of the Kootenais). We don't know anything about the surveyor's line, or the authority under which he acted, but we do know the line as to which we made the treaty, and it is a well-defined natural boundary, marked by a ridge of hills.

Senator Vest. No one had a right to run any line unless sent from Washington and until such is done the boundary as described by Governor Stevens must be regarded as the proper one.

Michelle. There is only one thing more I have to mention. It is about the railroad. I like to see the cars, but they kill some cattle and horses, and this is done sometimes through carelessness. I wish to have good engineers employed so as to avoid this.

Governor Crosby. When any stock is killed have the owners immediately report to your agent, giving him all the particulars, and you will find there will be no trouble in obtaining a settlement.

Senator Vest. Before leaving let me say that we are very glad to see you doing so well. We will tell our people how well you are getting along.

Governor Crosby. Of the Indians of this reservation I have heard very good accounts, and throughout the Territory, in which he is very well known, your agent, Major Ronan, bears an excellent character. And I wish to impress upon you that, while so many dishonest people are dealing with Indians you ought to appreciate such a man and do as he tells you. I also wish to say to you that, as you have told the great chief here from Washington that you wish to retain your reservation, which is large, you ought to remain on your lands and not interfere with the lands of white men, who are prevented from intruding upon your reserve. Had those bad Indians, who came here and created some disturbance some days ago, been unable to cross white men's lands and so prevented from coming you and others would have escaped considerable annoyance.

With these remarks and an interchange of expressions of good will the council was dissolved.

Document 19

Disagreements Over the Number of Land Patents Available in Bitterroot February 12, 1885

Source: Peter Ronan, *"A Great Many of Us Have Good Farms": Agent Peter Ronan Reports on the Flathead Indian Reservation, Montana, 1877-1887*, ed. Robert J. Bigart (Pablo, Mont.: Salish Kootenai College Press, 2014), pages 303-306.

Editors' note: Charlo was not pleased when he returned to the Bitterroot Valley and found out that there were only half as many land patents available as he had been told in Washington, D.C. Charlo also continued to worry about the efforts of Missoula County to tax the Bitterroot Salish Indians.

United States Indian Service,
Flathead Agency,
February 12th, 1885.

Hon. Commissioner of Indian Affairs
Washington, D.C.
Sir,

I herewith have the honor of enclosing a petition sent to me by Charlos, Chief of Flathead Indians, now residing in the Bitter Root Valley. It will be seen that Charlos still retains the idea that he was promised one hundred and four patents for lands, instead of the number surveyed for his Indians, fifty one, which I Still hold. In a letter addressed to you bearing date March 12th, 1884, I had the honor of alluding to this matter as follows:

"At one of the meetings at the office of the Hon. Secretary of the Interior, I stated that it was my opinion that the fifty one patents in my possession, were all that has been issued, but information was then offered that there had been issued one hundred and three or four, and that if they were not all in my possession, some would be found in one of the Departments at Washington. The Indians naturally returned with the impression that this information was correct, and it will require considerable tact to eradicate the idea."

Again in my special report in regard to a Council held with Charlos and his band of Bitter Root Flatheads, bearing date March 27th, 1884, that Chief stated in the Council that he "had been told that there were 103 or 104 land patents issued, while I stated there were only 51, and that if he had sufficient money he would return to Washington, and ask the Hon. Secretary if his words were to be depended upon, I informed him that it was a private and unofficial gentleman (Captain John Mullin [Mullan]) who had made the statement, and that the necessary data, not being immediately at hand, neither the Hon. Secretary nor myself were then in a position to contradict it, but that I had advised that the matter be examined into, and that as a result, I had a letter with the Hon. Secretary's own signature, which was equivalent to his own spoken words, and that therein I was notified that 51 was the correct number. I then produced the letter which was read by a few of the tribe capable of So doing, having in addition my remarks sustained by the rest of the delegation which visited Washington."

The letter above alluded to bears date at the Office of the Secretary of the Interior March 1st, 1884.

In regard to the wishes of Charlos, as stated in his petition I will offer a few suggestions.

1st. As the Indians desire to accept the patents in my possession, a proper map of the Bitter Root Land District should be furnished, so as to be able to properly show the boundaries of the same, and if the original patentee is dead the next of Kin, or in case no heir survives, then the patent be transferred to any Indian, being the head of a family, whom a majority of the Indians of Charlos Band may select, with the consent of the Department or Agent whichever may be deemed most advisable.

2nd. Charlos is correct in stating that under the Garfield Agreement several Indians removed to this reservation, abandoning their right to the Bitter Root patents and have made permanent homes here, and the lands that have been granted to them in the Bitter Root Valley is [sic] now unoccupied and will still continue to be owned by them, they holding said land under patents containing a clause preventing them from alienation. It would in my opinion be well to transfer such lands to any Indian of Charlos' band who might select to live upon and cultivate the same.

3rd. In connection with Circular #133, dated Washington July 28th, 1884, published for the information and guidance of Indian Agents in relation to the appropriation of $1000.00 "to enable Indians to make selection of homesteads and the necessary proofs at the proper land office" without payment of fees or commissions on account of entries or proofs, I respectfully submit, that in as much as the Register and Receiver of the Land Office are located at Helena, 150 miles distant from the Bitter Root Valley, and the Indians desirous of entering homesteads as provided in said act of Congress are poor and unable to defray the expenses of such a long journey, it would be a matter not only of justice in aiding them to take advantage of its beneficient provisions, but of economy (as the Indians would look to the Government to defray such travelling expenses for the reasons stated) that such entries and proofs be made either before some attorney authorized by the Land Office to perform such duties at Stevensville, in the Bitter Root Valley, or before the Clerk of the U.S. Court at Missoula, and a sum sufficient to defray the actual expense thereof be placed to my credit in order to accomplish the same, and upon presentation of the proper vouchers the expenditure of said sum be allowed.

4th. While at the office of the Hon. Secretary of the Interior, last winter, in conference with Charlos Band, complaint was made by the Indians to the Hon. Secretary that each year they were annoyed by the County Commissioners, and other officers of Missoula County, who claimed that the Indians of the Bitter Root Valley were amenable to taxation, and that said tax would be levied and payment of same enforced. The Hon. Secretary stated emphatically to the Indians that they would not be forced to pay taxes, and I trust this matter will be carefully looked into that I may be advised how to proceed should the county officers attempt to force payment of taxes from Indians living in Bitter Root Valley.

In conclusion I would state thirteen families of Charlos' Band have already removed to the Agency in compliance with arrangements made by me, under instructions from the Hon. Secretary of the Interior, and that houses are now under course of construction for them, and I expect to have them comfortably settled and cultivating the soil of the Reservation this season, and that more families will continue to follow until a large majority, if not all of the tribe will finally settle here. But I would suggest that the petition of Charlos be acted upon so that the Indians will have nothing to complain of in the future, in regard to their rights to the lands of the Bitter Root Valley. It is my humble opinion that this course will have a tendency to show the Indians that they can place reliance upon the promises and good will of the Indian Department and its servants, and when their rights in the Bitter Root are secured, they will be prepared to dispose of the same as the Department may direct and remove to the Reservation.

Very respectfully
Your obt. svt.
Peter Ronan
U.S. Indian Agent.

Enclosure in handwriting of Jerome D'Aste, S.J.:

Stevensville, Feb. 7th, 85

Major P. Ronan
U.S. Indian Agent
Major

Last winter I and some of my Indians came back from Washington to Bitter-Root valley with our hearts gladdened thinking we had secured for our families and tribe a home, in this valley, having been promised by the Government one hundred Patents. But we have been Sadly disappointed when, after coming home we heard from you that only fifty one Patents were offered to our people. Waiting in vain for the fulfillment of the Government's promise, I refused until now to receive the Patents already issued for some of my people. I felt bad in thinking, that by receiving those Patents I would exclude a good many of my people from having land in this valley, and that for the only reason that they were not here to give their names as willing to remain here, at the time of Garfield's treaty, and thus secure a farm. But now that I see that not only we are refused what we have been promised, but that white people are trying to take from my people even the few farms we are in possession of in this land of our forefathers, I beg of you to protect us in our rights. Knowing that you have taken so much interest in the welfare of the Indians under your charge, I hope that you will be willing to make the Government acquainted with our needs and wishes.

1. I with my people came to the conclusion to accept the Patents issued so many years ago for some of us. But the lands so patented having been surveyed when most of the Indians were off on the Buffalo hunt, only a few Know where the lines of their respective farms are. Hence I ask that the Government appoint some trusty man to find out for us the lines of such lands, not leaving the whites to take advantage of our ignorance.

2. In the second place we ask, that since we see very little hope of getting the other Patents promised in Washington, last year, at least, the Patents issued for those Flat-Heads, who agreeably to Garfield's treaty, moved to the Jocko, be turned to some of our people who got no land, because they were not here to represent their lands at that time.

3. In the third place I ask that some of our people who for several years are farming on lands which were not surveyed for them, be by the Government protected against those greedy whites, who having come here only lately are trying to jump these lands, though the Indians are living and have improvements on them. There is a case in particular, on eight-mile creek, where a white man, P. Lafountain, pretends by force to take the land from an Indian who has been farming several years and has a house on it. I would ask that the Government

would send some trusty man to inquire into the matter, and if found that the Indians have the first right to those lands, that said lands be surveyed for the Indians and Patents issued to them.

4. In the fourth place, since I have been promised, in Washington that we would be exempted from paying taxes, we ask that the Government should look in this matter and see that we be not bothered by County Officers, as they began to do with some of our people.

Thanking you for the help you obtained for our people by getting them wagons, plows, harnesses and provisions, and hoping that you be willing and able to assist us in our present needs, I am with all my people in whose name I send this petition.

Yours Respectfully
Charlos Chief of the
Flat-Head Indians
His signature +

Document 20

Chiefs Meet with the Northwest Indian Commission April 21-29, 1887

Source: Excerpts from Jno. V. Wright, Henry W. Andrews, and Jared W. Daniels, "Report of Northwest Indian Commission," in "Reduction of Indian Reservations," House Executive Document No. 63 (1888), 50th Congress, 1st Session, serial 2557, pages 43-46, 69-74.

Editors' note: In the agreement signed at this meeting, the Salish, Upper Pend d'Oreille, and Kootenai Indians of the Flathead Reservation accepted the removal of the Lower Pend d'Oreille and Spokane Indians from Idaho and Washington to the reservation. Two sections of land on the reservation were to be "set apart" for the Jesuit fathers and the Sisters at the St. Ignatius Mission for "as long as they are used for said [educational] purposes and no longer." The last article of the agreement provided for a new saw and grist mill and blacksmith shop for the northern part of the reservation. Unfortunately, the agreement was never approved or funded by the U.S. Congress. The commission received a very impressive welcome at St. Ignatius Mission. In the transcript look beyond the condescension of the white negotiators at the concerns voiced by the chiefs. Chief Arlee was particularly upset about the government paid judges and policemen taking over the law and order powers of the traditional chiefs. The speeches by the Indian students were likely written by their teachers. The chiefs complained about the gambling cards and whiskey neighboring whites sold to tribal members. The railroad had promised free rides to Indians five years earlier when it obtained permission to go through the reserevation. Now the railroad had stopped giving free rides to Indians.

Report of Northwest Indian Commission.
Flathead or Jocko Reservation.

Having concluded our work with the Calespels, we left Sand Point, Idaho, on the 21st day of April [1887], and arrived at Arlee, a station on the Northern Pacific Railroad, on the night of that day. We found in waiting for us Mr. Thomas E. Adams, the clerk of the Flathead Agency, with a conveyance, and we proceeded immediately to the house of Maj. Peter Ronan, the agent for this agency.

On the morning of the following day Chief Arlee, of the Flathead tribe, paid us a friendly visit. The agency is situated near the south border of the reservation.

The Saint Ignatius Mission, 20 miles from the agency, was deemed, from its more central position, the best place for the Indian council.

It required time to give the different tribes notice of time and place of meeting, as some of them resided upwards of 90 miles from the agency.

The following Tuesday (April 26) was therefore agreed upon as the day of meeting, and messengers were dispatched to notify the various tribes.

Before leaving Sand Point we sent a dispatch to Agent Ronan, notifying him of our coming and of the day we had named for the council.

On Tuesday we were conveyed in private conveyances by Agent Ronan to the Mission, being accompanied by Clerk Adams, Dr. [John] Dade, agent [sic] physician, and the Government interpreter.

This gave us an opportunity to see a large part of the reservation, more especially that part occupied by the Flatheads, who mainly reside on this part of the reservation. The Pend d'Oreilles reside near the Mission, and the Kootenais still farther off near Lake Pend d'Oreille.

Saint Ignatius Mission is located in about the center of the Indian population of this reservation.

The Commissioners were driven through the Jocko Valley and along the foot-hills skirting the valley, which is traversed by fine irrigating ditches constructed for the use of the Bitter Root Flatheads of Charlos's band, who are now settled by Agent Ronan, and who occupy cozy houses, surrounded by well-fenced fields, which the Indians were engaged in planting and seeding.

An account of the trip by an eye-witness says: "Turning off from the line of the Northern Pacific Railroad at Ravalla Station, and while driving across the divide leading to the Mission, the party were met by a large band of armed Indians, headed by the Indian police, dressed in their bright uniforms. Upon meeting the Commissioners the Indians ranged themselves upon each side of the carriages and fired a salute, giving a wild whoop of welcome, regardless of the plunging and rearing of the excited horses attached to the carriages in which the gentlemen of the Commission were driven. Arranging themselves on each side of the carriages, alternately firing their guns and ringing out their fierce whoops, the carriages dashed over the hills, followed and preceded by the wild escort."

On arriving at the Mission the party were welcomed by loud strains of music, pealing out from twenty-three brass instruments, drums, fifes, and clarionets, the soul-inspiring notes of the Star-Spangled Banner, rendered in excellent style by as many Indian boys from the veranda of the college.

In the evening, while discussing their cigars, the Indian band, composed of boys whose ages range from 11 to 18 years, gathered under the windows and gave a serenade. After rendering several airs, such as Hail to the Chief, Bonnie Blue Flag, etc., Judge [Jno. V.] Wright stepped to the door and made the following remarks: "My young Indian friends, in behalf of my associates of the Northwest Indian Commission and other gentlemen present, I return thanks for the beautiful serenade we have just listened to with delight and astonishment. Your performance is indeed astonishing, and furnishes an evidence of the talent which the Great Creator has given you to acquire and master music with your other educational accomplishments. As the thrilling strains echo and vibrate this night under our windows, beneath the shadows of the grand old Rocky Mountains, it furnishes a good contrast to a few years ago, when these gorges, glens, and lonely valleys echoed only to the howl of the prowling wolf and other wild animals or the terror-striking war-whoops of your ancestors. What a deep and lasting debt of gratitude you owe to the pains-taking patience of the good Father and the kind protection of a liberal Government, who have made it possible for you to advance from savage barbarism to education and civilizing pursuits, and also to the mastery of music, the inspiring strains of which touch and thrill the hearts of your visitors of another race.

"Again, I thank you and bid you good night. May you all live to manhood and to old age, a pride to your race and a source of gratification and joy to the fathers of St. Ignatius Mission, to whose attention, teaching, and devotion you owe your present elevation and refinement of character and morals."

The Commission, by invitation, visited the various workshops and mills connected with the industrial system of the mission schools.

These consisted of a saw and grist mill, printing office, tin shop, shoe shop, museum, saddle and harness shop, carpenter shop, and blacksmith shop. Specimens of industry were exhibited which demonstrated the capacity and skill of the boys. Everything is conducted in an orderly and systematic manner. On the farms the boys are also taught and practiced in all the details of the cultivation of the soil.

We were entertained by recitations in the various studies at the boys' school. An Indian boy, aged fourteen years, read an address to the Commission as follows:

"Honorable Gentlemen of the Indian Commission:

"Allow me to thank you for your kind visit to St. Ignatius Mission, and to welcome you in the name of my companions to our school. We look upon you as the chosen representatives of our Great Father in Washington, who so kindly cares for the children of the Indians and spares no expense to educate us in the same manner in which white boys are educated. In honoring you we mean to honor our Great Father, and to show him our gratitude for the great benefits which we are receiving from his fatherly kindness.

"We have learned from our father superior how kindly you have spoken to all the Indians west of us, and especially how pleased you have shown yourselves to be with the progress of the Indian children of the Cœur d'Alene school.

"We hope that you will be pleased with us also. It will encourage us in our efforts to learn, and it will also be a source of gratification to our teachers. However, we are but poor and timid Indian children, not quite at home in the ways and manners of white boys, and we hope you will kindly overlook our shortcomings."

To this the chairman replied as follows:

"My Young Friends: Every friend of the Indian and every generous human heart would rejoice to see what we have seen since we came on this reservation. The degree of progress which is manifested here gives promise of a bright future for you and your race. In the name of the Commission I thank you for the address of welcome you have made us, and I can say without flattery that you compare well and favorably with other schools we have visited in our various travels. You are greatly favored indeed. I can assure you that I never attended a school, and I doubt if any white man present ever attended one, with better school facilities than this. Some of you no doubt dislike to be at school. This should not be so. All whom you see here had to go through the same process through which you are going. Continue on in the way you are now traveling and your course will be onward and upward. The great Government whose flag floats over your building is your friend. No pains will be spared to advance you. We promise you all the encouragement and aid in our power, and we will look forward to the day with pleasure when the Indians of the Jocko reserve will be an educated, industrious, and independent people."

After being shown through the girls' school, which was perfect in all its arrangements, and hearing the various classes recite, we were satisfied that nothing was wanting. A little Indian girl read to us the following address:

"Honored Sirs: We are rejoiced to see you in our midst and bid you a cordial welcome. We must sincerely thank you for the honor that you bestow upon us to-day by your presence and the interest you thus manifest in our regard. We are confident, honored sirs, that you wish to promote the welfare of the Indians. It is this and your great condescension in deigning to visit us that gave us the courage to present ourselves before you and show you the little we know. We are but little children of the mountains aiming to become one day useful and industrious. We can not be learned, but we wish to be good, to please those who take an interest in the cause of our education and to repay them for their kindness to us."

To which Judge Wright replied:

"We are well pleased with what we have seen and heard. You have most excellent advantages provided for you here and you show that you appreciate them. You should continue to do so. If you do your advancement is assured. Respect, love, and obey these good sisters who have devoted their talents to your service and you will grow up wise and virtuous women, an honor to your families, to your school, and to your race.

"We thank you for your kindness of welcome, and will be happy to do all we can to advance your prosperity and happiness."

We give these particulars more for the purpose of laying before you the actual situation of the Indians and the rapid progress they are making than for any other purpose. Each tribe of Indians should be dealt with according to its actual condition, and these we found so different that we have endeavored in this report to accompany a history of our negotiations with such facts and circumstances as may throw light on their present state and condition.

The council met in the evening of the 26th. The three tribes, Flatheads, Pend d'Oreilles, and Kootenais were fully represented. The large school room was filled to overflowing, and many women and children occupied seats on the stoops and verandas outside the council room and grouped around in the boys' playground.

All classes were represented, from the oldest to the youngest, from the well-clad, thrifty looking farmers in business suits to the wild followers of the chase, some in gaudy blankets with broad, beaded belts, others in gaily-trimmed buckskins with beaded leggings. It was, however, noticeable that the civilized dress largely predominated, both with males and females. Some had their dwellings around the mission and the agency, while others had come long distances to meet the Commission.

The dwellers around the Pend d'Oreille River and around Flathead Lake, the tillers of the soil from Hot Springs and Camas Prairie, the Indian cattle-kings from Crow Creek and the Muddy, lonely wigwams in narrow gorges, far-away glens by sparkling water-falls, and wild, remote spots outside of civilized intercourse had been notified of the coming of the Commission.

The object of the visit was made known and the duties and power of the Commission clearly stated. There was but little difficulty in obtaining the consent of the confederated tribes to the removal of the Calespels and such portion of the Spokanes as might desire it to their reservation. They also consented that any other non-reservation Indians might be removed to their reservation on such terms as might be agreed upon by the United States. This was done on account of reliable information received by the Commission as to a small band of Kootenais whom it appeared had received but little attention from the Government or its agents.

Our information with regard to these Indians was derived from Rev. Louis Jacquot, of De Smet Mission, Cœur d'Alerne [sic] Reservation. The Cœur d'Alenes in their agreement with us also gave their consent to the removal to their reservation of all non-reservation Indians in that part of the country. These Kootenai Indians live in northern Idaho, along and near the international line. They are called Lower Kootenais, or Flat Bows. A part of them are in the United States and a part in Canada (British Columbia). Those in the United States number about 200. Up to this time they have had no treaty relations with the Government and have received no aid. No agent has ever visited them officially. Their country is being slowly taken up by whites, and they are now confined along the bank of the Kootenay River. They are very destitute, having nothing to rely upon for a support but fish, berries, and game. The land on which they live, beginning at Bonner's Ferry, is one vast swamp, unfit for cultivation. At times it appears as one vast lake. He said they were very poor and miserable, and that they expressed their surprise and sorrow that no attention was paid them. The statement of the priest touching the condition of these poor people excited the sympathetic interest of the Commissioners, and it was determined to call the attention of the Department to it.

We have heretofore given an account of the schools and other facilities afforded the Indians on this reservation by those in charge of the Fathers and Sisters of St. Ignatius Mission. The Indians highly appreciate these advantages and manifested the most intense anxiety that they should be fostered and continued.

It was the earnest request of the Indians themselves that article II [providing two sections of land for the fathers and sisters for school use] was incorporated into the agreement. In addition to these, after a careful inspection of the buildings for schools and church purposes, the various mills, shops, barns, agricultural implements and products, together with the farms themselves, all of which has caused an expenditure of from seventy-five thousand to one hundred thousand dollars by the society in charge, we felt that it was nothing but absolute justice that this provision should be made. The Jocko Reservation of itself is a most desirable place for Indians, and, with St. Ignatius Mission and its appliances for educating and civilizing the Indians, it appears to be perfect. Without the advantages afforded by this mission in the past and in the present, it is certain that these Indians would be far from that promising condition in which they are now found.

The land covered by the agreement is already occupied with the various improvements of the society, with an occasional Indian settlement, which latter are fully protected by the last clause in the article.

The prospect of an early removal of other tribes to this reservation and the consequent necessity for houses, fences, and, together with the fact that a large portion of the tribes now on the reservation live at a great distance from the agency where the mill is located, and the earnest desire expressed by the Indians for the erection of another saw-mill, accounts for article 3. Our own observation and knowledge, together with the statement of the agent, satisfied us of the necessity for this provision.

A large number of bridges have to be kept up on this reservation in order to facilitate travel from one portion of it to another, and this was also a consideration making this provision necessary.

The Commissioners beg leave to express their obligations to Rev. Leopold Van Goop {Gorp], S.J., and his assistants at St. Ignatius Mission, for courtesies and valuable assistance. We are also under great obligations to Agent Ronan and his clerk, Thomas E. Adams, of the Flathead Agency, for their kindness and valuable services to us; Major Ronan, whose long experience as United States Indian agent, and his constant vigilance over the interests of the Government and welfare of the Indians in strict obedience to his instructions from the Commissioner of Indian Affairs, offered us every facility in his power. Having concluded negotiations at the Jocko Reservation, we took passage on the Northern Pacific Railroad for Duluth, Minn., the nearest point on the Northern Pacific to reach the Lake Superior band of Chippewa Indians, at Boise Forte and Grand Portage Reservation.

* * * * * * * * *

Council with Flatheads, etc., Flathead Reservation, Mont.

The Commissioners met the various bands of Kootenais, Pend d'Oreilles, and Flathead Indians at St. Ignatius Mission on Tuesday, the 26th day of April, 1887.

There were present the Commissioners, John V. Wright, J. W. Daniels, and Henry W. Andrews, the chiefs and head-men of the various tribes, and many other Indians.

The council was opened with prayer by Father Van Gorp, of the Mission.

Judge Wright, then spoke as follows:

"My friends, as Commissioners of the United States, we shake hands with the Flatheads, with the Pend d'Oreilles, and the Kootonais. We thank you for assembling so promptly on our call, and we thank you for the imposing and friendly greeting which you have us on yesterday. We have traveled over much of your beautiful reservation, and it has filled us with delight and admiration. Nowhere can there be seen a more beautiful reservation. Your vast and fertile plains, watered with clear and health-giving streams, skirted with grand mountains, impresses us with the belief that you are indeed blessed beyond most Indians. But what has pleased us more is to find you living in comfortable houses, surrounded by good farms, and all striving to make a support and bring yourselves and your families to independence. We visited your schools on yesterday; and there we saw your children well clothed and well provided for, and exhibiting such progress in learning that it makes our hearts glad, and gave us assurance that in a few years your children will be intelligent, moral, and self-supporting. It was our earnest desire to visit you at an earlier day, but business of great importance with other Indians in different States and Territories detained us so that we could not come until this time.

"You have a large reservation, and although you have many Indians on it, there is much more land than you and your children will use for many years to come. It is doubtless known to you that the white people have been coming this way for many years, and that they much desire to have your reservation opened to white settlement. It is not right that great bodies of land should be permitted to remain unoccupied and uncultivated. It is a part of the policy of the Government of the United States to reduce Indian reservations to proper size when they are out of all proportion to the number of Indians living on them. In order to avoid this trouble the Government desires, where it can be done, to settle Indian reservations with Indians, and open to settlement abandoned reservations. We have not come to open your reservation to white settlement. It is not a part of our instructions to do this, but it is a part of our business to get your consent to the settlement of some other Indians on this, your reservation.

"The Spokane Indians who reside around Spokane Falls, in the Territory of Washington, are poor, and otherwise in a bad condition. They are in the midst of the white people, and are exposed to many troubles. Many of them have no homes and no land. A part of our business was to induce them to remove from that place, and take homes on the Colville, Cœur d'Alene, or this reservation. We have recently come from Spokane Falls, stopping with the Calespels at Sand Point, in Idaho.

"A few of the Spokanes expressed a desire to remove to this Reservation, but the most of them prefer to go to the Cœur d'Alene Reservation. The Cœur d'Alenes, in the councils we held with them, gave their consent, and agreed, that not only the Spokanes but Calespels and other Indians might come and live on their reservation. The Calespels desire to come here, but before removing them it is our duty to get the consent of the tribes on this reservation. The Calespels or Pend d'Oreilles are you know are of the same blood of the Pend d'Oreilles here. They are very poor and have very poor lands. They are wild and have no advantages, no schools, no churches, no agent, and indeed nothing but the poor living they make by hunting and fishing. The Great Father has pity on them and he thinks you should also pity them and allow them to come and live with you. In the agreement which we made with the Spokanes and Calespels, we provided for giving them homes and houses, farming implements and provisions to give them a start. What we want is that you shall give a cheerful consent to this arrangement. It will do them great good and it will also do you good. It is plain that if your reservation were settled up with Indians the white people would quit asking for it, and even if they continued to ask they could not get it, as the Government is your friend and will spare no pains to protect you and advance you in your pathway to civilization.

"There is another thing I wish to say to you. Some of your chiefs have told us that you are much in need of a saw and grist mill on this side of the mountain, which lies between here and the agency. We know it is a long way from many of you to the mill, too far to be of service to you. We therefore propose, if you so desire, to agree that a saw and grist mill shall be built and a miller and blacksmith furnished so as to accommodate those who live on this side.

"Some of you have also told us that you desire to make provision for your schools and the farms and buildings attached to them. This we will also do if you desire it. If you wish that the fathers who have built the houses and opened the farms may continue to use them for these purposes, we will put in the agreement according to your wishes if they are reasonable. I have now explained as well as I can the nature of our business, and we would be glad to hear what you have to say about it."

The three leading chiefs, Arlee, of the Flatheads, Michael, of the Pend d'Oreilles, and Aeneas, of the Kootenais, after a moment's consultation, replied.

Chief Arlee said:

"The land belongs to me. I am Arlee, chief of all the Flatheads. We are glad to see you here. We expected you last fall but you did not come. We heard that you passed by on your way west. You have now returned and we are glad. We have much to talk about to you, about our country and the railroads, and about our judges. We wish to talk about many things. I was in Washington. I shook hands with the Great Father. I will tell you all. We will meet again to-morrow. What you have said is all good. We are glad you have come."

Chief Michael said:

"We heard you were coming many months ago, and then we heard you had gone by us and we were afraid you were not coming. We are glad to meet the Great Father's Commissioners. You come as friends. We have heard what you say and we understand all. My people will all agree to what you say. We wish to do what our Great Father wants. We will throw no brush in his way. We have pity on the Calespels. They are my kinsmen. We say yes; let them come. We say the same to the Spokanes. We are willing to give them homes on our lands. We wish the land lent to the fathers. They have led us on the good path. They teach our children and make them good. We will not sell our land, but we will lend it to the fathers for schools and churches."

Chief Aeneas expressed similar views for his people.

Judge Wright. Shall we proceed now?

The Chiefs. No; we will council together to-night and meet you again to-morrow.

The council then adjourned.

Friday, *April* 29.

Council met as per agreement; prayer by Father Van Gorp.

Judge Wright. We have prepared an agreement in accordance with what was said on yesterday, which will now be read to you and fully explained.

Commissioner Andrews here read the agreement, at which the closest attention was given as requested by the Commissioners, and each article plainly and fully interpreted to the Indians.

Chief Arlee. We don't wish the land sold to the fathers.

Chief Michael. We did not understand yesterday that the land was to be sold to the fathers.

Judge Wright. The agreement does not say that the land is sold. You only agree that the land and houses may be used by the fathers as long as they use it for school and church purposes, and no longer.

Chief Michael. Now we understand you, we are all willing to lend our land to the fathers.

Chief Arlee. We are willing to lend the land; this is all right. We are satisfied with it. I now have something to say. I want to make some complaints. My people do some hunting; there is game on our reservation and my people hunt and kill deer and other game; we want ammunition. Why is it that our Great Father will not allow us to buy powder, shot, and cartridges? We are peaceable, and we will do no harm; we will do only good; we will not shoot the Indian nor the white man; we want to know why our Great Gather [sic] will not let us have cartridges. Is it that he is afraid we will kill his people?

Another thing. The white men make cards and they make whisky. They gamble with the cards and drink the whisky. If whisky and cards are bad, why don't the white people quit making them? They tell us they are bad. Why do they make them and use them? If these things are good and not bad, why will not the white man allow the Indians to have them? I wish you to tell me this. I want to say more. I wish to say another thing about the railroad. When the Great Father sent a commission to ask my people to allow the railroad to be built on my land, he told them if they would allow the railroad to pass through he would let me people ride free without paying money for it. Now he has got the railroad and he won't let us ride. The cars run over my cattle and my horses and they will not pay me for them. I want the pay. Where is the money? We can not get it. They run the cars over my people and kill them. I want the railroad taken off my land. I want it moved away over the land of the whites, I don't want it on my lands. I tell my people not to hurt the road, nor to tear it up. You need not be afraid, we will not trouble the road. I want it taken off my land.

I do not want white men to come on my land and cut the trees and dig up the minerals. We do not wish them to do this. We want them kept off. Some of them bring their cattle on my land and eat up the grass. We don't want this. We want the grass for our own cattle. We want our reservation marked all around so that white men will not come on it. We do not want the judges and the policeman. They do not act right. They do wrong. We want the head-men of the judges to decide the cases. We don't want all three to decide. The head-man ought to decide. How is it when one judge is one way and two the other? I want you to answer this question. We don't want any judges or policemen. We want the chiefs to rule the people. Is it right for the judges to have sick men whipped? And women? They have whipped sick men and they had a woman whipped who was pregnant. She told them she was in that way, but still they had her whipped. And she had an abortion. Do you think that was right? When the judges decide a case does anybody else have anything to do about it? Can there be any appeal? They say they have made laws. We don't want their laws. Let the chiefs make the laws for the people. This is the way Indians do. What do the whites do with a man who commits murder? Do they hang him? Tell me what they do and what we should do. I want to know.

Judge Wright. When we get through signing the agreement I will endeavor to explain all these things to you as fully as I can. They are all important questions and I am glad you have spoken of them. We are very glad you have so readily consented to the agreement. You have shown your respect for the Government. And you have shown your good sense. It will be pleasing to the Great Father to hear of the way you have acted and how well you are doing. It is gratifying indeed, that of all the Indians here there is not a single one who opposes the agreement. A large majority of you are here, and no doubt the balance will all agree as you have done.

Chief Michael. We all understand the agreement; all of my people will sign it. I am Chief of the Pend d'Oreilles.

Chief Aeneas. All of my people are not here. What I do all will do and agree to. I am a friend to the white man. I am a friend of the Great Father. I live a long way from here. My people live a long way. We are poor. We have no mill near us. I think it is 90 miles from where I live to the agency. We have no sawmill to give us lumber; we have no carpenter, no blacksmith, and no farmer to show us how to work. I want you to ask the Great Father to give us these things so we can support ourselves and our children. This is all I have to say.

Judge Wright. The Calespels have agreed to come to this reservation, and I understand they intend to settle not very far from where the Kootenais are. We have agreed to build a saw and grist mill for them, and you (Aeneas) and your people can get your wheat ground there, and also get lumber with which to build houses. In the agreement we are making here to-day we also provide for the building of a mill on this side, and you can also have the benefit of that, as the agent no doubt will put it where it will accommodate the largest numbers and the most needy.

Chief Aeneas. That will be all right.

After the agreement was signed **Judge Wright** spoke as follows:

"My friends, the business for the transaction of which this council was called has been completed. You have done well. You have shown your good sense. Your respect for and confidence in the Government, as well as your kind feelings toward your less fortunate brothers, the Spokanes and the Calespels. All this we will carry back to the Great Father, and we know he will be well pleased with you and your actions this day. You will never by sorry for what you have done. You will always be glad." Addressing Chief Arlee Judge Wright said: "I will now endeavor to explain to you the things which seem to trouble your mind. You complain that your people are not allowed to buy cartridges. I will tell you why this is so. The Great Father knows that you and your people do not use your guns to shoot white men or to shoot one another. This is not the way with all Indians. Some tribes want guns and ammunition to use in wars against one another and to hurt the whites. It was because of these that the law was passed which forbids selling ammunition to Indians. There are many Indians in the United States besides you. The laws must be made general — must be made for all — as it is not always in the power of the Government to find out where there should be an exception made.

"You seem also to be dissatisfied about the railroad which runs through your land. You say that in order to induce you to give the right of way through your reservation you were promised free passages on the road. This is so. I have read the speeches which were made to you when the right of way was asked, and you were told that you should have free rides on the road. For some reason, I do not know what, it was not so written in the agreement which was made with you. It may have been that it was forgotten. I do not know how it was done.

"For a long time your people were allowed to ride free. At the last session of Congress a law was passed forbidding the granting of free passes. It did not say that free passes should not be issued to Indians, but the railroads said they thought it included Indians. I did not think so. We think when the railroad managers come to look into the question, and when they find that you were promised free rides, they will in good faith stand up to the promises made at the time. Your agent, Major Ronan, tells us that he has already received a letter from the company telling him you will be permitted to ride free on the reservation. We think the Government will see that you have your rights. You also complain that the railroad trains kill your cattle, and that you get no pay for it. In all countries where railroads are this sometimes happens. It can not be provided against. We understand from the agent that you have been paid, and I am sure you will be paid in all proper cases.

"It sometimes requires time and delay. This is the way with the white people also. Because of these things you ask that the railroad be removed from your land. This can not be done. The railroad is of great importance to you, as it is to all the country. By it you get cheap and safe travel, and it brings you things you need and could not get here without great cost. You ought to be glad you have a railroad, and not sorry; not interfere with it, but do all in your power to render it safe and certain. Other Indians where we have been, who had no railroads, have asked for them, and want them to run through their country. This should be the way with you. As to your timber, mines, and grass I have to say that no white man has any right to come on your reservation and carry off your timber or dig for minerals without first getting lawful permission. The Government will protect your reservations in this regard. It has protected other Indians, and it will do the same for you. You need have no fears about this. Neither are white men allowed to drive their cattle or other stock on your reservation to eat your grass.

"If this occurs report it to Major Ronan and he will see to it. Your reservation is so large that it can not be fenced in on all sides so as to keep stock off, and if white men's cattle stray on to your lands and are not driven on you should not hurt or injure them. If they are driven on report it to your agent and he will attend to it for you. As to your judges and policemen, you should be glad that you have them. It is a good thing. White people have judges and police officers all over their country. They are not given to hurt you, but to protect you against outsiders and against bad men among you. They are for the protection of the weak against the strong. There must be some power to decide when men can not agree, and somebody to see that the decisions are carried out. As you advance you will more clearly see the advantages of having good judges and good policemen. You should all respect and obey them. If necessary you should aid them. If they do wrong it can be corrected, but you can not get along without them. Among the whites all are made to obey them, even the Great Father and all other high officials. If the great chief of the whites obeys the laws the chiefs of the Indians should also. A good chief will make his people obey the judges and submit to the law. It is a bad chief who does otherwise. The Freat [sic] Father will not respect a chief who gives his people bad advice or sets them a bad example.

"You have three judges. We are told that they are good and sensible men. We know them, and we say that they are good men; all of them. When they try a case they should all talk together and try to do exactly right. If two think one way and one another way, the two must govern. This is the way with the white people. No man is perfect, and all men, however good, may make mistakes; but when the judges decide, that is the end of it all and all should stand by their word. The Great Father has given you these judges and laws to protect the poor and weak, for he feels as much for the poorest and weakest Indian as he does for the greatest chief among you. The use of whisky and cards is an evil to both the white people and the Indians. Good men among the whites advise their people not to get drunk and gamble. Indians should not do it. It is the cause of most of your troubles. Wise men among you know this, and he is a bad chief who advises his people to drink and gamble. The Great Father will not respect or favor such a chief. As to white men coming on to your reservation to live, I say that if your women will quite marrying white men you will have nothing to complain of on this account. Every one having Indian blood in his veins has equal rights on the reservation as long as he behaves himself, but men who do not obey the laws and regulations will not be allowed to remain; they will be sent away. This is the law. Some of the whites impose [oppose] whipping as a punishment for crime. All do not. You should not whip a sick man or a woman. This is wrong. It is unusual and cruel. I learn that you are mistaken about a pregnant woman having been whipped, and I am glad to hear it was not so. I think you should treat your women better than you do. You make them do much hard work that you ought to do yourselves. It is enough for a wife to take care of the children and the housework, and attend to the garden, and things like that. The hard work you ought to do yourselves. Among the whites the women are respected and protected, and we hope to see the day when you will do the same. Wherever we have been we have seen the women too much imposed upon. We would be glad to see this different.

"Among the whites, when a man murders another the law says he shall be hung. A man may kill another in order to save his own life, and if one man provokes another so as to put him in a great passion and in that passion he kills the other the punishment is less; but all who kill are punished, unless done in self-defense.

"But let me say to you that if you will all behave yourselves, and when you have troubles submit them to your judges and obey them, you will not have these troubles to talk about. If you will not do right you must be made to do, and punishments will follow. The good Indians have no reason to fear laws, judges, or policemen. It is only the bad who have these things to dread. This reservation is not for the Flatheads alone. It is for all of you and those who are to come in it. You should all be friends and have the same heart. This will make you strong. If you become divided, you will be weak. A big bunch of sticks all bound together by one cord is not easily broken; but take one stick at a time and all can soon be broken. This is the way with you. You have a good agent. The Great Father looks on him as one of the best in the service. That is the reason he has been agent so long. He tries to do right by the Great Father and right by you. Major Ronan does everything he can for you and he gives your people everything the Government sends here to you. He will not cheat you nor tell you a lie. We have seen what he has done for you, and what he is doing now. It is your duty and for your interest to respect and obey him in all things. He knows better than you what is best to be done for you and what is not best.

"If Major Ronan were to do an intentional wrong he would be sent away before many sun's rise.

"And now I have answered all your questions, and I hope you are satisfied with my answers. Soon we go away from you and I may not see you again, but it would give me great pleasure once more to visit your rich and beautiful reservation and find you all living on good farms, in good houses, well furnished, your lands well fenced, and your hills covered with stock. All these you can have if you will but do your duty and take advantage of the opportunities offered you."

Commissioner Andrews then addressed the council:

"My friends, as we are about to part, after having discharged the duty imposed upon us, and I trust to your entire satisfaction and to the satisfaction of the Great Father at Washington who sent us to your beautiful reserve —

perhaps never again to meet — you to return to your homes and we to visit the Indians of a far distant State, I take the liberty of addressing a few words to you.

"There is no question before the Great Council at Washington in which the good men and women of the country take one-half the interest that they do in the Indian question, and that interest is not lessened as the years go by; but as the rights of the Indians are more fully understood, the people are demanding that the Great Council shall respect those rights and give to the Indians a part, at least, of what is their just due from the Government. In this connection I can assure you that the Indians of the Great Northwest, of which you, the old and brave confederated bands of Flathead, Pend d'Oreille, and Kootenai Indians of the Jocko Reserve form such a large part, are not neglected by the Great Father and his Council, but in all their talks your rights and condition are duly considered, all your known wants supplied, and your future welfare and happiness closely studied.

"I know of no tribes of Indians in the United States, or elsewhere, who have so many things to be thankful for as the Indians of the Jocko Reservation, in the Territory of Montana. You are blessed with the finest climate to be found in America. You have on your reservation the grandest prairies of the Great Northwest; you have the purest streams of living water that man has ever seen; you have the most magnificent ranges of mountains in the world; you have one of the very best men in the service of the Government as your agent, Major Ronan, known as well in Washington as he is in Montana, as the great friend of your race, and I only repeat what I have heard many honest members of your tribes say since we came among you, and I have no doubt every Indian on the Jocko Reservation joins in the wish, 'we want him always.'

"You also have to guide you to the happy hunting-ground of the great hereafter good and noble fathers of your church, who voluntarily left their homes and loved ones in far distant lands to spend the remainder of their lives in promoting your present and future welfare. They have also established here at Saint Ignatius Mission schools for the education and civilization of your children, which are not excelled by any schools for the education of white children anywhere in the United States.

"Where, then, I ask, is there a people more blessed than you? With all the comforts of civilized life, with good health and such happy surroundings, with such brave and manly men as Arlee, of the Flatheads; Michael, of the Pend d'Oreilles; and Aeneas, of the Kootenais, as your chiefs, what more can you ask to make your lives one continuous scene of happiness. Then, my friends, place your hands upon the plow, raise up the wheat, the corn, the oats, and the potatoes, and your hearts will be glad. But do not, I pray you, raise up the whisky bottle to your lips, for it will make your hearts sad. Whisky is your curse, as it is the curse of the white man; it has brought down to early graves more brave, strong, and noble sons of the forest by far than the bullet ever did; it destroys the Indian's manhood while living, and takes from him all the happiness God intended he should enjoy. You had better by far be bitten by rattlesnakes and die of their poison than to drink the whisky sold in this northwestern country and die from its poison.

"We are now about to take our leave of you, and should the Great Council at Washington approve the agreement which we have this day made with you, you nor your children will, I trust, never have cause to regret that the Great Father sent us to you."

Document 21

Son of Chief Eneas Murdered at Demersville

August 1889

Source: "The Kootenai Indians Again," *The Inter Lake* (Demersville, Mont.), August 30, 1889, page 4, col. 3; Peter Ronan, *Justice to Be Accorded to the Indians: Agent Peter Ronan Reports on the Flathead Indian Reservation, Montana, 1888-1893*, ed. Robert J. Bigart (Pablo, Mont.: Salish Kootenai College Press, 2014), pages 80-83.

Editors' note: Somehow the local Demersville newspaper was offended that Kootenai Chief Eneas would want justice for the murder of his son. Eneas thought that if Indians were punished for killing white men, white men who killed Indians should also be punished. The killing of Chief Eneas' son, Samuel, in Demersville was a tragic affair and the historical records include many contradictory sources. Some of the events leading to the murder were either aggravated or caused by alcohol. The local whites seemed to be very anxious to blame an Indian for the killing, but this was probably a self-serving falsehood. Eneas' statement emphasized his diplomatic efforts to protect his tribe while also avoiding further bloodshed. He controlled his anger, despite the provocations from many of the Upper Flathead Valley whites. Ronan had Eneas' side of the story published in a Helena newspaper and his 1890 annual report to the Commissioner of Indian Affairs. In response to this report, the Commissioner of Indian Affairs decided the killing may have been "totally without justification" and asked the Secretary of the Interior to have the United States Attorney for Montana investigate. He also instructed Ronan to cooperate in the investigation. The Commissioner of Indian Affairs then received various communications from white officials blaming the Indians for the conflict and asking for protection from the Kootenai. The Commissioner requested that the U.S. Army investigate the conflicting claims. A grand jury was convened but there was no record of anyone being punished for Samuel's death.

The Kootenai Indians Again.
Chief Aeneas Accompanied by Fifty or Sixty of His Tribe Visit Us.

Last Wednesday, Chief Aeneas, of the Kootenia tribe, came to Demersville with some fifty or sixty of his followers, all painted and decorated in the latest

Chief Eneas
Source: Archives and Special Collections, Mansfield Library, University of Montana, Missoula. (photograph number 81-284)

Indian style, to find out if possible who killed his son, and who the guilty parties are that have been selling the Indians whiskey. They held a conference at the town hall and two Indians named Louie, and Antwine, swore that certain parties had sold them whiskey. Warrants were at once issued for their arrest. Only one man was arrested however, and he was afterwards released. Chief Aeneas had agreed on Wednesday night that he would be on hand at 10 o'clock a.m. with the two prosecuting witnesses and further, that all who accompanied him should leave their arms behind. After waiting for some time after the hour agreed upon, and no chief showing up, a messenger was despatched for him to come at once. Word was soon brought back that the Indians had all left, and that no signs of their presence were visible. The people of this valley are getting somewhat weary of this continuous outbreak of the Indians, and think its about time that something was done to hold them in check. The Cliff House fed about fifty of these redskins Wednesday noon, and there has never been an Indian excitement here yet, but what has cost Mr. Clifford from $50 to $200.

* * * * * * * * *

United States Indian Service,
Flathead Agency,
September 9th, 1889.

Hon. Commissioner of Indian Affairs
Washington, D.C.
Sir:

With the hope of bringing certain criminals to justice, that live in the settlements at the Head of the Flathead Lake, I shall go to the County Seat of Missoula County, where the Grand Jury is now in session, and bring before them the following statement made to me by Eneas, Chief of the Kootenai Indians of this reservation. It refers to the events and cause of the last sensational reports published through the country of an Indian uprising in that region, and is as follows:

Chief Eneas:

Three Indian boys of my band were gambling near Oust Finley's place on Mud Creek on the reservation. They lost everything they had even to their blankets. They then started for the Head of the Lake going up the East side, and avoiding my home which is on the West side. On the way they passed a creek where there are some white settlers, about one mile from Demersville. At that place a whiteman who was on foot took a horse away from another whiteman who was riding the same. The fellow who was set afoot begged of the Indians to loan him a horse to ride home, which they did and turned back with him. The Man's name is Joe Morant and he is a settler at the Head of the Lake. He gave the Indian boys whisky upon which they got drunk. When they got to Demersville they were drunk from the whisky obtained from Morant. At Demersville, they got into trouble and a whiteman drew a pistol on one of them but a fight was prevented by outsiders. I (Eneas) was camped near Chief Michel's place, and the day after the Indian boys mentioned started for Demersville, I moved my camp to go home. I camped for the night near the Steamboat landing at the Foot of the Lake. My son-in-law, Louie having loaned a horse to the Indian boys he took the steamer to Demersville to get him back. Before getting on the steamer Louie asked my son to take his horse and ride up to Demersville and meet him there. When I got to my home at Dayton Creek, my son and another Indian rode to Demersvill[e]. They had no arms when they left. They camped the first night with some Pend 'd Oreilles and Kootenais on this side of Demersville. In the morning they found the three Indian boys, the party altogether being six Indians. They sat around the store all day at Demersville. In the evening, two of the boys who previously got whisky from Morant were approached by a whiteman who came out of a saloon, and who is known to the Indians by the name of Jack Sheppard. He asked the boys if they wanted to buy whisky. The Indian boys replied that they had no money; they then reported to their companions that a whiteman offered to sell them whisky. My son-in-law Louie had money and he gave the boys four dollars to buy with. They found Jack and gave him the money. Jack pointed out a place on the bank of the river where he would deliver the whisky. True to agreement Jack returned with two bottles of whisky, which they carried to the other Indians. They all went away from the vicinity of the store to a more secluded spot and commenced drinking. One bottle was drank by six Indians, and my son after drinking said he was hungry and started to the hotel to get something to eat. My son in law Louie followed him. Louie heard a white man talking loud to my son through an upstairs window, ordering him to go away or he would shoot him. Lou[i]e took my son by the arm and tried to take him away. Louie said he heard some one come down stairs who came out the door and while he (Louie) held my son the white man shot him. When my son fell, Louie stated that the man who shot him told him to get away quick or he would be shot. Lou[i]e could not run as he is lame but he turned and saw two white men with guns who told him to get away, and followed him as he hobbled off, for about a hundred yards. Two of the Indian boys who got the whisky started that night after the shooting, for Tobacco Plains, and the other three Indians started back to my home on the reservation. They told me that white men killed my son at Demersville. I sent a whiteman called "Savia" [Francois Gravelle] who is married to a Kootenai woman to get the body of my son. When "Savia" returned with the dead body he told me that the white people at Demersville wanted me to go up there. The morning after the Killing a camp of British Kootenais arrived at Demersville from Tobacco Plains, and they recognized the body as being that of my son. The whitemen told them also to tell me to come to Demersville. I did not wish to go but was advised by a white man who lives in the Lake country to go. It was sixty miles from my home to the Agency and I started for Demersville without letting you (the Agent) know as the distance was so far. I took some of my people along, but sent word ahead that I was coming with no hostile intent, but simply to inquire if my son was killed by whitemen or not. If so to ask that the murder might be punished, and the men who sold the whisky might also be punished, as that was all the cause of the trouble between my Indians and whitemen. I camped on the night of my arrival at the house of Baptist Le Bow [J. B. LeBeau], who is a white settler and lives on this side of Demersville. In the morning I sent another man to let the people know I was coming to talk with them as a friend. When I got to Demersville the people seemed excited and afraid that I came there for revenge. I assured them through an interpreter as best I could my friendly intentions. I could not get any good council with them. I knew that not one of my Indians who had the trouble had a gun or a pistol with them when they left my camp for the Head of the Lake. I do not know where any of them could have borrowed or purchased a pistol or a gun. I told the people if they could tell me where any one of them got a gun or pistol then I might think my son was killed by an Indian. One of the Indians sold a horse to a white man. I asked that white man if he traded a gun or a pistol for the horse — he said no! I asked to see the ball which killed my son, and was answered that the ball was sent to the Agent (not so it was no[t] sent) and by him it would [be] sent to Missoula. Louie, my son-in-law told the whites at Demersville, in answer to a question that he saw the gun plainly in the hands of a white man which killed my son — that it was not a pistol but a gun which looked like a Winchester. Louie also claimed that he could recognize the man who held the gun, and was asked to do so if he was present. Louie pointed out the man but he was not arrested. That man lives in a house at Demersville, but Louie does not know his name, but can point out the house. Finding that I could not learn anything about who killed my son; whether it was a white man as claimed by the Indians; or by an Indian as claimed by the whitemen. I came home to my place at Dayton Creek. The whites wished me to stay one day longer but I felt it would be useless to do so.

I now leave it in the hands of the white men for investigation, and I trust they will do me the justice to investigate this killing. My Indians claim it was done by whitemen, the white men claim it was done by Indians. God Knows! I do not. I now throw myself upon your sense of justice to all.

A great many of my people have been killed by white men; two of them were hung by a mob. I know of no punishment or even a trial that was ever given to a white man for killing any of my Indians, and I now think it time to show that there is justice to be accorded to the Indians as well as to the whites. If this matter shall be brought before the Court at Missoula I am ready to be there and also to do all in my power to bring in witnesses who might be required.

Eneas Chief of Kootenais
his X mark

Respectfully submitted

Peter Ronan, U.S. Indian Agent.

Document 22

Charlo and General Carrington Negotiate about Bitterroot Lands October 1889

Source: Excerpt from Henry B. Carrington, "The Exodus of the Flatheads," manuscript, Carrington Family Papers, MS 130, Manuscripts and Archives, Yale University Library, New Haven, Conn., chapter 7, pages 1-12, chapter 8, pages 1-4.

Editors' note: This manuscript is the only detailed description of the negotiations between Charlo and Carrington in 1889. Carrington gave a meticulous account of the parleying, but only quotes Charlo at key points. Unfortunately, Carrington's manuscript just represented his view of the bargaining. It would have been very useful to get Charlo's description of the events. Presumably the specific incidents referred to were generally accurate, but Carrington added his own biased interpretation of Charlo's motives and inflated Carrington's skills as a negotiator. "Sic" has not been used except in a few typographical errors.

Chapter VII.
Negotiations with Charlot's Band.

Before leaving Washington, the Commissioner [Henry B. Carrington] obtained from Lieut. General Scofield a letter to the Commanding Officer of the Department having headquarters at St Paul, requesting that the garrison of Fort Missoula, four miles south of the City of Missoula, be authorized to render assistance in case of an emergency requiring military aid. The precaution proved to be unnecessary, but a visit to the post, upon completion of the preliminary investigations at the Jocko Agency, added a moral support to the negotiations that immediately ensued.

The services of blind Michel [Revais] and Eneos Francois, "The Mountain Lion," also a good interpreter as well as one of the patentees of land in the Bitter Root Valley, had been secured, and the journey was made in two days.

A large flag was flying from a tall mast before the Stephensville hotel, upon the arrival of the party, and many citizens as well as Indians had assembled in the vain expectation that a few hours, or possibly a few days, would complete the work prescribed by the Act of Congress. The fact that in addition to the signatures of all Indians interested in the lands, the examination and appraisement of two hundred quarter sections, with their improvements were to be made, did not abate the expectation of many, that the Indians might all be removed before the ensuing winter months of 1889.

On the following morning, early, Michel was called upon to procure suitable transportation to Charlot's cabin, as the first business to be transacted in the valley. To his suggestion that the trip should be made on horseback as the road was bad, or delayed until after Charlot came to town, it was a sufficent reply, that "as Charlot hauled supplies to and from town in a wagon, any other wagon, or a buggy, could make the trip, even if more leisurely, and with some discomfort, but the promise to Charlot must be kept.["] A bright young Flathead, well-painted, well mounted, and well equipped, was enlisted as a guide to the Chief's cabin, and a start was made. Over rocks and bogs, around stumps and fallen trees, through sloughs of uncertain depth, the journey was conducted and after ascending a slight hill confronted by a formidable gate bars, Charlot was seen in *negligee* Indian apparrel, fixing a plow, near a corn stack in front of his home cabin. A few acres of wheat stubble in front, half an acre, perhaps, of corn stumps, and a smaller spot of meadow, with old harrows, wagons, broken wheels, a few farm and garden tools, a very small smoke house, and one half-covered tepee, or lodge, constituted the immediate surroundings, while a rude rack which supported some old harness, three lean horses, a few hogs, some chickens, more dogs, and a cow crumping dry corn fodder in the angle of the fence, constituted the other visible farming resources of the Flathead Chief. It needed no words to confirm his sad refrain, so often repeated at Washington, to Garfield, to Vest, and at Jocko, that "Charlot, was poor."

Close by Charlot's side, as the buggy passed the entrance after Michel had taken down the bars, stood little Victor, his bright grandson, named after the "Great Victor." The introduction, with tender of a cigar and a light, and the assurance that the first thing done upon reaching the Bitter Root Valley, had been in accordance with the promise made at Jocko, and to invite him to a conference in the village, was followed by an invitation to enter his cabin, where acquaintance was made with his family. Beyond this invitation, no business was mentioned and the talk was purely social, or about his farm and crops, and what he had laid up for the coming winter. Upon looking at some photographs, he asked that he might have one for Victor and he placed it upon the shelf above an enormous fireplace. Piles of robes and blankets along the sides of the cabin designated resting places for the entire family at night; and with a parting present of cigars and the request that he send for such bacon, sugar, tea, and tobacco as he needed, the interview closed. Without folling [sic] to the bars, he said to Michel, "Tell the White Chief that he is the first white man from Washington that ever visited Charlot's cabin," that "he promised, when at Jocko, and he did not lie!" He started two sons for Stephensville very promptly, and their return with the supplies promised soon became widely known, so that the next day found Indians from various directions flocking into town, for similar manifestations of the white man's presence and regard.

One incident connected with the visit to Charlot, was so impressively suggestive as not to be omitted. While carefully reining the horse through the roughest part of the journey, as Michel could not drive, and, to follow the mounted guide was of chief concern, a sweet voice, hummed the hymn, "Nearer, my God to Thee: nearer to Thee!" It was Michels. To the inquiry, "Do you know that? Where did you learn it?" and the request "Let us sing it through, together?" he answered, "I forgot! I did'nt know I was singing it aloud! we cant sing it here." The response, "This is the Great Spirit's temple, over head, and these great pines are supporting the arches. It is just the place to sing, as the mockingbirds and whippoorwills all about us are doing," brought a smile and a good hearty outburst of the melody.

Conversation about the death of his wife, and the misconduct of his son who had been put in jail at Missoula for bad conduct when drunk, was followed by an expression of sympathy for him when alone in his cabin near the Agency. He promptly replied, "I am never alone. I say prayers, and sing hymns, and fear nobody; for the Great Spirit who is everywhere, hears me, and if I cant see him, I know he is near, just as I know you are near, but, cannot see you. All the noises in the woods are from the great Spirit, and the birds know just what to do, because he made them, and they cant see him, more than Michel can."

In all subsequent negotiations, and conferences, even when Charlot seemed most obstinate, violent, and threatening, Michel never lost faith in the success of the mission nor that his people would all be gathered at Jocko. He "had prayed for it, all his life, and his father and Francois' father, who helped the white men when they first came to the Bitter Root Valley, would know of it, somehow, and be made happy."

Early on the next day, Michel was busy in giving invitations to all whom he met to come to the appointed place for interviews; and although the Agreement was upon a table by itself, and now and then, a signature was witnessed, no pressure was brought to bear upon any, save the simple announcement of the general purpose of the visit, and the "hope that considerable sums of money would come to the patentees as well as the re-union of all the Flatheads, if all acted together for the good of all." It was known that the visit to Charlot had been simply a friendly call, and before noon, he appeared in person both to return the call and acknowledge the gifts received at his cabin. He came, with hair carefully oiled and braided, wearing the same suit when he wore when visited General Grant [i.e., President Chester A. Arthur] in 1885 [i.e, 1884]. When asked to permit his picture to be taken, in exchange for the one given Victor, he hesitated. When asked to get his people before St Mary's church, and have all taken together, he was pleased with the suggestion and in a very short time more than a hundred assembled. One old man, on crutches, Stephen James, and a very old woman shouldering a pappoose in a cradleboard were among the first to take positions. Other s....s and poappose and several leading men of the tribe, including those who visited Washington with Charlo in 1885, soon completed the effective historic group, while the church in the immediate back-ground, and the three lofty peaks still farther away, supplemented all that was needed to give enduring interest and value to the scene.

Upon return to headquarters, many Indians followed. One brought an "early Rose" potatoe as a present, weighing six pounds and twelve inches in length. Gigantic applies, more than five inches in diameter, were so decidedly extraordinary in size, that two were immediately mailed to the President, as samples of the valley fruit. The gathering of so ma[n]y of the tribe, of all ages, led to the announcement of an early next day service at the St Mary's church. All the benches were filled soon after the bell rang, and nearly every foot of the floor was packed with kneeling forms, intermingled with children of all ages and sizes. The streets and stores had been crowded by Indians, most of them in their best attire, and after the service, the large room at the hotel, set apart for the purpose, and on level with the sidewalk, was filled as closely as men, women and [c]hildren could be squatted together, while the windows were obscured by others whose faces pressed against the glass to see if they could in some degree understand what seemed like some strange patomime occurring within.

From the first, diary notes were taken of these interviews, to be compared, afterwards, with the interpreters recollection, and both questions and answers were written as the interviews progressed.

During the succeding days of constant conference, the citizens generally did all within their power to prevent the idle young men and the weak old men from getting whiskey. The assurance that if a saloon keeper sold or, gave strong drink to an Indian, he would be sent at once to the Missoula jail, and the hire of a wagon for such a possible contingency, may have been an additional inducement to good order; but the citizens generally seemed to feel that the future of the valley might depend on success in this final attempt to effect the removal of the Flathead Indians from their midst. Mr. J. R. Fauds, Editor of the Rocky Mountain Gazette, was most assiduous in his appeals to the public to maintain good order and support of the movement then in progress.

Charlot was constant in his attendance, often passionately demanding the "literal execution of the Stephens Treaty," as "all that he would submit to"; but at every interview some of his people signed the contract, regardless of his protests. Repeatedly, he declared that "he never would sign, but kill himself first." When Vandenberg, his chief companion in the visit to Washington, with his son, stepped to the table and signed, and the immediate approval by the much beloved and worthy Father [Jerome] D'Aste, followed, Charlot seemed impressed by the loneliness of his position. There was a sense of honor in his words and bearing, that was at times almost majestic, as he repeated the fierce threat against his own life, adding "the women will call Charlot a coward and a liar, if he change his promise and sign."

Suddenly, he arose, and thus appealed to his own history, in his own behalf.

"Where is the white man who can say that Charlot is not his people's friend? The Nez Perces went to war with the white man. Chief Joseph filled the mountain passes with his soldiers and then came into my lands, where he never belonged, to kill my brothers the white men. Chief Joseph held out his hand to Charlot, the son of the great Victor, and this is the way he talked. 'The white man is a liar! He talks smooth to get peace and sign papers, and when the Indian lies down to sleep, with no arms, the white man tears up the paper. White man steals the Indian's land and white man lies. He kills all the game, and spoils all the rivers. He hates the red man. We will drive the white man away. We will live as our fathers lived. The white man shall bury his dead, and never come back again.'"

After a few moments pause, Charlos, continued:

"Then I put my hand behind my back, and this is what I said to Joseph. 'Charlot, never lies! Charlot never betrays his friends. You are in the land of the Flatheads, where you never had a home. You want to go through the land of my fathers to kill my friends. If you will go through the valley in peace, Charlot will say, — yes — but will not take your hand, for it is the hand of the white man's enemy. You may go through; but if you steal a calf, or a little chicken from Charlot's friends, Charlot and his soldiers will strike you as his fathers knifed the Blackfeet, on all sides, and spare nobody! Go Joseph! Charlot has no more words for Joseph."

Chief Charlot's account of his services, was not exaggerated in his earnest but calm, recital. Immediately after his interview with Joseph, he organized a full company of his braves, who were armed by the government, and he personally conducted the exposed white families to Fort Owen and other places of security and protected them until additional troops arrived in the valley. Mr. Amos Buck, of Stephensville, who took part in the defense, informed the

Commissioner, that "but for Charlot's heroic intervention, and against superior numbers, all the families of the valley would have been massacred."

At one visit, standing in the midst of three encircling groups, all upon the floor, when pipes passed freely and the dense smoke almost obscured recognition, the chief waved before his face a soiled copy of "Governor Stevens Treaty" which he always carried with him, and with aggressive, defiant emphasis, demanded,

"Will the white man, at last, and now, do what this paper says? Is the white man like the Blackfeet, who only steal, and kill, and lie? Charlot will sign no more papers."

Suddenly returning the paper to his bosom he drew forth a white and a red handkerchief. These he spread in silence to his right and left, upon the floor, and with solemn mein continued his appeal.

"See, white Chief. There's no blood, not a drop, there," pointing to the white emblem at his right. The Flatheads never shed the blood of a white man. They shed their own blood to save the white men. "Charlot, the son of Victor never lies."

Pointing slowly and scornfully to the red emblem at his left, he raised and wrung it as if soaked with blood, and replacing it upon the floor, again broke forth with a ringing voice that brought crowds from the street to the open windows.

"See there, believe Charlot. That is like the Blackfeet, soaked with the white man's blood. They are liars, thieves, and murderers. I hate the Blackfeet and cut out their hearts." Suiting action towards, he stamped upon the red emblem, in great fury, while every feature betrayed malignant hate, and he made gestures in pantomime, of the sweep of the scalping knife and deadly thrusts. Then he told little Victor to put it in the stove to burn, as the Blackfeet ought to burn.

Then, his face relaxed its sternness as he lifted the white emblem and gently placed it in his bosom, saying in sibfdued [sic] tones, as if only speaking his thoughts, "Charlot, son of Victor, loves the white man, and puts this where the white man is always safe, against Charlot's heart. Charlot, speaks the truth."

The climax of these numerous conferences respecting the removal of his band to the Jocko Reservation, was of peculiar interest, from its semi-religious aspects and deserves [literal?] record. After many interviews, when concession on his part seemed almost hopeless of attainment, and an unusual number of his people crowded the room and adjacent street he again announced, in more excited terms than ever, that "he never, never, signed the Garfield Agreement"; that "whoever said so, was a liar, and he didnt want to talk to liars!"

It seemed for a moment as if the indignant chief had finally resolved to end the interview, whatever his people might individually do. After a brief silence, the Commissioner stepped into the adjoining room, but quickly returned, holding in his hand the *original* "Garfield Agreement," saying, as he approached near the Flathead Chief, "Charlot, I am your friend! Charlot has spoken the truth! I want the interpreter to tell all Charlot's friends that any man who says that Charlot lies, is himself the liar. Here is the paper with Charlot's name written by a white man, but no cross (X) opposite Charlot's name, because Charlot refused to sign the paper when Second Chief Arlee and Third Chief Adolph signed. Charlot is not bound by that paper. The Stephens paper was good, a great while ago, but Charlot needs a new paper, better than either, and the white man and his red brother are old enough to make a new treaty, and let the treaties of dead men be forgotten."

Charlot looked about him and seemed to study the faces of his people. The Indians, for the first time began to talk among themselves, and were not interrupted for several minutes. The vindication of Charlot's statement, that "he never signed the Garfield Agreement" brought exclamations of surprise; and refilling their pipes, they watched his every motion. Suddenly, but with dignity, Charlot again arose and seemed burdened by a sense of injured honor in case he should sign the paper. He spoke, with earnestness, "I said I would never sign the paper" and with a fierce motion as of putting a knife to his breast, added "I would kill myself first. Charlot never changes! The women would call Charlot coward and liar, if he changed. I told you twice, and more than twice that I would kill myself before I would sign, and prove myself a liar. You pinch me too hard. It hurts!"

"But, Charlot," was the reply, "Father D'Aste and myself will, if you kill yourself, be very sorry and mourn for you and your people. But when Charlot's people cry for bread to feed the hungry, or for blankets to keep them warm, can Charlot rise from the grave, when they dig and find him, to answer their cries? When Victor meets him in the spirit land and asks "why Charlot left his people 'can he answer Victor without trembling? No! Charlot will not kill himself! He will stay and lead his people to peace and happiness."

"Charlot, let me ask you something. Think hard, before you answer. Does Charlot, never change?"

"Never," was the impassioned reply.

"But, Charlot, you say that you never change! Once you were a little pappoose, like those in the corner, stretched out on cradle-boards

[Here a page is missing from the surviving manuscript.]

in the Stephensville stores, to come to this room and ordered them to supply nearly sixty families with flour, bacon, coffee, salt, tea, and sugar, with no cost to you and the s....s came and loaded the ponies with all they could carry, you said, "White Chief told the truth and the dream was a lie!"

Charlot, the Great Spirit never tells lies! His whispers are true. To conquer and drive away a bad spirit is a greater victory, according to the good Book, as Father D'Aste will tell you, than to take your enemy's village and all his braves. Only the Great Spirit — never changes! When Charlot said, I never change! I wondered if the Great Spirit had entered into Charlot's body, and was speaking through Charlot, 'I never change.'"

"Charlot. You tell your young men who gamble, drink fire-water, fight, and steal, that they must change from bad to good. Go now, and think by yourself. To-morrow will be another Sunday, and after the sun rises all will say prayers in the Church. Stay away, and do not come here, until the Great Spirit whispers something to your heart that will bring peace and plenty to all your people. Tell all these people to go away; and Father D'Aste, and your white friend will ask the Great Spirit to give us all the same message because he loves all his children alike, and wants us to be happy in peace and never have war any more. Charlot, our talk is done!"

After a brief pause, Charlot moved his left hand toward the door speaking as if to himself, but understood by his people, and with something like awe in their silent movement, all left. Some went silently to the cabins and tepees near the church. Others mounted ponies and as quietly disappeared.

When the last one had left, Charlot, having wrapped his blanket closely about his person, extended his right hand, and withdrew, with these simple words. "Goodbye! Charlot will think, all night, and do what is right, if he can."

Chapter VIII.
The Flatheads Unite Under Charlot.

It was after 2 O'Clock when Charlot thus dismissed his people and retired to his temporary quarters near St. Mary's church. In addition to the usual Saturday market attendance, the prospect of an early settlement of the Indian land question had attracted farmers, ranchmen, and a few speculators from distant parts of the valley and from Missoula. Several of the poorest Indians from distant tracts, both men and women, squatted themselves on store steps, or on the sidewalk along the course of the bright little stream that ran in the gutter, past the council room, on the way to St Mary's River.

At about 5 O'Clock, Indian women appeared at the door and the windows, evidently in great terror, reporting that "two of the young men who had secured liquor, were cutting each other with knives," and imploring help. An interpreter was at once sent to Charlot with orders to stop the fight and restore order among his people. The gravity of the situation was instantly understood by the Chief. It was a strange episode to occur so soon after the conference of the morning. The offenders were knocked down by him instantly and the flagellation, with his stout whip, was so furious and determined that an appeal from the women and a request to remove them without further punishment, alone suspended the growing excitement. It fitly closed a day of intense and dramatic sensation.

Saturday night passed with unusual quiet in the Indian camp. On the following morning, at a very early religious service, the Indians assembled with peculiar quietness, as if the shadow of some impending calamity rested on the entire congregation. The silence at headquarters was unbroken and the curtains were drawn down. The order of the previous day that "no Indians returns until Charlot should so direct" was observed, although several had sent word by the interpreters that "they wished to sign the paper." It was not until 11 O'Clock that one of the interpreters who had passed through a side door to the hotel office brought word that Charlot was sitting upon the door step without, with no one in company except little Victor, while Vandenburg and others were across the street near Buck's warehouse watching his movements. Presently, a light rap at the door, un-answered, was followed by a second, and then a third more decided rap. Michael partly opened the door and asked Charlot "What he wanted?" Upon his reply that "he wanted to open his heart" he was invited in, and the room was again, almost instantly, packed with his people.

In simple words, with no reference to the incidents of the previous day, he made a full statement of the poverty and wretchedness of the Flatheads of the valley, especially naming several very aged men and women who could not help themselves and whom the young men would not help. He said that "the young men would hunt and sell their game for fire-water, and he could not stop it," that "they followed the words of bad white men and stole what they wanted to eat, without working for it." He dwelt tenderly upon the burial place near the church, asking "if it would be dug up by white men when his people went to Jocko?" Upon being told that "it would be protected, just as well as the other burial places near the white man's churches," he made very explicit inquiry as to what would be their priviliges and holdings at the Jocko." He was informed that "he would have his own choice of land so far as possible, but that good cabins would be built for all and that whatever he thought best for his people would be put upon paper when he was ready to explain their greatest needs."

He then stepped forward, with extended hand, and replied. "The Great Spirit said to me last night, 'Trust the white Chief.' Charlot loves his people! Charlot will change and do right! Charlot will sign the paper, and then, the white Chief can write down what Charlot wants."

A pen was placed in his hand, with the brief word "Charlot is a great Chief. He has conquered the evil Spirit, and will make his people happy! Everybody will be happy!" He then affixed his (X) to his name. His entire demeanor altered, in an instant. Sullen moroseness and passionate action were exchanged for every indication of contentment and peace. A murmur of satisfaction pervaded the room, Blind Michael could not restrain his tears of joy, and Charlot at once spoke again, "Charlot will make everybody sign!"

But he did not lose sight of the promised "List of good things," and seating himself upon the floor began his recital. He "wanted all to be written *twice*, so that he could have a copy and be sure that all was just as the talk had promised." His first inquiry was "if, when his own land was sold, he, and not his people generally would have the proceeds?" *Next*, "He wanted a new wagon and harness." *Next*, "that upon reaching Jocko, every family having young children should have a fresh cow." *Next*, "to have for himself and family the Arlee house and land, which had been improved and were nearest the Agency and the warehouse of supplies." This was promised also, "if just arrangements could be made with Arlee's widow." *Then*, he explained, with pantomimic effect, that, "the sun got very hot over head at noon, and the snow and rain were sometimes very bad," and "he wanted a two-seated, covered, spring-wagaon [sic], for visiting his people and getting them settled at work." This was promised, "conditional upon approval at Washington; but, otherwise, it would be charged to him, because the other Indians who had such wagons had always bought them by sale of stock, or furs." He was also informed that "such groceries as were immediately needed would be furnished them without cost, in addition to such as had been already distributed to the most needy."

Document 23

Commission Tries to Buy Part of Flathead Reservation March 25, 1897

Source: "Council Is Ended," *Daily Missoulian*, March 25, 1897, page 4, col. 2.

Editors' note: The negotiations on Flathead in March 1897 were the opening salvo for the Crow, Flathead, Etc., Commission which was trying to convince the Flathead Reservation tribes to sell part of the reservation. Charlo and the other tribal leaders refused to sell any land. This newspaper article summarizied the negotiations from the viewpoint of the white men involved. No transcript of the 1897 meeting or account from the Indian side has been found. See also article from September 27, 1898.

Council Is Ended
Commissioners Have Two Big Talks with Reservation Indians.
Chief Charlos Opposed to Relinquishing Any Lands
— Another Pow-Wow Next Summer.

United States Commissioners Col. J. B. Goodwin and Benjamin F. Barge, in company with Indian Agent Major Jos. T. Carter, came to Missoula last night from St. Ignatius Mission, where they held their second preliminary council with the Flathead Indians relative to securing some of their lands. Chief Charlos was at both councils and the propositions laid before the Indians were submitted through an interpreter, although a great many of the Indians understand the English language. The councils held at both Arlee and St. Ignatius Mission were for the purpose of the commissioners laying before the Indians what the government wanted and would do in case they will relinquish part of their domain, and now that the commissioners are away the Indians can discuss the matter among themselves and when the next council is held the latter part of spring or early in the summer they will be in a position to decide intelligently.

Both commissioners are favorably impressed with Chief Charlos and while he is not in favor of relinquishing any of the lands of the Flathead reservation they think before the next council is held the chief will have changed his mind and look upon the proposed purchase as one looking to the betterment of the Flatheads. The majority of the Indians on the reservation are Pend d'Oreilles, next in number the Flatheads, and the others Kalispels, Spokanes and Kootenais. The Indians, the commissioners say, are in good condition and without doubt the most intelligent they have yet visited.

Col. Goodwin, wife and two sons leave today for Fort Hall, where they will join Commissioner Chas. G. Hoyt, who is now negotiating with the Bannack and other tribes. Commissioner Barge will return to the Flathead agency with Indian Agent Carter and visit certain portions of the reservation where there are large numbers of the Indians, enquiring into their condition and gleaning a description of the valleys, etc.

Document 24

Chief Charlo Rejects Land Sales

September 27, 1898

Source: "An Eloquent Old Man," *The Anaconda Standard*, September 27, 1898, page 10, col. 2.

Editor's note: The commission that met with Charlo and the other tribal leaders in 1898 was called the Crow, Flathead, Etc., Commission. Fortunately transcripts of the January and April 1901 meetings between the Commissioners and chiefs have survived and are reproduced later in this volume. Despite the refusal of the tribal leaders to consider the sale, the commission kept up their efforts to obtain Flathead Reservation land by persuasion or coercion through the early years of the twentieth century. This article lauded Charlo's speech at the meeting but did not give a transcript of what Charlo said. See also article about earlier negotiations in March 25, 1897, above.

An Eloquent Old Man
Chief Charlot Tells Commissioners His Opinion of Them.
A Big Pow Wow Was held
Conference Between the Head Men of the Confederated Tribes and the Treaty Commissioners on the Reservation.

Missoula, Sept. 26. — The meager reports that have been received here concerning the conference between the head men of the Confederated Tribes and the treaty commissioners on the Flathead reservation have not given much idea of the details of that important meeting. It was known, as reported in the Standard at the time, that the proposition of the treaty commissioners for the opening of the reservation for settlement had been rejected by the Indians, but further than that not much was known. It is now learned, however, that the meeting was one of the most interesting ever held on the reservation. Its chief feature of importance was the address delivered by Chief Charlot of the Bitter Root Indians in reply to the commissioners. The old man was very eloquent, and those who heard his address, even with the loss of effect that always follows translation, say it was a remarkable effort. It produced a marked effect upon the Indians and it must have afforded the old chief considerable satisfaction to be able to tell the commissioners what he thought of them and to relieve his feelings of the wrath that has been accumulating for these many years.

The proposition of the commissioners, as it is understood here, was that the Indians cede to the federal government a strip of their land 25 miles wide, running east and west along the northern border of the reservation. This would include that part of the Flathead valley that lies within the reserve, the Flathead lake and the Mission valley as far down as Crow creek — about 640,000 acres in all. For this the commissioners agreed to pay the Indians 60 cents an acre. Of this sum the red men were to receive 5 cents per acre in cash and the remaining 55 cents was to be expended for them by the government in improvements and stock. All of the Indians know, of course, that the sum the government has paid to the Nez Perces, the Crows and other tribes who have ceded to their government their reservations. They know that the average sum that has been thus paid has been about $3.75 per acre, and when they were offered the insignificant sum named above they were justly indignant.

Charlot made the principal reply to the commissioners. He said, in the first place, that he and his people had no confidence in the commissioners. He did not believe that the commissioners ever came from Washington. He did not think that they had any authority any way. He and his people had treated with commissioners too often, and they were through with that business until some of the promises that had been made by the previous commissions had been fulfilled. When he had any treaty to make he wanted to go to Washington and make it with somebody that would speak with authority and would keep his promise. He referred eloquently to the sufferings of his people as a result of the broken promises made by commissioners, and said that he would deal no more with them. He said: "You think this land is good. So do I. You want it. I propose to keep it for my people, their children and their children's children. You want to give us a cow apiece for our land. I am afraid that the cow would hook me."

The old chief became very ironical as the address progressed and he paid his respects to Professor Barge of the commission in strong language. He told how the professor and his commission had brought all of the Indians together at the mission and then had not come to meet them at all. To Professor Barge he said: "I thought that I had cut your tongue out, but I see that another is growing." He refused to treat with the professor at all.

It looks now as if the whole matter was as far from any practical settlement as ever. It is of much importance to the people of this section, and it is to be hoped that a commission will some day be named that will be more successful in treating with the Indians. It may be that the department is at fault for not giving the commissioners sufficient authority. Anyway, there is something wrong somewhere. If the matter could be properly handled, there is no doubt that some satisfactory arrangement could be made with the chiefs and their people. They certainly have not been properly treated.

Document 25

Charlo and Kakashe Complain About Agent Smead August 25, 1900

Source: "Letter and Statements of Flathead Chiefs Sharlo & Ki-ki-is-see," enclosure number 1 in Cyrus Beede to Secretary of the Interior, August 25, 1900, U.S. Department of the Interior, "Reports of Inspection of the Field Jurisdictions of the Office of Indian Affairs, 1875-1900," National Archives Microfilm Publication M1070, reel 11, Flathead, 6597/1900.

Editors' note: These statements include Chief Charlo's and Baptiste Ka-ka-shee's complaints about their treatment by Agent W. H. Smead and Flathead Agency policies in 1900.

Statement of Sharlo, Chief of Flathead Indians

I spoke to agent Smead about cattle and horses of white men on the reservation and told him it was his duty to keep them off. He replied "Sharlo, You have no brains. You are opposed to me. He said I was just like a horse." I said "if I am a horse you ought to take care of me and when you call me a horse I think you are not a fit man to be the Agent." Another time I told him where some white men had driven cattle on the reservation and suggested that the Agent have them removed — the Agent said "Wait a little while." This was over a year ago but the agent did nothing to remove these cattle. The half breeds and the Agent stand in together.

Last year Agent Smead and Alex Dow the trader rounded up all the horses and cut the Stallions; when they found horses without brands on they appropriated them. The chiefs tried to stop this rascality but we were powerless. Smead said he had authority from Washington to round up the horses & take those which were not branded. Many of these unbranded horses belonged to old people & children living on this reservation, who had not been able to round up & brand their horses. Eighteen of our head men tried to stop this round up of Smead & Dow but we couldn't stop it. They brought these horses to Alex Dow's field, about 200 & Alex Dow Killed them & fed them to his hogs. Agent Smead said he would take the money Dow gave for these horses & divide it up among poor Indians, but none of the poor Indians ever got any of it.

Sharlo, his x mark

Witnesses to mark, Oscar Anderson, L Geis

I hereby certify that I acted as interpreter for Sharlo & that the preceding statement was written at his dictation & that he fully understands the contents thereof.

Paul Shawaway
Interpreter.

* * * * * * * * *

Statement of Ki-Ki-is-see Chief of Flathead Indians

Last spring I came to this agency & saw a band of cattle in a field near there about 100 — They told me they belonged to Agent Smead. Their brand was H. I told the agent there was a thief stealing horses near the foot of the lake. Smead asked me if I knew the man. I said yes, his name is Owl, which is all the same as thief. I said two men can prove he is a thief. Agent Carter had driven him out once, but he came back again. Smead said he would see about it but the man is there yet. I told him about last May.

Agent Carter used to do something but Smead does not help the Indians at all. I could give much more information if there was time to look around & get names.

Ki-Ki-is-see, his x mark

Witnesses to mark, Oscar Anderson, L Geis

I certify that I acted as interpreter for Ki-Ki-is-see and fully explained to him the contents of the above statement & that I wrote it at his dictation.

Paul Sha wa way
Interpreter.

Document 26

Reservation Chiefs Reject Sale of Northern Part of Reservation April 18, 1901

Source: James H. McNeely, et. al., to Commissioner of Indian Affairs, April 18, 1901, letter received 22,670/1901, land division, RG 75, National Archives, Washington, D.C.

Editors' note: Fortunately, this letter included the transcripts of the January and April 1901 meetings between the Crow, Flathead, Etc. Commission and the Flathead Reservation chiefs. The commissioners repeatedly threatened the chiefs: "The time will come when he [the Great Father] will take these matters into his own hands and do what he thinks best for them [the Indians] without a council." Chief Charlo replied, "You all know I won't sell a foot of land." They made plain their unwillingness to sell the northern part of the reservation. The chiefs pointed out that the government had not kept the promises it had made in earlier agreements and also realized that selling land was not in the best interests of the tribes. Kootenai Chief Isaac pointed out, "You told me I was poor and needed money, but I am not poor. What is valuable to a person is land, the earth, water, trees, &c., and all these belong to us. Don't think I am poor."

Hon. W. A. Jones,
Commissioner of Indian Affairs,
Washington, D.C.
Sir: —

We have the honor to report that this Commission held a general council with Indians of this Reservation at St. Ignatius Mission on the 3d instant. This council was called at the request of a number of Indians who were not satisfied with the result of the general council held in January last at the same place, and who were not represented at that time. Two or three days prior to the date first named (April 3d) requests were made of us for a further postponement of two months, with the statement that Chief Charlos had forbidden these Indians to act, or even talk to the Commissioners about an agreement, stating that he and others intended to go to Washington before any agreement was made. These requests we did not see our way clear to grant, and hence informed the Indians that the council would be held according to public notice.

The different bands were fairly well represented at the council, but it was plain from the start that the same opposition (Chief Charlos and the cattle-men) had complete control of the influential Indians. We have good reason to believe that quite a sum of money was used in defeating our propositions, one Indian having gone so far as to tell an employe at the Agency that he was approached with such an offer and asked to work against the Commission.

The portion of the Reservation selected by the Commission as the most advantageous for the Indians to dispose of was a strip off of the north end containing some 450,000 acres. With the exception of the Kootenais, who do little or no farming, that portion is very little used by any number of the other Indians. It is nearly all taken up by white men married to Indians, and a few half-blood cattle-men, most of whose rights on the reservation we believe are questioned. The tribes as a whole receive no benefit from the use of all this land, and we are informed that Charlos and his band, who are our chief opposition, have not been on the land referred to for twenty years. A number of these cattle-men sell live stock every year to the amount of many thousands of dollars.

For these reasons your Commission deemed it for the best interest of the Indians as a whole to dispose of this land, and we still hold the same opinion, although we consider it unwise to try and negotiate with them further at the present time and under the present circumstances, as they have rejected all our propositions. We are still fully satisfied that a large majority of them realize the conditions and are in favor of selling, but are held back by the leaders whom they have been so long accustomed to obey.

Under the circumstances we would ask that the work here be discontinued for the time being, and would respectfully make the following recommendations for the general good of these people, believing, too, that they would have a tendency if adopted to break up the opposition to an agreement, which we are satisfied would improve the condition of these Indians materially.

Recommendations.

1st. — That this Reservation be surveyed and allotments in severalty be made to all entitled to them, at once.

2d. — That the rights of white men and half-breeds who are now using the northern part of this reservation be determined, and that if possible the tribe in general be remunerated by the parties so using the land held in common by the Indians.

We would further state that the Agent [W. H. Smead] is in full accord with the above recommendations.

We would respectfully ask for further instructions.

With this report we transmit copies of proceedings of the two councils held at St. Ignatius in January last and on the 3rd of this month respectfully.

James H. McNeely, Commissioner and Chairman.
Charles G. Hoyt, Commissioner.
B. J. McIntire, Commissioner.

Flathead Agency,
Jocko P. O., Montana,
April 18, 1901.

* * * * * * * * *

Enclosure number 2:

The Council with Flatheads, and other tribes of the reservation, assembled at A. L. Demers' store, St. Ignatius, on Thursday, January 3d. 1901. Commissioners Hoyt, McIntire and McNeely, and Agent Smead were present representing the Government. The Kalispells and Kootenais were not represented.

Agent Smead introduced the Commissioners and stated object of the Council.

The Indians selected Joseph McDonald as interpreter, and Michel Revais, the official interpreter, acted for the Commission.

Commissioner Hoyt, addressing the Indians, said he was glad to see so many present. Since last council two of the Commissioners and the Agent have been to Washington and learned the wishes of the Great Father. We asked to be sent back here for the Indians' benefit. They can make a better deal with the Commissioners than to go to Washington. We heard last night that some one had reported that allotments could not be made unless a majority of the Indians consent. This is a mistake, as the Great Father has a right to do as he pleases for the benefit of the Indians. He has a right to make them allotments at any time. The time will come when he will take these matters into his own hands and do what he thinks best for them without a council.

At the last council we offered a certain price for a part of the reservation, and have heard since that the Indians didn't think the price was high enough. We have now prepared an agreement by which, if the Indians will accept, they will get all the land will bring. The Indians can sell the land themselves. Say we figure on the northern part of the reservation — everything north of the line between Missoula and Flathead counties — a line just North of the Sub-agency at Ronan. Fewer full-blood Indians live there than any place else on the reservation. Say we arrange to sell in this way, a commission of three Indians will be appointed, with their Agent a member. Then, if any persons want to buy a farm they can come to this Indian commission and say, we want to buy this land, on which no Indians are settled. No home will be taken from an Indian without he consents and is paid for improvements. This Indian commission will then put a price on the land for so much money. Then if the buyer will pay the price the money will be sent to Washington, and when enough is paid in there, 1/2 of which will amount to ten dollars for each Indian here, old and young, this will be paid to them. After ten years the Government will buy the remainder of the land, at an appraised price to be settled by the Secretary of the Interior. Half of the money received is to be paid to the Indians in cash as fast as it amounts to ten dollars each, and the balance is to be expended for the benefit of the Indians, under direction of the Secretary of the Interior. If people who want the land will not pay the price fixed in cash the land will not be sold, and nobody can buy more than enough for a home, not for speculation, and must live on it, except timber and grazing land.

The Flatheads are sensible people. Many of them are educated. We have presented this matter on business principles. If I want to buy a horse from Michel I have to pay his price. In this way the Indians will get all they think their land is worth. This agreement continues ten years and then any unsold land will be bought by the Government at a fair price.

The rights of any Indians like the Kalispells who haven't been sure of their rights will be established. Indians and half-breeds living on the reservation, whom the Indians wish to live here, will be granted full rights. The agreement provides for paying the Flatheads $6000.00. for letting the Kalispells of Camas Prairie remain on the Reservation.

Duncan McDonald asked: "Who are meant by Flatheads?"

Hoyt's reply: All others except Kalispells — Chief Michel's band. The $6000, to be paid to the other Indians for allowing the Kalispells to remain with full rights on the reservation, is to be expended in buying stallions for improving the breed of horses. Also $10,000.00. is to be paid to the Kalispells for expenses in removing to this reservation. Also $5,000.00. to pay the Kootenais for removing onto the unsold part of the reservation if they wish to leave their present homes.

Also allowing Charlos' band $1200. for certain things that he says were promised him for removing from Bitter Root Valley to this Reservation, this money to be expended for cattle for Charlos' band.

Charlos — "If these things had been paid for I would have had a larger band.

Hoyt — We will provide so he will be satisfied. The agreement also provides that no Indians will be required to move from their homes unless they wish; none will be forced to move, and if they do the Government will pay for their improvements what they are worth. Mr. Hoyt repeated the provisions of the proposed agreement and stated that the Commission of Indians would be paid $25. a month each for their services.

This is a business proposition which the Indians ought to think over. It is intended for their best interests.

Mr. Hoyt then introduced Commissioner McIntire, who said he was pleased to meet with the great chiefs and part of their people. He appreciated the discomforts of coming long distances in such cold and snowy weather to attend this council. Their homes are in the same country as his and he trusted that they would be friends. He wished to see the Indians of this reservation prosper to the greatest extent. It is necessary that they shall have money. The northern portion of the reservation is very thinly settled by Indians. For this reason the Great Father has selected it to be sold. There is a great amount of land there for each Indians — more so than in the Southern part. Most of the land in the Northern part is not occupied or used by Indians. The Great Father wishes to sell part and give money to the Indians. They have no annuities or other sources of income. He wishes to provide for Indians, food, clothes, houses, cattle, etc. When the treaty is made they will not only have all the land they need, but money besides. They will fix prices on their land. The Great Father thinks they have a right to set prices on land as they have on a horse. We think that this is the last offer to be made to the Indians. That this is the last Commission that will be sent to them. *[Handwritten insert in original document: "?? This plan was emphatically condemned in I. O."]* Indians' rights will be protected. They can select homes where they please. If they remove their improvements will be paid for. Land in Northern part of the reservation brings them in little or nothing. If land is sold they will not only have money but the value of their other property will be increased. On the Yakima reservation Indians are prosperous, since lands were allotted, by leasing or working themselves. The Great Father wishes the Indians to fix values of land without white influence. We shall now be glad to hear from Chiefs and head men and report what they say to the Great Father.

Chief Charlos — You all know that I won't sell a foot of land. Washington is not far from here and when we want to sell we can go there. Washington is our father, and why does he want to take our land from us ("by force," according to Duncan McDonald's interpretation?) I know by the papers who has a right to represent Washington, and demand that they be shown. (The agreement was here shown) I want to see credentials with big seal on.

Duncan McDonald explained by stating how one Corey, who represented himself as a special agent, several years ago swindled people on this reservation, which made Charlos suspicious.

Charlos — I have been told when any commissioners come here to require him to show his credentials.

The commissioners all said they possessed credentials but didnt have them here.

Commissioner McIntire said that Agent Smead knew the commissioners, and that they were authorized to treat with these Indians. He asked whether Charlos would take the Agent's word.

Charlos said he would not. *["!!" handwritten in original.]*

McIntire — If Charlos refuses to negotiate without seeing the seal, the Commission will report the refusal to the Great Father. We will produce it as soon as we can get the commissions.

Charlos — The boundary lines have been surveyed three times, and the reservation has been set aside for the Indians forever.

Agent Smead assured Charlos that the commissioners were all authorized to treat with these Indians. He said he wouldn't allow anybody on the reservation under any circumstances unless duly authorized. He had seen the papers of all three commissioners. He had known Commissioner McIntire ten years. He had been to Washington and talked about these commissioners. They are from the Great Father, and sent here to treat with the Indians. He said that the commission would be glad to listen to all chiefs and head men.

Duncan McDonald — Charlos forbids them to speak.

Commissioner McIntire — Ask them whether they wish to talk of the matter amongst themselves tonight.

Commissioner McNeely — This is entirely agreeable to the commissioners.

Agent Smead — I think it wise for Indians to hold a council tonight amongst themselves, and consider the commissioners' proposition very carefully. Don't arrive at a wrong conclusion. The commissioners are servants of the Great Father in Washington. He sends them to you. Treat them with respect. They want to do what is best for the Indians. The Great Father is the Indians' friend. He may not send another commission to treat with you. Don't make the Great Father angry with you. If you don't understand the agreement ask the Agent or Commissioners. Send for the agent if he can help you or explain anything.

The Council then adjourned to re-assemble tomorrow, (Friday) at ten o'clock forenoon.

* * * * * * * * *

Friday, January 4, 1901, 11 a.m.

Agent Smead called the Council to order. He asked the chiefs for the conclusion of their council last night.

Charlos — When we were in Judge Joseph's house we studied and talked about the matter and looked all about the reservation. We have been mistreated and so concluded not to sell any part of the reservation. Other Indians besides himself have got the worst of it in dealing with the Government. We have not got pay for our lands in Bitter Root Valley. We have talked with this Commission and do not wish to do them any wrong. The Flatheads have always been a peaceful tribe. There is no white men's blood on their hands. We saw the first white man in my grandfather's time and have always treated them right.

Commissioner McIntire — Is there anything wrong about the Commission's proposition?

Charlos — Our tribes and other tribes have been deceived by the Government, and for this reason we have no confidence that we will be treated right, judging by the past.

McIntire — Do you still dispute the authority of this commission?

Charlos — I do still doubt it.

McIntire — If the Great Father does just as he proposes will you be satisfied then?

Charlos — If I could go to Washington myself I would talk the matter over with the head men there.

McIntire — Don't you know that the agreement if made goes to the Great Father before it becomes final, the same as all treaties?

Alexander Matt made an explanation to Charlos of the commissioners' meaning, and still Charlo repeated that he did not wish to sell the land.

McIntire — Does he refuse to sell under any circumstances?

Charlos — Yes.

McIntire — Do any other Indians wish to talk now?

Judge Lewissohn — Three commissions have been here. I have been all over the reservation and talked with the Flatheads, Kalispells and Kootenais. They have never got what they were promised and we are all afraid to make a treaty.

McIntire — Do you understand the proposed treaty, and do you think it a fair proposition?

Lewissohn — I don't think you went at it in the right way. If you want to buy land why don't you come with money?

McIntire — Do you want to sell under any circumstances?

Lewissohn — No.

McIntire — Do you take us for boys who don't know what to do or how to do it?

Lewissohn — No.

McIntire — Do you mean to say that you won't sell even for money?

Lewissohn — It depends on the chiefs, and what they decide to do the tribes will follow.

McIntire — Have the chiefs instructed you what to say?

Lewissohn — No; I form my own opinions. Many others of these people hold back.

McIntire — Hasn't the Great Father made a fair proposition if carried out?

Lewissohn — If we could see the Great Father and he would tell us what to do we would study the matter over seriously. A few days ago the Agent went to Washington and I would have liked to go with him but he didn't ask me. In making our old treaties we knew this time would come and we would be asked to sell our land. When the Stevens and Garfield treaties were made we thought the reservation was ours forever. Then other tribes were brought in here to live on our reservation.

McIntire — Does anybody else wish to talk, mixed bloods included? Any person has a right to talk here. The reservation is going to be thrown open; it is only a question of time, *["!!" inserted in original]* and educated Indians, who have considerable at stake, ought to express themselves.

Duncan McDonald — I wish to talk to the Indians in their own language and will not refer to the Commission but the Government. They think the Government is a big wolf, from their point of view. When they made a treaty with Governor Stevens he had a sweet mouth. He made a line around the reservation but it has since been made smaller; a slice of land down by Paradise was cut off. Stevens promised things that the Indians have never received. Afterward Garfield held a council with these Indians with the same result. He was plausible like this commission. Charlos' land in Bitter Root Valley is still unsold. Washington has lots of money while these Indians are living from hand to mouth as best they can. Indians are starving while waiting for money promised to them. The Flatheads have always been friendly to whites and have clean hands while the Government has been kicking them around. Other tribes that have fought the Government have been treated much better than the Flatheads. The Indians feel this way and are afraid to sign an agreement, for fear they will be treated as heretofore. In a few years the Government will want to make another treaty and buy more land.

McIntire — Will you please express you own opinion of the fairness of the proposed treaty?

Duncan McDonald — Poor Michel and Charlos have been treated cruelly. Promises made to them were similar to yours. When half-breeds wish to talk, full-blood Indians say they must not.

Joseph McDonald — Indians don't understand the $10. proposition.

McIntire explained it to the interpreter (Jo McDonald) who in turn explained to the Indians.

Alex Matt (educated half-breed): The Indian chiefs wish to seld [send] a delegation to Washington and prove for themselves whether the Government wishes to make a treaty. That is the reason why they don't want to make a treaty now. They also wish to collect their back pay, and to tell the authorities themselves what was promised to the Indians. He also expressed himself in favorable terms toward this Commission and its proposed agreement.

McIntire — We have listened to the Indians' proposition to go to Washington. The Great Father has sent us here to treat with you, but you have refused to recognize us. It would do no good to go to Washington. The law provides for you to treat with this Commission and with nobody else. We will say to the Great Father that you have not treated us with proper courtesy and respect. You have denied our authority and papers, and said you do not believe the Agent's word. *["!" inserted in original.]* We do not come here to beg you but to state facts for your own good.

We will also report to the Great Father that a large portion of your land is being occupied and used by cattle-men who are not Indians and have no rights on the reservation. Their right, if they have any, will be settled. We believe that it is largely through the influence of these stock=men that no treaty has been made. You can't accuse us of not being plain in our talk. We will try to make good our words in this and other matters.

The full-bloods and half-bloods are poor, yet they are satisfied to go to the stock=men and get a few cattle on shares and be their slaves, instead of owning their own land and receiving pay for its products. The northern part of the reservation is occupied mostly by cattlemen who are getting rich at the expense of the Indians.

Agent Smead then spoke — I have been your agent three years, and when I see the poor way in which the Indians live I feel sympathy for them. I wrote to Washington about affairs on the reservation and called attention to the conditions. A few things were sent here but not enough to take care of the poor and sick. I asked for good stallions to improve the breed of horses, and for cattle that the Indians could sell. The answer was that the Indians had no money like other tribes who had sold land that they didn't need. Last month I went to Washington, after talking to Charlos and other chiefs. I saw the authorities at Washington and pleaded for the Indians. The answer was that the Flatheads had been neglected but the fault was with the Great Council which didn't appropriate enough money. Our hearts are with the Indians. I told the authorities at Washington that the Indians didn't want to sell the reservation or any part of it. They replied that if there is a small part of the reservation that the Indians can spare they might sell to this Commission. Also that the Indians said they had not been offered enough for land. The Great Father wants to pay all that it is worth and the Indians ought to be paid the full value. If Indians will sell land they will have money, cattle, stallions and other things that they need. This is the reason why the Commission is here today.

I am sorry to see them sell any part of the reservation. It is like a man selling part of his farm. — he dislikes to do so, where he has lived all his life, but if he is in need of necessary articles and has no other way to get them, he had better sell and buy what he needs. The question is, hadn't you Indians better sell part of the reservation and buy what you need? I have figured that the land that the Government wants to buy ought to bring a million dollars, or nearly $700.00. for every man, woman and child on the reservation. One-half would be paid in money, the other half to be spent by the Secretary of Interior for blooded horses, cattle, houses, etc.

Under this agreement you would sell this land yourselves, through three of your number and your Agent. The money would be divided twice a year so long as there is land to sell. Unsold land would belong to you. At the end of ten years the Government would buy the unsold land in the ceded strip and pay you its full value. This money would amount to a great deal. A man, his wife and two children would receive about $2800.00.; with four children $4200.00., half cash, the other half to be spent to buy articles that you need. In addition, your remaining lands would be surveyed and allotted. Any old person could rent his or her share and receive cash. Allotments could be made on the ceded strip or on the unsold portion of the reservation.

Other Indians who have sold their lands — the Crows, Nez-Perces, Blackfeet, Bannocks, Shoshones, Umatillas, etc., have money and think it was a good thing to sell. You have the opportunity to do this today, and don't you think that you had better do it? I, as your Agent, have explained the agreement honestly. Think it all over, and if you don't sell I will not be angry with you. If Charlos and his poor people had money I wouldn't advise you to sell. It is now for you to decide for yourselves.

McIntire — Does any other Indian wish to talk? There was no response.

Agent Smead read an extract from the Stevens treaty of 1855. He also referred to the General Allotment act. Both of these empower the Great Father to allot lands and sell surplus lands without the consent of Indians. *["?" inserted in original.]*

Lewissohn — I am sorry that we can't go to Washington. Indians go there to see about big things. We are afraid of each other. *["Distrust" inserted in original.]* You don't want me to go to Washington.

The Council then adjourned without date.

* * * * * * * * *

Enclosure number 1:

Proceedings
Of a General Council Held with Indians of the Flathead Reservation at Saint Ignatius, Montana, April 3, 1901, (Wednesday).
at Predieux & Demers' Store.

The Council assembled at 3 o'clock p.m. Present, Commissioners McNeely (chairman), Hoyt and McIntire; also Agent W. H. Smead.

Interpreters, Michel Revais (official for the Reservation), Gustave (Statah) for the Kootenais, Louis Camille, Ed Dishon and Maud S.

Commissioner Hoyt — This Council has been called for the Indians' benefit. We had a council last January, but the Kootenais and Kalispels were not here. The Commissioners thought they would go away and not return, as no agreement was made, but some Indians came to the Commissioners and asked them to have another council, and we wrote to Washington and asked if we should come and have this council. Washington told us to come back again. This council is for the Indians and not for the Commissioners. We come at the time the Indians asked us to come — the week before Easter Sunday. We are here for the good of the Indians, and want to talk over the same matters as last time.

Some Indians on the upper part of the Reservation have their money from their Bitter Root lands. Chief Charlos has his money. We heard that Charlos wanted this council put off, and that he said he was going to Washington. Charlos can't go there without a permit. If he goes without, the President will not see him. We don't think the President will issue him a permit. Some time ago the Commission asked the President to let some of these Indians go to Washington, but he said No. He said if they went to Washington they would have to come back and made a deal with the Commissioners. We can't put off a council because Charlos or any other Indian wants us to do so. Our orders are to deal with all the Indians and not with one. Washington don't believe that Charlos or any one else has a right to stop these Indians from making a deal. If the Kootenais want to sell part of their land, the Indians at Charlos' end of the Reservation have no right to say they sha'n't. Charlos has received his money and he has no right to stop the Kootenais and other Indians from getting money for their land. Charlos doesn't seem to take an interest in his Indians as I don't see him here to-day.

It won't be a great while until the Government will allot these lands. *["?" inserted in original.]* Washington has a right to allot lands at any time it thinks best for the Indians. It would be better for the Indians to sell part of their land before the Government allots. They can make a better deal now and get more for it than to have the Government sell it for them. This is the reason we have come back. It is better for the Indians.

We have the same plan as when we were here last time. I want to make it as plain to you as I can. The land we have in mind is the northern portion of the Reservation, north of the Sub-Agency. We want to allow the Indians to sell that land at a price they make themselves. The Indians now have three Judges. We want to appoint three Indians more to put prices on those lands, these Indians to be paid for their time the same as the judges are paid for their time. These three Indians are to go over the land and put prices on the different parts of it. Then, if some one wishes to buy a quarter=section he goes to this Indian Commission and asks the price of it. These three Indians then find out which piece of land the man wishes to buy, and they and their Agent put a price on the land and tell the white man the price. If he won't pay this price he can't buy it. Some pieces of land will be worth more than other pieces. If the white man pays the price asked, the money will be sent to Washington. As soon as there is enough there, the Secretary or President will send it out and have it divided amongst the Indians. Half will be paid to the Indians in cash and the other half will be spent by the President for things that the Indians need. The money should be distributed at least twice a year. The Indians will get the benefit of all money paid in. Nobody else will receive any of this money except these Indians. I want to have this plain, as we were misunderstood the last time. Some Indians thought they would receive only one payment. The Indians will receive payment after payment as long as money is received.

Commissioner Hoyt repeated what Agent Smead said in his talk at the last council:

"I have figured that the land ought to bring a million dollars, or nearly $700 for every man, woman and child on the reservation. Half would be paid in money, the other half in blooded horses, cattle and other articles that the Indians would need. Under this arrangement you would sell land through three Indians and the Agent. The money would be distributed twice a year as long as there is land to sell. This money would amount to a great deal. A man, his wife and two children should receive about $2800. Half would be in cash and half in articles that you need. After ten years, if there was land left, the Government would buy it and the pay the Indians for it."

Com'r Hoyt then said: We have other provisions in the Agreement, and called for questions.

A Pend d'Oreille Indian replied that he thought everybody understood. (The foregoing was interpreted into Kootenai and the other dialects.)

Commissioner Hoyt: I now want to talk about the Camas Prairie (Lower Kalispel) Indians. They made a deal some years ago at Sand Point, Idaho. The great Council in Washington never said Yes to that agreement. No agreement is good until the great Council says yes to it. Washington has always been very sorry that the big Council didn't say yes to that agreement, and we were instructed to put a provision for the Camas Prairie Indians in the new agreement. We have put in, that Washington is to send Michel's band $10,000. This money is to be used to buy cattle and other things that Michel's Band needs. It is in this paper, and anyone who can read can see it. It doesn't come out of land sales, but is to be sent from Washington. It is to make right the old agreement.

In addition, Washington is to spend $6000 for all three of the tribes in what they may need.

In addition, Washington is to spend $1200 for Charlos' Band for things he claims were heretofore promised but not paid.

If this deal is made, the Kootenais may have to leave where they are and come to this part of the Reservation. They don't have to move unless they want to, but will probably want to do so. If they do move to another part of the Reservation south of the line of division, it will be a hardship and expense to them. So we have put in the agreement that if the Kootenais move they are to have $5000, either to be paid in cash or things they need, as the President chooses. This is outside (to Kootenais) of proceeds of sales of lands. They will get their full share of what is paid for land and this in addition. Mr. Hoyt asked —

Question: Do you understand?

Answer by several, "Yes."

Com'r Hoyt: All these Indians are poor and need money and things that money will buy. The Kootenais, Kalispels and nearly all the Indians need money. If they do, why not exchange land that they don't need for money that they do need?

We have offered a fair proposition. We think it the best ever offered any Indians. I have been dealing four years with Indians, and it is the best proposition that I have ever seen. *["!" inserted in original.]* It leaves the sale of land entirely to yourselves. You and the Agent put a price on land, and if a man doesn't want to pay the price he can't have it. If he does pay the price, the Indians get the benefit of every cent he pays. Nobody can take any advantage of you under this agreement.

Chief Isaac (of the Kootenais): Do you intend to make good arrangements with us?

Com'r Hoyt: The best we can.

Chief Isaac: Are you chief?

Com'r Hoyt: We represent the Chief at Washington.

Chief Isaac: I am chief of the Kootenais, and anything I tell my Indians to do they all do. You're off (wrong). When they treated for this reservation, the treaty wasn't this way. Three men were the head men, and when they granted this reservation they didn't grant it to sell. When these three men gave us this reservation it was a big country. When they made lines, white man's place was outside of the reservation. When treaties were made with other Indians they were to get money in their hands, but they never got it. Where is it? All I got was hearsay. I never got money in my hands or saw it with my eyes.

Before we make a new treaty we want to know the boundary lines of this reservation. That is the next thing we ought to work on. Making bargains for the reservation is out of our line. We want to quit making bargains until we find our lines. To-day and afterwards I don't want to hear any more stories, but want the truth. My body is full of your people's lies.

You told me I was poor and needed money, but I am not poor. What is valuable to a person is land, the earth, water, trees, &c., and all these belong to us. Don't think I am poor. Why do you tell me I am poor? Does stock, land, timber, etc., make me poor? I don't consider myself poor, because I don't need anything. Therefore, don't think I am poor and you won't make any bargain with me. We haven't any more land than we need, so you had better buy from somebody else. Maybe some poor people are willing to sell land. Forty-six years ago we made a deal with people who talked the same language that you do.

That is all I have to say, and you had better hunt some people who want money more than we do.

(There were expressions of approval from Indians.)

Com'r Hoyt: The first thing in the agreement is a provision to have the land surveyed. Does anybody else want to talk?

Judge Kackashee: I heard Isaac talk, and I believe none of the Indians want to sell land.

Chief Michel (of Lower Kalispels): Of course the words of the Washington Chief are good and we can't break them. He sympathized with us poor Indians and told us to take good care of our land and not squander it, and said, if you do, you will be poor. We know these were his words. You say he said the words you told us, and we can't answer them.

Com'r Hoyt: Anybody has a right to talk.

An Indian: Children don't want to talk after the head-men have talked.

Com'r Hoyt: We are glad to have heard this talk. Have taken it all down and will send it to Washington. We have offered you a fair agreement as Washington told us to do, and we don't know what Washington will do now. We have offered you a fair agreement and told the truth. We have the best of feeling toward the Indians here, and have carried out all our instructions from Washington. We shall be glad to furnish more provisions to you this evening and to-morrow.

Judge Lewissohn: Everybody understands well, and the three Indians who spoke told the truth, and all other Indians agree with them. It takes too long to receive our money. We intend to go to Washington, as we now have plenty of money to go with.

At 6 o'clock p.m. the Council adjourned sine die.

Document 27

Chief Charlot Protests Opening of Flathead Reservation January – March 1905

Source: Samuel Bellew to Commissioner of Indian Affairs, January 12, 1905, letter received 4,318/1905, finance division, RG 75, National Archives, Washington, D.C.; "Flathead Council Is Now in Session Considering Future Conditions," *The Daily Missoulian*, February 5, 1905, page 4, col. 5-6; "Council Continues on Reservation," *The Daily Missoulian*, February 6, 1905, page 2, col. 2; "Flatheads' Council Comes to End," *The Daily Missoulian*, February 9, 1905, page 2, col. 2; "Chief Charlot Is Going East," *The Daily Missoulian*, February 10, 1905, page 4, col. 4-5; "Charlot to Have Place of Honor," *The Daily Missoulian*, February 21, 1905, page 1, col. 5; "Chief Charlot Returns from Capital and Will Call Council," *The Daily Missoulian*, March 18, 1905, page 3, col. 1-2.

Editors' note: Charlo and the other chiefs were outraged that the government was proceeding to allot the Flathead Reservation without the consent of tribal members and leaders and went to Washington to stop the opening. No transcript of Charlo's negotiations in Washington has been found to see his argument against opening the reservation. The *Missoulian* reported the tribal council and Charlot's resulting 1905 trip to Washington, D.C., in detail, but the early reports made it sound like Charlot was only seeking to secure a small timber reserve for the tribe. As the last article made clear, Charlot and the chiefs and headmen were totally opposed to the allotment policy and opening the reservation to white homesteaders.

Department of the Interior,
United States Indian Service,
Flathead Agency, Jocko, Mont. Jan. 12, 1905.

Hon. Commissioner of Indian Affairs,
Washington, D.C.
Sir:

Charlo, Chief of the Flatheads, desires to visit Washington, taking with him Judge Antoine Moise and accompanied by Ed. Deschamps and Pascal Antoine, as interpreters.

The object of Chief Charlo's visit is to protest against the opening of the reservation: It has been explained to him several times, both by Special Agents who have been here, and myself, that Congress had decided to open the reservation for settlement and to allot the Indians land in severalty, but in face of all this he is still unbelieving and clings to his understanding of the Stevens treaty made in 1855, with his father and at the making of which he was present, and says he will not believe nor consent to it until he is told "face to face by the President."

Should he then be convinced that the reservation will be opened in spite of his protest, he desires to urge that action be taken to preserve some of the timber land for the exclusive use of the Indians, instead of having it all sold as provided in the bill; also that the Indians be protected in their water rights by legislative enactment, that there may not be the same trouble here that he claims exists elsewhere where lands have been alloted and the balance opened for settlement; there are a number of other minor points that he wishes to discuss with the "President."

Charlo is the recognized hereditary Chief of the Flatheads and has considerable influence with them, especially the full-bloods, and should his opposition be placated, considerable petty annoyances might be avoided and the assistance, instead of ill-will of himself and following be gained.

Very respectfully,
Samuel Bellew
U.S. Indian Agent.

* * * * * * * * *

Flathead Council Is Now in Session Considering Future Conditions Head Men Are Present to Hear Chief Charlot's Plan Regarding an Appeal to President for Setting Aside of Timber for Exclusive Use of Indians.

From authentic sources it is learned that the great council among the confederated tribes of the Flathead reservation at present in progress has been called at the behest of Chief Charlot, who has an important matter to place before the head men and chiefs of the different tribes.

The old chief, who for many years was the recognized head of the tribe and whose father, Chief Victor, signed the Hellgate treaty of 1852 [sic], is desirous of making a trip to Washington and laying before President Roosevelt, personally, a grievance which the Indians have against the bill providing for the opening of the Flathead reservation.

As the measure stands today, through a probable oversight on the drafter of the bill, and through whose efforts the measure became a law of the land, no provision has been made to retain any of the timber lands on the reservation for the use of the Indians.

Chief Charlot, who is recognized as one of the leaders among the Indians of the United States, has given the bill opening the reservation his careful consideration and he has discovered that no provision has been made reserving the Indians any timber rights whatever.

His idea is that within the next few years there will be a scarcity of timber for firewood purposes on the reservation; that when that time arrives the Indians who have been allotted their lands in severality, will be compelled to buy their firewood from the white men who become the owners of the timbered area. To obviate this condition he thinks a personal appeal to the president will result in much good and that a law can be passed during the present session of congress which will carry a provision to the effect that a forest reserve will be created providing that certain lands on the reservation will be the exclusive property of the Indians. This will give a timber supply to the Indian residents of the reservation that will last for many years to come.

Generally speaking, according to the information secured in Missoula yesterday, the project is meeting with approval among the members of the confederated tribes and it is believed that the Indians on the Flathead will raise enough money to send Chief Charlot and his interpreter, as well as a number of other Indians to the national capital to ask for legislation along the lines above suggested.

The old chief was one of the most bitter Indians on the reservation in opposing the opening of the reservation, but when he was shown the clause in the Stevens treaty which provided that the president could allot the land in severality to the members of the tribe when the proper time arrived, he acquiesced, and although the news was most astounding to him, he made no comment further than to say: "That makes sweat," and he then gave up the lands which he had been taught for many years past was the exclusive property of the Flatheads and the other confederated tribes.

It is believed that Chief Charlot will win all of the other Indians over to his views and that he will leave within the next two weeks for Washington, there to make a formal protest to the "great father" and to place in his hands the petition from the members of the different tribes on the Flathead reservation for a timber reservation to be the exclusive property of the Flathead reservation Indians, and on which there will be no poaching by the white men after the reservation is formally opened.

* * * * * * * * *

Council Continues on Reservation
Flathead Indians Have Not Concluded Their Discussion Regarding Timber.

The council of Flathead Indians and chiefs of allied tribes is still in session. Those engaged in the deliberation of the questions which have arisen, maintain absolute silence regarding the proceedings. No white men are permitted in the council tepee and even Agent Bellew is ignorant as to the secret proceeding. That there is friction among the headmen of the tribes, is evidenced by the fact that so much secrecy is being maintained. Chief Charlot is known to wield considerable influence among the older men in the council and he is in earnest in his efforts to secure from President Roosevelt a forest reserve which shall forever remain the exclusive property of the Flathead Indians. Chief Charlot's plan is to go to Washington in person and present the Indians' side of the question prior to the issuance of the proclamation declaring the reservation open for settlement.

Charlot has frequently complained regarding the failure of congress to provide a protection for Indians' firewood and building logs and at the time runners were sent out to summon the chiefs in council, Charlot stated his plan. Since that time the question of the rights of selection of land in severalty has come up in connection with the enrollment which is now in progress.

It is intimated that Charlot stands for allotment of land to full bloods only and that the privilege extending the right to all who have any trace of Flathead blood in their veins, is extremely opposed by the old chief. Charlot is said to be a brainy man and the final result of the council may mark an epoch in the checkered career of the Flathead and allied tribes. The whites look for an announcement tomorrow.

* * * * * * * * *

Flatheads' Council Comes to End
Result of Conference Is Safely Guarded by Those Present.

The great council of the Flatheads, which has been in progress near the mission for the past several days, and at which a number of matters of interest to the confederated tribes have been considreed [sic], has come to an end but whether or not Chief Charlot has carried his point and will be sent to Washington as a delegate from the tribe to lay his proposition for a forest reserve for the use of the Indians in the future before the president can not be learned in Missoula, although it is generally conceded that Charlot has won out in his proposal and will go to Washington if the consent of the d[e]partm[e]nt can be secured. It is stated, however, that the government has flatly refused its permission.

Another important matter which was before [t]he council was the considering of who among the mixed bloods are eligible to enrollment and who will come under the head of members of the tribe eligible to allotment of land when the reservation is opened for settlement. Quite a large number of claimants, who allege they are entitled to enrollment, have not yet been adopted into the tribe according to the custom which has been in vogue for centuries and as a result of the conference a number of adoptions may be made in the near future, but this is opposed by Charlot.

While Charlot is no longer recognized as the hereditary chief of the Flatheads by the government, he is nevertheless considered as the dean of all the chiefs of the confederated tribes and what he stands for is generally considered good enough for the other chiefs and head men to follow. He is vigorous and determined in the pushing of any project he may undertake and his friends in Missoula — and he has a lot of them, too — are all sanguine in their belief that the old man will do considerable good if the government will allow him to go to Washington and personally talk to the "Great Father" concerning plans he has which will result in benefit to the members of the confederated tribes.

* * * * * * * * *

Chief Charlot Is Going East

Ruler of Flatheads Determined to Tell President of Tribe's Needs.

Chief Charlot, hereditary chief of the Flathead tribe and dean of the chieftains and head men of the confederated tribes on the reservation, accompanied by his interpreter, Antoine Paschell, is in the city on his way to Washington, where he will personally lay certain matters before President Roosevelt in regard to the opening of the Flathead reservation. All of these matters were discussed at the big council which was held near the agency last week, the story of which has already been published in the Missoulian.

Yesterday, through an interpreter, Chief Charlot talked interestingly and stated that he expected to accomplish considerable good by his trip to Washington. He is one of the most able Indians alive today and he thoroughly understands all of the conditions which prevails in the political world. He knows that President Roosevelt, by reason of his resident in the west, is better acquainted with the conditions which prevail in Montana than any other man who has ever been in the presidential chair, and by reason of this fact he expects his petition will not fall upon deaf ears.

For some time past the old chief has been endeavoring to secure permission from the department to go to Washington, but this has been refused him. On account of this refusal the council last week was called. At the council enough money to send him and his interpreter to see the "Great Father" was pledged and Charlot has gotten this far on his journey. He will remain in Missoula for a few days, until another message is sent the department asking that Agent Bellew be also allowed to go to Washington with the chief. If this request is refused then Charlot and his interpreter will make the journey together.

There seems to be little desire on the part of the department to absolutely prohibit Charlot from going to Washington, the messages which declined to authorize the trip advising him that owing to the short session of congress, he will be able to accomplish but very little in the righting of the wrongs he alleges and the plans for the betterment of the condition of the Indians which he proposes. In this matter he is advised to wait for a more propitious time.

However, Charlot is of the opinion that there is no time like the present to do a good deed, and if advices authorizing Agent Bellew are not received in the city within the next few days, the journey to the national capital will be begun by the noted Indian.

In addition to the forest reserve which is desired by the Indians and which has already been exploited in the Missoulian, Chief Charlot has other projects which he desires to bring to the attention of the president. One of these is the preservation of the water rights which the Indians have acquired on the reservation. Quite a large number of Indian ranchers have learned the value of irrigating ditches and at no little trouble and toil they have brought the water upon their lands. As it is these water rights are not of record; the Indian has the right of use and no more, and the recommendation will be made to the president that a special act of congress be passed guaranteeing the right of irrigation and preserving the rights already in use to the Indians who have acquired them. In addition, as there are a number of excellent reservoir sites on the reservation, some action will be asked from the national government to guarantee their use to the confederated tribes.

Another matter which Charlot discussed yesterday was that in the Flathead opening bill no provision is made for the care of the poor, crippled, blind and infirm residents of the reservation — and there are quite a number of them too — and he will ask that some provision, such as the county uses in the care of its poor, be provided for the Indians.

Charlot asserts that the Indians will all have some money coming to them when the reservation opens, but he and the others who were promised money when they gave up their lands in the Bitter Root valley thirty years ago have had experience which they do not relish and are still awaiting the money which was promised for the sale of the lands which they relinquished. He thinks the same methods may prevail with the opening of the Flathead, and if it does, then the old and infirm members of the tribes will starve to death while they are waiting for the money which has been promised.

Charlot is still hale and hearty and is very vehement in his opinion that good will result from his visit to Washington. He is one of the few members of the Flathead tribe who cannot speak the English language, keeping an interpreter with him whenever he is away from the reservation. He is very pronounced in his views in regard to people of mixed blood being allowed allotments on the reservation and asserts that the white men have already gotten enough graft from the Indians; that they should not be allowed to come to the Flathead because they have a little Indian blood in their veins and, through their superior business judgment and knowledge of soil, select the cream of the lands of the reservation. This is another matter he will bitterly oppose when he gets to Washington and talks with the "Great Father" regarding the woes of the Flatheads and the procedure which should be following in their rightment.

For a while Charlot was in consultation with an attorney of Missoula yesterday and, though his trip to Washington may be made in opposition to the wishes of the Indian department, it can be depended upon that he will keep well within his rights and will secure an audience with the president, even should his petition be turned down again, as it was on the occasion of his last visit to Washington, when he, in company with a number of the reservation stockmen, lodged a protest against the collection of the grazing tax which is exacted from all of the stockmen of the reserve who own in excess of 100 head of horses or cattle.

* * * * * * * * *

Charlot to Have Place of Honor

Special to The Missoulian.

Washington, Feb. 20. — Chief Charlot arrived Saturday with Pascale, his interpreter. To-day they called upon Congressman Dixon at the capital.

Mr. Dixon is arranging an interview for them with the president and commissioner. Charlot says he will not believe the reservation is to be opened until the president tells him so. He will remain several days.

Mr. Dixon is arranging with the inauguration committee to give Charlot a place of honor in the parade.

* * * * * * * * *

Chief Charlot Returns from Capital and Will Call Council
Famous Flathead Will Protest Against Opening of Reservation and During Interview with President Stated His Reasons Which May Result in Investigation.

Chief Charlot and Interpreter Michael returned from Washington yesterday afternoon on No. 3. The old chief was so weary when Missoula was reached that he decided to stop off and rest for a day before continuing his journey to the reservation.

Interpreter Michael says the inauguration ceremonies were particularly interesting and that Chief Charlot enjoyed them, though he was not in the parade. The chief had a short talk with the president, explaining his views. He met Senator Carter, Congressman Dixon, Judge Knowles and other Montanans.

The interpreter says it is a mistake to suppose that Chief Charlot went to Washington to insist upon a timber reserve being set aside for the use of the Indians. That was attended to before he and Charlot reached Washington, Mr. Dixon having had the bill amended to include a timber reserve for the Indians. The fact is, Charlot does not want the reservation opened at all, and will do all in his power to prevent its being opened. He says that under the plan of allotment provided for in the bill too many breeds are getting a finger in the pie. He has no objection to the half-breeds of the three tribes on the reservation getting land, but there is an innumerable host of quarters and eighths, and many with just a trace of Indian blood who have been enrolled and who will be given land. Again, there are a number of Nez Perces on the Flathead reservation who claim to have been transferred there and they also demand enrollment and land. Indians from other lands are there who demand enrollment, but it not known whether any of them have succeeded in their desire or not.

Charlot asked for a congressional committee to investigate, and the interpreter says that while this may not be given, there will be a special agent sent to Montana and that he may be expected some time during the coming summer. Meantime, Charlot will call a council, which will be held on the reservation some time next month. He will endeavor to get the council to petition the government to delay the opening of the reservation until such time as a commission can examine and report upon the feasibility of opening the land to settlement. If it be decided that the reservation must be opened, Charlot will then endeavor to have only a portion of the reservation opened. He is bitterly opposed to the Indians being forced to select lands. He says that it is unfair to make Indians lose their tribal rights and become white men. They are unfitted as a rule to become farmers and need the assistance the government now gives them. Charlot says it makes no difference what the other Indians may decide to do, his band, removed from the Bitter Root valley, now in the southern portion of the reservation, along the Jocko, will never consent to receive lands in severalty. The whites took their land, good land, and forced them to go on the reservation, where they did not want to go, promising them that the land should be theirs and their children's forever, and that land they expect to keep, unless the government goes back on its solemn pledge.

The interpreter was asked how Charlot enjoyed his trip and in reply said that the old chief didn't enjoy all of it. He was thinking, thinking all the time. He is getting old and dislikes traveling. He would not have taken the trip had he not been convinced that he could stop the reservation being thrown open to settlement. He doesn't care for a timber reserve, or for a farm or for anything else in particular, except to retain the reservation as it is.

Asked if in the council held before Charlot went to Washington it was not decided that the Indians would be satisfied with the plan to open the reservation, provided they were given a timber reserve, he said that no such an argument was reached. Charlot did not believe that the reservation was to be opened until he reached Washington. He says he can't understand it. Although the treaty provides that the reservation can be opened, Charlot says he never knew that provision was in it, and can't understand how it got there.

When the old chief reaches the reservation he proposes to make a personal canvass of the situation. He says that while he may not prevent all the reservation from being thrown open he believes he can stop all of it from being opened to settlement. He remains implacable. He will never consent to have his people alloted land in severalty.

Document 28

Kootenai Chief Koos-ta-ta's Work Horse Stolen

March 9, 1906

Source: Koos-ta-ta to Samuel Bellew, March 9, 1906, Flathead Agency Papers, letters received, 8NS-075-96-323, National Archives, Denver, Colorado.

Editors' note: One of Koos-ta-ta's work horses was stolen by a tribal member and then sold to a white man who would not return the horse until legally forced to. Koos-ta-ta was not able to put in his crop with only one horse and did not have the money to purchase another horse.

Dayton Mar. 9. 1906

Mr Samuel Bellew U.S. Indian Agent
Flathead Agency Montana
Dear Sir:

I just made a trip to Kalispell to get my work horses that was stolen from me by Gingra, and could not find the man, so I showed my letter that I had from you to the officers in Kalispell and they said it was no good, and said that Doc Hull knew that I could not gain Possesion of my horses. Now I have made three trips after my horse and it has cost me several dollars expences, and I still failed to get the horse, it has been proven that this horse was stolen from me and I shouldn't be out the money that I have to gain possession of a horse that is my own property that I never sold or traded to any one. I will soon be ready to put in my crop and this particular horse is one of my only team I have to work and if I am unable to get him will have to buy one to go with his mate to make me a team and it will cost me $100.00 to buy one as good as this one is, and at this time of year I am unable to get the money to buy one with and if I am not able to get my horse will have to ask you to help me to buy one as I will have to have another horse to put in my crop.

Now as you are my Agt I want you to try and get me my horse as I have failed my self.

Yours Respectfully
Chief Koos-ta-ta

Document 29

Sam Resurrection Complains About the Allotment and Opening of the Reservation August 1908

Source: "Sam Resurrection Is Angry," *The Daily Missoulian*, August 16, 1908, page 12, col. 4-5; "Sam Resurrection in Jail," *The Daily Missoulian*, August 18, 1908, page 2, col. 1; "Sam Resurrection Is Released from Jail," *The Daily Missoulian*, August 22, 1908, page 10, col. 4.

Editors' note: Sam Resurrection was the most prolific Flathead Reservation leader between 1907 and 1919 period who complained about the allotment policy forced on the tribes. He made repeated trips to Washington, D.C., and Helena, Montana, to petition for a revocation of the policy. The written sources give a distorted representation of Resurrection's abilities. Sam Resurrection was probably much more eloquent in Salish than in his letters written in English. Resurrection signed almost all of the constant complaints during the early twentieth century against the forced allotment and opening of the reservation. Even though the government ignored his protests, he never gave up his crusade to have tribal voices heard. Tribal elders at the turn of the twenty-first century remembered Resurrection positively, despite his failure to halt the allotment and opening of the reservation. The newspaper coverage treated his campaign against allotment as a joke and emphasized his problems with alcohol. The tribal history based on oral sources being compiled by the Salish–Pend d'Oreille Culture Committee in St. Ignatius, should help correct the biases in the condescending letters from the Commissioner of Indian Affairs and the Flathead Indian Agent, and the bigoted reporting of contemporary white newspapers. See the biographical sketch of Resurrection in Salish-Pend d'Oreille Culture Committee and Elders Cultural Advisory Council, Confederated Salish and Kootenai Tribes, *The Salish People and the Lewis and Clark Expedition* (Lincoln: University of Nebraska Press, 2005), pages 126-127.

The 1855 Hellgate Treaty did include an article allowing the President to assign lots to individual tribal members or families who would locate permanent homes. The article also referred to the 1854 Treaty with the Omaha which allowed the remaining land after allotments were made to be sold to non-Indians. The transcript of the negotiations for the Hellgate Treaty, however, did not indicate that this article providing for allotments was explained to the

Indian chiefs. Resurrection's letters made plain that the tribal leaders believed That allotment without the consent of the tribes was a violation of the 1855 Hellgate Treaty.

Sam Resurrection Is Angry
Flathead Veteran Has Many Grievances Which He is Anxious to Adjust.

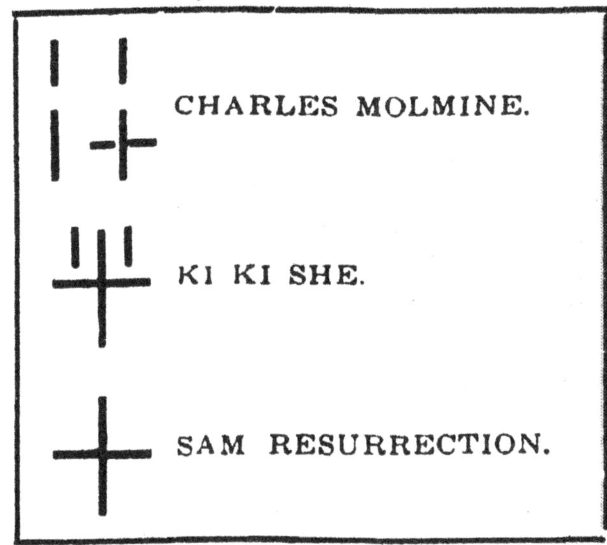

These are the signatures that are appended to a couple of remarkable letters that are to be sent eastward soon by chiefs of the Flathead tribe who are opposed to the opening of the reservation and who have other grievances that they wish to have adjusted right away.

Sam Resurrection is in town from the reservation and he is on the warpath. Sam is one of the Flathead chiefs and he has a long list of wrongs that he proposes to redress if it takes all summer. In the first place, Sam is dissatisfied with almost everything and he realizes that he is the man who must make conditions right. His principal grievance is that Charlot, hereditary chieftain, is no longer fitted to govern the tribe. "Charlot is old and blind. He does not know. The white man says we do this and we give you hundred dollars. Charlot says 'Give me the money' and he don't know what it is the white man will do. We cannot have him for chief. Sam Ressurrection is a smart man. He is the man for chief."

If he can get the reins of government and the tribal war bonnet to wear, Sam will take care of all the other matters the minute he gets the authority; he has the signatures of a lot of the tribe — he says — to his declaration of rights, but in order that no time may be lost, he is getting the work started along other lines.

He is planning to stop the opening of the reservation right away and he is going to make the Northern Pacific restore the old free-ride contract with the Flatheads. He came to town yesterday with a gripsack, eight inches long, stuffed with documents. He consulted several lawyers and then came with his interpreter to The Missoulian office, where he made an extended speech and submitted two letters which he is going to send, one to President Roosevelt and the other to General Superintendent Gilbert of the Northern Pacific.

When he had concluded his speech, he asked through his interpreter: "Is that good talk?" Upon receiving assurance that it was a gilt-edged stemwinder of a talk, the interpreter remarked: "You bet. He smart man. He ought to be chief, that man."

Sam has two propositions to make to the Northern Pacific. One is that the Flatheads be restored their right to free rides between Umatilla and Billings and the other is that, in lieu of this restoration, the Northern Pacific pay the tribe $3,000,000. Either will be satisfactory.

The letter to Presi[d]ent Roosevelt gives a history of the relations between the Flatheads and the white men. Sam, in his address, declared that "Mr. Columbus was a good man. I never see Mr. Columbus, but Flatheads don't fight him." And then he goes on with an accurate review of the treaties and contracts that his tribe has made with the government. It is an interesting communication and is given herewith:

The First Letter.

Theoder Rosevelt, Washington, D.C.

I am writing you a few lines, dear friend Roosevelt. I want to let you know how long we see the first white man, we see Columbus its 416 years, that's the first time we see whites and the flatheads never fights white mans, and thats why we always say that is our friends and our hundred years ago we see 7 white men Louis Clark at Larsses Hole, and now when we see them we were very glad we put all our blankets on the ground and they walk on it and come and see us we were very glad and talk them good and talk to us good one of them. Mr. Stevens fifty-three years ago and he see the three chiefs name was Victor Martin Flathead and Alexander Michel and they make the treaty here Stevens told the three chiefs this would be our reservation as long as there were any Indians here these two people did not tell the Indians that the president would sell the reservation. After that they send three men here Garfield was the head man when he got here he asked the three chiefs what kind of treaty they made with Stevens the chiefs told Garfield this would be a reservation as long as there was any Indians Garfield told them that was right he thought it ought to be that way. Certainly two years ago you send a man here that came here and did not ask no permission and went ahead and surveyed you must recalect Stevens

Sam Resurrection
Source: Sélis–Qlispé Culture Committee, St. Ignatius, Mont.

and Garfield made a treaty with the indians out signed a contract and we have got that contract yet. They don't like to make a treaty and then have the whites to come here and give us a piece of land and sell the rest. There three people Joe Dixon Major Blue Totain they are working hard to throw the reservation open. The appraicors are fooling the land away Johnny Matt and Angus McDonald they put $1 50 cents one acre they don't want the appraicors they want some one else that don't want to give away the land. I want to know what kind of a law you got when my mail comes here the major opens them and read them Those men come here and made a treaty and we would like to stay by the contract make arrangements with you this spring there are three tribes here the flathead ponderay and Cootnay the three tribes will sign a contract. They have been working for two years ago to open the reservation and then it would of the tribes satisfied the three tribes don't know what they are doing the whites are trying to fool them those three men that name that made the treaty with us and we have got the writing here to show for it and we believe that these three people told us right. this is from yours truly signed bye chief

Shall Moolmine,
Patie Ka Ka She,
Sam Resurrection.

The letter to Mr. Gilbert is more peremptory and is as follows:
F. W. Gilbert, General Superintendent, St. Paul, Minn.

Sir, My Friend — It has been 27 years since we made a treaty with you to put you road our country you were to give us so much money and a free ride over the road from Umatilla to Billings. The Chieves that made this treaty and also the agent, Major Ronan, are dead. Us that are living still remember this treaty. When Ronan, died we have had three agents since, Carter, Smead and Samuel Bellew. Ronan took the right away from us without our knowledge. These last three agents, we have never spoke to them about the treaty. If this right is not given back to us we figure you out in debt to us to the amount of $3,000,000. Please ans by return mail. Yours truly.

Chas Molmin,
Ki Ki Chee,
Sam Resurrection.

This petition is by the prominent chieves of Flathead.

* * * * * * * *

Sam Resurrection in Jail

Flathead Chief Gets Full and Loses Tribal Documents and Heraldry.

Sam Resurrection, lord of the Flatheads, is in jail. Worse than that, the tribal records, important documents, Sam's coat of arms, and all sorts of valuables are lost, along with a valise that was the pride of Sam's young life. Sam was arrested yesterday morning by Officer Therriault on the request of an attorney, in whose office Sam had created a scene. The Flathead chief, full of indignation over the prospective opening of the reservation and loaded to the guards with a vitriolic brand of firewater, entered the lawyer's office and began to accuse the legal light of having appropriated his satchel with its priceless records and heraldry. Sam continued his tirade and a cell in the county jail was the only recourse of the lawyer, who did not care to sit all day in the surf beat of broken English and Indian profanity.

Sam Resurrection is of the opinion that nobody loves him. He thinks he is the victim of a conspiracy and that President Roosevelt is the instigator of all his troubles. He thinks that a minion of the government stole his valise, for he is now of the belief that the Missoula lawyer didn't get it. Sam recently addressed a letter to the president, along with other chiefs of his tribe, and he firmly believes that the loss of his documents came as a direct result of that epistle, which, although it has not yet been given official attention, he is sure has aroused official wrath. Sam can see his lands and the lands of the Indians who call him chief, or would like to call him chief, or whom he would like to have call him chief — according to how the reservation folk arrange their affairs of government — snatched rudely away and usurped by whites. Sam can see nothing but dark clouds on the sky of his future, and he is sore. Nobody loves Sam, he is sure of that. Today Sam will be sobered up and, if he manages to get out of jail, the sun may shine again for him, but now — last night, at least — Sam Resurrection was moodily morose.

* * * * * * * * *

Sam Resurrection Is Released from Jail

Sam Resurrection was yesterday morning released from the county jail, where he had been locked up for several days on a charge of having been drunk and disorderly. Sam didn't know what to do with his liberty at first. He left the jail and, within a few minutes, returned and stood around the place until the janitor, not recognizing the chief, locked him up again. Several hours later Sam Resurrection was again released and this time he did not stand upon the order of his going. Sam has not yet fully decided as to whether or not he will go to Washington to lay his grievance before President Roosevelt. First of all, Sam will institute search for his famous grip, which he lost early in the spree that landed him behind the bars.

Document 30

Chief Charlo Repeats His Objections to Opening the Flathead Reservation October 6, 1908

Source: L. E. Milligan to Secretary Garfield, October 13, 1908, and Charles to Secretary Garfield, October 6, 1908, from file 70,266/1908 Flathead 308.2, Central Classified Files, RG 75, National Archives, Washington, D.C.

Editors' note: Pierre Pichette, a blind tribal member, sent this letter to the Superintendent of the Montana School for the Blind, in braille. The letter represented yet another effort by Charlo to have his complaints about the opening of the reservation heard in Washington, D.C. The letter is very hard to follow, but readers can get Charlo's general points.

Montana School for the Blind
Boulder, Montana, Oct. 13, 1908.

Secretary Garfield,
Department of the Interior,
Washington, D.C.
Dear Sir:—

A blind Indian Boy on the Flathead Reservation has sent me the enclosed appeal from Chief Charles [Charlo], to be forwarded to you. I have translated Chief Charles' letter litterally, and also enclose a brief typewritten summary of his claims.

Trusting you can find time to give this rather remarkable letter your personal attention, I am,

Very respectfully,
L. E. Milligan, Supt.

* * * * * * * * *

October 6, 1908.

Secretary Garfield,
Department of the Interior,
Washington, D.C.

We respectfully appeal to you for a conference between a representative of your department and the Confederated Tribes on the Flathead reservation.

The Treatise which the Government has made with the Confederated Tribes, have been violated in the following respects:

1. White settlers have located on the Flathead reservation without the consent of the headmen of the tribes and we are powerless to dislodge them.

2. A new boundary line has been surveyed across the lower end of Flathead Lake cutting off part of the reservation, without consulting the Confederated Tribes.

Charles [Charlo],
Flathead Chief.

* * * * * * * * *

October 6. 1908

Secretary Garfield,

We kindly appeal for through a council of the confederated tribes. Some oppositions were found very necessary to be controlled and promises made and offered to the confederated tribes through the treaties is found also very necessary to be attended by the Department, for as to our considerations we kindly ask help for them to be upheld by the Department.

No. 1. It is very well understood and familiar by all that it is prohibited for settlers to enter into the Flathead Reservation and settle without a consent of the head men of the Confederated Tribes, and as we considered over it many such people that has no rights at all in the reservation are found to be referred and while others hired a lawyer to compose rights for them. And why did not they furnish evidences or witnesses to prove and compose their rights before the Head Men of the Flathead Reservation.

Now we kindly ask a question. Is a lawyer authorized to introduce and compose the rights of such people that we know has no rights at all in the reservation? It has been done before by a lawyer and it seems to us that those people without any rights were taken and thrown into a grinder by the lawyer and at last dropper [dropped?] out turned into Indians.

No. 2. For the new line situated so the furthest end of the northwest part of the Flathead Reservation. It has been announced to us so we all know very well the main boundary line of our reservation we have been considering by the new line which runs across dividing the Flathead Lake. The question is why and how was that new line located. Was it authorized without a consent of the Confederated Tribes to be situated and as for the part cut off from the reservation by the new situation line already mentioned, is it purposely done to be a loss to the Indians of a part of the reservation?

No. 3. Treaties of the Confederated Tribes. First treaty was made and signed by Governor I. I. Stevens and the Head Men of the Tribes.

Second treaty was made and signed by Governor Garfield and Head Men also.

Third treaty was made and signed by General H. B. Carrington and the Flathead Chiefs.

And through those treaties offers and promises were given for the benefit of the Indians and they were very gladly accepted. And we having been considering that why and how are not those offers delivered to the Indians yet. Or are these three men not authorized to make such treaties with the Indians, and if they are authorized it is time for the Department to attend to them and direct them as they were promised.

On your arrivance on 1907 on the month of July and that friendly speech you made before the Indians promising your help as to whatever you may be able to, so we do not hesitate to ask for your kind help, also we wish you to favor us for you to deliver our writings to the United States President. We also ask of him his kind help to acquire these matters controlled.

Our writings is concluded with wishes for your kind people help and hoping to hear a joyful answer to our desires.

Yours affectionate friend,
Charles [Charlo], Flathead Chief.

Document 31

Charlot's Complaints About Agent Morgan

March 31, 1909

Source: Mr. Charlot to Secretary of the Interior, March 31, 1909, and Fred C. Morgan to Commissioner of Indian Affairs, May 8, 1909, from file 27,058/1909 Flathead 154, Central Classified Files, RG 75, National Archives, Washington, D.C.

Editors' note: The first letter is an example of the efforts of Chief Charlot and other tribal leaders to get Washington officials to pay attention to their complaints about Agent Fred Morgan's reform efforts on the reservation. The original is hard to follow so paragraphs and some periods have been added to the manuscript. On the same day this letter was written to the Secretary of the Interior, Charlot also wrote an identical letter to the Commissioner of Indian Affairs. The second letter reproduced here is Morgan's explanation and defense of his actions. Morgan's letter is more literate and readable than Charlot's, but it represented only one side of the story and must be taken with a grain of salt. Morgan was making a special effort to end adultery and drinking on the reservation. He thought that Indians trying to protect their rights were agitators and particularly complained of Pascal Antoine and Henry Matt. He also noted that tribal objections to allotment and the recent murder of four Indians by a Montana game warden added to the unhappiness of many tribal members.

March 31, 09

Secretary of the Interior Washington D.C.

as I become sensitive enough I lenriad and was infoned by my father flathead chief Victor aboud their Kindnesses and well behaviars and kinds treatments to the whites. the first white peoples seen by the flathead tribe was at Rosses hole. the flathead Chief at that present time was three eagles. these seven whites were seen by the flathead. they were permetted enter in to the camting ground of the tribe without harm or damage under the acts of the head Chief. as they arivearrened safly. robs were spread out for them to sit on. flathead Chief three eagles then said to his tribe and children that such people as these whites not to be Killed or interfered and always be Kind friends and treat them right always.

after the death of three eagles, Peter Sh-De-moo was then appointed by the tribe to be head Chief. while Peter Sh-De Moo was head chief of the flathead he gave equally at advises to his tribe and children as three eagles. then after death, Peter Sh-De-moo, my father was appointed head Chief of the flathead. he also firmly Kept the Kindnesses of the two dead chiefs and after the death my father I was appointed head Chief of the flathead for the first dead head chief was my arand father second dead Chief was my uncel third head Chief was my father Victor. so I firmly stand and keeped the Kindnesses of the three dead head chiefs to the whites, we flatheads at this present time do not mistreat or harm white at all for we Kindly Keep the words of the chieves and now we are surprised aroused by his acts and treatments to us.

first complaiments a prisoner under the care of a Govern. police escaped. the Indian Agent called the police in to the office and told him he has to be locked in Jail and police replied first said to the Agent we have to notfy the judges first. the Indian Agent said the Judges has no business aboud It. go or I will shoot you.

second complainments. the time when Baptist Ke-Ke-Shee and his interpreter were ready for their tripe to Washington D.C. on dudy the Indian Agent and half breed named Alex. Matte prevented the interpreter and Kept him in Jail for a day for not to been Christian. when Baptist Ke-Ke-Shee and his interpreter met togather again Baptist Ke Ke Shee took six other men along with him as far Missoula for he was afaraid that his interpreter may be arrested again. this six man stayed with him for several hours at missoula before he left. there six mans on their way home on the train one of them was Killed by the train. this event was the fault of the Indian Agent and Alex Matte if they would not prevent and arrest the interpreter no such thing would happen.

third complaiments one fool blood Indian man was Called in to the office by Agent and told why are you making so many talks about me. the man replied that he was not disoturbing any thing only helping his tribe and that he was rights to do so. and Indian Agent said to him that if he still Contioes such talking that he shall be reffared from the reservation. is the Indian Agent authorized by the department to refer Confedereted Indians from the reservation with out any wrongs found to the Indian.

we Kindly want you to investiagate in our Complainments for we are all anxious to get red of our Agent for we want Kind one that will treat us right

hoping our writing asking for your Kind help will be received with stasfation. Please notify us before long aboud our Complaiments.

I remain yours truly friends
flathead Chief Mr Charlot
Jocko P. O. Montana.

* * * * * * * * *

Department of the Interior,
United States Indian Service,
Flathead Agency, Jocko, Montana,
May 8, 1909.

Concerning Flathead
conditions.

The Honorable,
Commissioner of Indian Affairs,
Washington, D.C.
Sir:

Replying to Office letter of the 28th ultimo, Education-Administration, 27058-1909, EAF, I have the honor to submit the following:

> 1. What offences you refer to the Police Court. Would the case of a Government policeman who allowed a prisoner to escape come before it?

The Indian Court at this agency is conducted as nearly as possible in accordance with the Rules and Regulations. It is my desire and aim to at all times conform with the regulations. At times cases come up for which there are no provisions in these rules. Such cases I try to decide on their own merits, and to be just to all concerned. And for some of these cases I refer to the state laws.

In regard to the policeman (Paul Charley) who let the prisoner (Sohnia) escape, I have to state I was under the impression at that time that it was proper to refer the matter to the Indian Court. Since receiving your letter of inquiry and reading the regulations more closely it seems that the jurisdiction of the court is perhaps not broad enough to cover the conduct complained of. There was no punishment inflicted upon the policeman, it being my idea to have him disciplined by being put in charge of the jail for a short period of time, he remaining on duty as a policeman. At no time was he incarcerated. If the instructions under which I am working are not broad enough to allow me to use some discretion in regard to maintenance of discipline among those under my charge I would respectfully request full information as to what course to pursue in case of violation or infraction of the rules and regulations, or a disobedience of orders and instructions given by me. I did in the matter what I thought best for the maintenance of discipline. It is my desire to keep clearly within the scope of my authority in my efforts to conduct the affairs of this agency, but escapes from the jail are too frequent (there have been four since I assumed charge, but one of which has been re-arrested) and in this case the policeman was given particular instructions to guard his prisoner. This prisoner is the one who was since re-arrested, after an attempt on my life. He is now in Helena, awaiting trial before the Federal Court for assault. The offence for which he was arrested, and put in jail, was drunkenness. After his escape I learned that he was also guilty of adultery.

When Sohnia escaped from the jail the policeman was ordered to re-arrest him, but seemed to make no effort to locate him, and flatly refused to obey my orders. It was then that he was brought before the Indian Court, and detailed — not imprisoned — to look after the agency jail for six days. It was through wilful neglect on his part that Sohnia escaped. I am certain he could easily have found this prisoner, for a little later I learned where he was staying, and on going to the house and telling Sohnia to come with me he grabbed a rifle and pointed it at me, threatening to shoot. I succeeded in calming him, however, and, as above stated, he is now awaiting trial before the Federal Court.

For a more definite reply to that part of the question "what offences you refer to the Police Court," I will only say that at present there are in agency jail four persons serving sentences for living in adultery; one for desertion and non-support of his wife; and one for drunkenness. And these are not the only classes of offenders, as is shown by the reward offered by licensed trader G. H. Beckwith, for information that will lead to the arrest of parties or party who set fire to hay, buildings, etc., copy of which I enclose with this letter. But a couple hours ago I received word from Mr. Beckwith that last night some one broke into and burglarized his store, and that some of the Fathers' buildings at St. Ignatius Mission had also been entered. It is only a couple of weeks ago that three parties were convicted by the Federal Court for selling liquor to Indians, and one for introduction of liquor. I have three cases set for a hearing before the U.S. Commissioner tomorrow, for introduction of liquor. Besides Sohnia, whom I have previously mentioned, there are awaiting trial before the Federal Court at Helena one person accused of murder; two for horse stealing; and three for introduction of liquor.

> 2. What the facts are in the case of the Interpreter who was put in jail for one day at the time he was ready to come to Washington with Baptiste Ke-ke-shee. It is said that Ke-ke-shee thought it necessary, in order to prevent the re-arrest of the interpreter, to take six men with him as far as Missoula, and that one of these men was killed by a train while on his way home.

Office letter of December 12, 1908, Education 81329/08, JHD, Subject: Conditions on Flathead; encloses a copy of letter sent the same date to Rev. L. Taelman, S.J., St. Ignatius Mission, in answer to a letter from him relative to moral matters on the reservation, and instructs me "to act with discretion, and not to involve them (the mission people) or Father Taelman in such investigation as you will make of the charges which he has preferred, unless it becomes necessary in the interests of justice."

The evil of which the Father complained was widespread on the reservation, there being many more than the cases which he reported. In the past there had been no attempt to punish such offenders. While I feel that among the very old Indians, who have married according to the Indian custom, and lived together for many years, there may be some excuse, yet there is none for the young educated Indian who knows better, and who, in many cases, deliberately deserts the wife to whom he is legally married, and without even procuring a divorce, lives in open adultery with another woman.

Most of these cases I have taken up. It was necessary to confine some of the offenders in jail. A few of these have been making all manner of threats (I have been reliably informed by an Indian, who did not want his name mentioned, that three different parties had stated they would shoot me on sight) and doing all they could to interfere with my work. As to whether or not I am succeeding in my efforts to suppress this evil I would respectfully request that your Office write Father Taelman for another report. I will state, however, that the mission people have in no manner been spoken of, or brought into, my work for the abatement of this evil.

Jackson Sundown was an offender whose name was not on the list submitted by Father Taelman. He was the interpreter whom Kakashee intended taking to Washington, and who had accompanied Kakashee on such a trip a short time previous. I informed Kakashee that I would not permit Jackson to accompany him as interpreter, as he was living in adultery, was a leader among the gambling and drinking element, and not a proper person to represent the tribe in Washington. Kakashee then stated he would take another interpreter. When the party left the agency I instructed a policeman to see that Jackson did not go with Kakahsee. Jackson's confinement in jail was for but one night, and due to a misunderstanding of my order by the policeman, as the next morning I learned that he had placed Jackson in jail. I immediately released the latter. He then went to Missoula, where he took the place of the interpreter whom Kakahsee had promised me to take, and accompanied Kakashee to Washington.

Missoula is but 27 miles from the agency. The Indians who accompanied Kakashee there I believe went solely for the purpose of getting drunk, for, as nearly as I can learn, all returned in an intoxicated condition. Two, Pascal Antoine and Kaltome, came home on train No. 5, which is due at Arlee at about 11 P.M. Instead of coming to this station they got off at a small flag station called Schley, some distance below Arlee. Both were drunk. They had a small quantity of liquor with them. They were seen hanging around the station, and ordered away by the station agent, who told them that there would be a train in a short time, and it was a dangerous place for them to loaf. From all appearances Kaltome wandered back to the track, laid down and went to sleep, was run over by the train and one leg cut off. This must have happened about two A.M., and he laid there until about four or five A.M., when he was found by parties going home from a dance. They immediately notified this office, and in company with Dr. Heidelman, the agency physician, I went to the cabin of Lassaw, where Kaltome had been taken. While the injury was being dressed Pascal Antoine came in drunk, creating some disturbance, and wanting to fight. It was necessary for me to arrest him and bring him to the agency jail, where he was imprisoned for the second time since his return to the reservation, he having been been [sic] absent for about five years. I understand that he was on the Sisseton reservation, got into trouble, and was ordered off by the Agent there. There was some talk that it was Pascal who was responsible for Kaltome being on the track; that there were injuries on Kaltome's head, and finger marks on his throat. However, a careful investigation by the physician and myself did not reveal any such marks.

I will also state that Pascal Antoine is one of the principal agitators around the agency, attending councils, creating dissatisfaction among the older Indians, who normally are very peaceful in character. I think the information received by your Office was inspired by this man, Joe Pierre, and Henry Matt. Joe Pierre served a sentence in jail for returning to the reservation drunk at the same time as Pascal Antoine and Kaltome did, he being one of the men who accompanied Kakashee to Missoula. He (Kakashee) is also an old offender. On several occasions he has been found helplessly drunk by the policeman at St. Ignatius Mission, where Kakashee resides, and on account of his extreme age, and feeble condition, has been taken care of by the policeman until sober.

Henry Matt has been in four drunken fights within a year, two since I assumed charge. His last offence was drunkenness, and severely beating one Emmanuel Curley, at St. Ignatius Mission. For this he was arrested. The cases against Pascal Antoine, Joe Pierre and Henry Matt were tried by the Indian Court during my absence, Special Agent Thomas Downs being present and officiating in my place. I would respectfully suggest that your Office ascertain his opinion of those cases, and the incidents at that time; also, his opinion of conditions on the reservation at the time I assumed charge.

Henry Matt, although I have no absolute proof in all cases, has been creating trouble and dissention ever since his imprisonment. At the time of his punishment he stated that the Government had no right to punish him, and made the boast that he would have Special Agent Downs fired for his part in the trial. He did not deny his guilt; he simply contended that — in his own words — "the Government had no right to punish one of the leading men on the reservation."

Referring again to Office letter submitting list of Indians living in adultery, furnished your Office by Father Taelman, you are advised that in this list are the names of John Gongras and Emily McDougal. I warned Gongras against this practice, and as the woman was not a member of this tribe I ordered her off the reservation. She returned, and was again ordered to leave. Returning again (to Polson) she was brought to the agency by the policeman stationed at that point. She stated that she intended going home as soon as some money, which she expected, came. As she was not a member of this tribe I did not know what jurisdiction I had in the case, being unable to find anything in the regulations to cover the matter. I was not sure that I could imprison her, but as she had no place to stay I told her she could remain at the jail until her money came. Later she stated she could get work at Evaro or Missoula, and I allowed her to go. She was away but a few days, however, when she returned, with a money order on the local post office, which was the money she had been expecting, she said. She had this cashed, and has left the reservation. I wrote your Office about this case, asking that I be wired as to how to proceed. After she had left the reservation I received a message advising me to take the matter up with the state courts.

I enclosed herewith copy of statement from her, taken by the clerk, Mr. Allen, just before she left the reservation. This shows one of the cases where I have conclusive proof of the efforts of Henry Matt to make trouble.

In the copy of the interview sent with Office letter of November 13, 1908, Land 69971-1908, WMW, the second complaint the Indians had was:

> That they did not want the reservation opened or allotted; that none of the headmen or chiefs agreed to the opening of their lands and want the country retained for their children in order that they may hunt and fish as did their parents.

The fourth complaint is:

> That Joe Dixon has signed the names of their headmen and many members of their tribe to a petition to have the reservation opened and allotted; and that the headmen and others whose names are attached to the petition did not sign it and knew nothing about it.

Here is the principal cause for dissatisfaction. The old time Indians, the full-bloods, are bitterly opposed to it. They are still holding councils (two the past week) trying to devise some means for preventing the opening. Your Office can readily understand what trying work it is to have to tell them that their reservation must be opened, and at the same time try to show them the advantages the opening will have for them; to tell them that their children, born after a certain date, cannot be allotted, and at the same time keep them contented. One of the sorest points with the old Indian, and a matter he cannot comprehend, is why, with a large amount of surplus land on the reservation, to which he claims absolute ownership, his (in his words) little babies are to be robbed of land rightfully belonging to them, in order that it may be saved for some incoming white man.

When your Office realized that such men as Henry Matt, Pascal Antoine, Joe Pierre, and others, in the furtherance of their own selfish interests, and their desire for revenge against me for punishing them for their misdeeds, are playing upon this discontent of the old-time Indian, you can more readily understand that no matter how hard I try to smooth matters for them, how patiently I listen to their grievances, it makes a difficult task more difficult, and renders it impossible to entirely elim[i]nate in the short time I have been in charge, all the dissatisfaction and discontent.

3. Whether Indians are expressing dissatisfaction with the conduct of affairs, and, if so, what their complaints are.

To this I must answer **Yes**. Justice to myself compels me to say that in the past the laws of the reservation have not been enforced. Offenders who are now being punished for their misdeeds, and who in the past had escaped punishment, are expressing much dissatisfaction with the conduct of affairs. I have shown heretofore the cause, principally, of dissatisfaction among the older Indians. Another reason is the election of a business committee to represent the tribe in place of the headmen who had formerly transacted tribal business. The council which elected this committee was composed of more than 300 representative members of the reservation and only 13 opposed the selection of the business committee. The mixed-bloods, who form a majority of all the Indians on this reservation, are represented on the committee, they comprising four of the nine members. A very few of the older Indians do not like this, they holding that the old full-blood should transact all tribal business.

Another cause was the reservation of reservoir sites by the U.S. Reclamation Service, and the request that the allottees in these sites relinquish and select lands elsewhere. Until about the first of April they had refused to do this, and it is due entirely to the efforts of this office that they were finally persuaded that it was for their best interests to do so. They were quite bitter against the Reclamation people. I had reliable reports that most of this feeling was caused by outside parties, they telling the Indians that the Reclamation Service would have to pay any price they asked, and as some of the Indians stated they would not relinquish unless they received $20,000.00 and $30000.00 for their relinquishments, I am inclined to think that this was so. At any rate, I had a talk with some of those parties, and informed them that if I could secure sufficient evidence as to who was doing the agitating I would revoke their licenses, and put them off the reservation. Two days later I received a letter from U.S. Commissioner Bailey, of Polson, copy of which is enclosed, showing that my talk had produced the desired effect.

The U.S. Reclamation Service is also having trouble in securing labor, caused largely by agitators near the agency, who are telling the Indians that if they will refuse to work they can force the Reclamation Service to pay higher wages. At present the force on the Jocko project is threatening to go out on a strike. The matter of wages paid by U.S.R.S. was brought to the attention of this office by the Indians, and it is our opinion that the wages paid are very fair; in fact, many white people are only waiting for an opportunity to secure work.

On March 24, last, your Office was written relative to the killing of four Indians on Holland Prairie by the Deputy State Game Warden, to which you replied under date of April 27, 1908, Land-Uses, 72298 and 24518/08. The Indians here insist that at the time the Stevens treaty was made they were told that they could hunt and fish at any time and place they saw fit; and now that they are told that this privilege only gave them the right to hunt and fish off the reservation in common with the citizens of the state, and subject to the state laws, they feel that they have not been fairly dealt with, and have been wrongfully deprived of their hunting grounds. Since this killing threats have been made that "they would get an equal number of white men."

Referring to the forepart of my letter, wherein I state that there is nothing in the Regulations governing certain cases that arise, I beg leave to inform your Office that under date of Apr. 21, last, I wrote your Office asking how to proceed in such a case; whether or not I had authority to go off the reservation and bring back to the reservation escaped prisoners from the agency jail, and also other Indians, members of this tribe, for offences committed here. Near Missoula is an Indian camp which is made a refuge for any offender against the rules of the reservation. I know that one, and possibly more, of the prisoners who have escaped from the jail are at this camp. I enclose copy of letter received yesterday morning from a member of this reservation, asking that I come and arrest some of the parties there. I respectfully request information as to what course to pursue in this case.

I agree with your Office "that a good deal of trouble can sometimes be avoided by giving the Indians straightforward explanations of any difficulties which may arise, especially of any act which might otherwise arouse their suspicions." It is almost unnecessary to inform your Office that the Indian is very suspicious, and that just at this time conditions are probably harder than they have ever been before. I assure your Office that it has been my endeavor to do the right thing, and to work for the best interests of the Indian; but try as I may, it is impossible, at this particular time, and with the conditions such as they are, to avoid some dissatisfaction.

In this letter I have tried to show things just as they are. If your Office desires further information I respectfully ask that an inspecting official be sent. I am confident he would uphold me in what I have done.

I wish to assure your Office that it has been my endeavor to do in every case what I thought right and proper, and with as little annoyance and embarrassment as possible to your Office.

Very respectfully,
Fred C. Morgan
Supt. & S.D. Agent.

[Enclosures 1 and 3 with letter are not reproduced here.]
Enclosure No. 2:

Flathead Agency, Jocko, Montana,
April 8, 1909.

I, Emily McDougall, certify on honor that while I was staying at the police quarters at Flathead Agency one Henry Matt told me that as I was not a member of the reservation Mr. Fred C. Morgan, the Superintendent, could not keep me there. He advised me to enter suit against Mr. Morgan for false imprisonment. Later Mr. McClure and one of his sons told me the same thing. A few days ago, while in Missoula (where I had gone to look for work) Henry Matt came to me and tried to persuade me to see a lawyer and sue Mr. Morgan. I told him to mind his own business; that I knew what I was doing. At no time while I was at the police quarters did I consider it imprisonment. Mr. Morgan told me I could stay there until I got my money from home, which I expected, and with which I intended paying my way home. Later he told me that if I could find work he would let me go, and this he did, as on Monday, March 29, 1909, I told him I thought I could get work at Evaro, but that if I did not I would go to Missoula. Mr Morgan loaned me a horse to go to Evaro, gave me carfare from there to Missoula, and a letter to the Salvation Army Captain asking him to help me find work.

(Sgd) Miss Emily McDougall.

Witness:
(Sgd) H. S. Allen.

Enclosure No. 4:

Missoula, May 3, 1909.

Indian Agent, Ravalli.

Please come out west of town right near Chinamans ranch as soon as you can. Tillie and Geb are making all the trouble they can for me, drinking every night and beat me and trying to sell my tent and horses. I do not even sleep in my tent at night. Cant on account of them making such trouble and trying to kill me. Tillie owns ranch by Mission and has a husband and son there named Joe and husbands name is Chimime and they think you cant do any thing with them and they are not afraid of any thing. I am not drinking myself at all and cant even get a chance to work in the day time or sleep at night for this woman making such trouble here in my tent. If you could please help me by getting this woman away I would be much obliged to you. You know I told you before if I had any trouble I would let you know so I am writing to let you know how she is acting now. She wants to take my boy away from by force and of course I do not want him to go with her. I want you to help me in this so she will leave my boy alone because she would soon kill him. Tillie was in jail here for 10 days and as soon as she got out again the same day she began to drink worse than ever. Black Sam came in and tryed to make them behave and they beat him with a stick and rocked him and nearly killed him right in my tent, so if you could come right away and help me I will be much obliged to you. Its white people live right near here that are writing and they know all about the trouble I have had.

(Sgd) Joe Gaive.

Copied May 8, 1909.
HSA.

Document 32

A Last-Minute Tribal Protest Against Opening Reservation December 28, 1909

Source: Chief Antease, et. al., to Secretary of the Interior, December 28, 1909, part of file 70,266/1908 Flathead 308.2, Central Classified Files, RG 75, National Archives, Washington, D.C.

Editors' note: Right up to the opening of the reservation in 1910, tribal leaders consistently protested against opening the reservation without the consent of the tribes.

Polson, Mont. December 28, 1909

To the Honorable Secretary of the Interior,
Washington, D.C.
Sirs:—

The Whites are flooding in here, and they are taking all kinds of privileges here hunting, fishing, and prospecting this Indian Reservation. This reservation has been set aside for the tribes before going here and not for the Whites; we released the balance of the country to the Whites and we have not interfered with them on the lands we agreed we would let them have, but with our White friends they never cease to crowd us, they are here now right amongst us contrary to the treaty. With the Whites it looks to us like the Government pays no attention to us but instead encourages the Whites to impose upon us. There is a few things which we will demand from the Government before the Whites come on this Reservation, in this we want a settlement with the Government in regard to two strips of land taken away from us by the Whites or the government itself, we don't know how the Whites do these things. But since the treaty there has been taken away from us two large strips of land, the one is where Kalispell is built; our line according to the treaty extended to Columbia Falls to the North but is now at Dayton creek. The Whites are on this Northern portion of our Reservation and we never received a cent for this part of our country; we want a settlement now before anything else takes place. We can't see why our country should all go to the Whites for nothing and us be satisfied, we are not satisfied the way these things are taking place. And there is another thing which we are going to explain to you and which we want you to explain to us, we are informed that the government has cut off of our Reservation a large piece of country and has turned it into a Forest Reserve, if this is the fact what are we going to get out of this part of our country? Are we obliged to let the government have the land for nothing or not? We would like to know the results on this strip of our country. The government knows and we know that our boundry line included the Swan River country, starting from Columbia Falls on the North East to the Skunk prairie on the South East. This part of our country has been taken away from us and we have not received a cent for the same, now we ask a settlement for these tow [sic] strips of our Country before the Whites get in here again. If they are going to take our country like this and us receive nothing, that is just like taking away our lives, and they might as well take away our lives and be done with it. We seek a reply on these questions, I am the chief Antease, acting according to the wishes of the Reservation people.

Awaiting your reply,
Chief Antease, ([blank]) His mark.
Kusto
Batse
George Chief Hat
Williams
Alex Andrew

Chief Antease is acquainted with the parties on this Reservation all the lines conserning it.

Biographical Sketches

These biographical sketches of Salish and Kootenai chiefs and interpreters draw on the written evidence in the historical record. They say something about the tribal leaders, but they are only part of the story. They need to be balanced by the oral histories now being compiled by the Salish–Pend d'Oreille and Kootenai Culture Committees in St. Ignatius and Elmo, Montana. When the oral materials become available, they can be combined with the written record to give a much more complete picture of these leaders. In the meantime, the reader must consider these biographical sketches with caution.

Chief Adolph
Bitterroot Salish
ca. 1809–1887

Chief Adolph or Red Feather was born in about 1809.[1] As a young man he earned many war honors, but only a few were described in detail in the surviving historical documents. Father Nicholas Point, S.J., pictured one battle where Adolph was wounded by two arrows which he pulled out himself. Despite the injury, Adolph went on to kill with his lance a Blackfeet warrior who threatened a sick Salish man.[2] It is likely that Adolph was the artist who drew two ledger art drawings of his war honors that were preserved by Father Pierre De Smet, S.J. These drawings refer to a number of other Adolph war honors, but they include minimal detail.[3]

According to Flathead Indian Agent Peter Ronan, about 1835 Adolph and Arlee led the Salish warriors who attacked a Gros Ventre war party that had just ambushed a Hudson's Bay Company party near the mouth of the canyon between the Missoula and Jocko Valleys. Two Hawaiians or Coriakas working for the Hudson's Bay Company were killed. The Salish killed about half of the Gros Ventre war party. Afterwards, the area was known as the Coriakan Defile.[4] In 1877, Adolph said the Nez Perce had killed his brother in about 1837.[5]

Adolph was a loyal follower of the missionaries and in 1856 was one of the Salish chiefs who visited St. Ignatius Mission, while St. Mary's Mission was closed, "to fulfill their religious duties."[6] Adolph was known as a stern disciplinarian who "never fails to reprimand any of his tribe who may deserve it" including spanking children who misbehaved.[7]

He did not speak at the 1855 Hellgate Treaty council, but did sign the treaty. Adolph also signed the October 1855 Judith River Treaty.[8] After Gov. Isaac Stevens' 1855 treaty trip across Washington Territory, wars broke out between the Lower Columbia Basin tribes and the United States Army. In 1859, Father Pierre De Smet, S.J., led a delegation of seven Upper Columbia chiefs to Fort Vancouver to negotiate with General W. S. Harney. Adolph was one of the chiefs who accompanied De Smet to Fort Vancouver and assured Harney that the Upper Columbia Basin tribes wished to remain in peace and keep out of the Indian-white wars of the late 1850s.[9]

In the 1860s, Adolph and the other Bitterroot Salish chiefs repeatedly complained that the government was not fulfilling the provisions of the Hellgate Treaty. In April 1865, Adolph was one of the chiefs who signed a letter to the Montana Governor objecting to the influx of white settlers into the Bitterroot Valley.[10] Two years later in June 1867, Adolph and the other Salish chiefs petitioned the Flathead Indian Agent because they had not received the promised annuities or a Bitterroot reservation.[11]

In August 1868, Adolph and the Salish chiefs again complained to W. J. Cullen a special Indian agent at Fort Owen. Adolph made a speech at the meeting that the Salish had not received the annuities promised in 1855 and the Bitterroot Valley was not kept as a reservation for the Salish. Adolph particularly pointed out that the Salish needed tools to establish farms in the Bitterroot: "We want farming tools. My hands! Look at them!! They are my tools. I scratch the ground with my nails. The Great Father wants us to make farms. He ought to send us tools."[12]

Adolph signed a May 1871 letter to the President about the government's failure to set aside the Bitterroot Valley as a reservation for the Salish.[13] In July 1872, Adolph was one of the Salish and Kootenai chiefs who signed a contract with James Fullerton, a Washington, D.C., attorney, to "demand and recover from the United States of America, all such sum and sums of money, debts, dues, accounts and other demands whatsoever, growing out of or in reference to annuities from or treaties with the United States."[14]

Congressman James A. Garfield came to the Bitterroot Valley in August 1872 to try and induce the Bitterroot Salish to remove to the Jocko Reservation. Garfield made generous promises of government aid in the move and establishing new farms in the Jocko. But after the government had failed to keep its promises in the Hellgate Treaty, Adolph was skeptical: "Only one thing. Charlois and I do not believe all we hear." Finally, Charlo, the head chief, refused to sign the agreement, but Arlee, the second chief, and Adolph, the third chief, signed.[15] Chief Arlee and his extended family moved to Jocko a year or two later, but Adolph remained in the Bitterroot with Charlo until the end of the 1870s.

When the hostile Nez Perce Indians came through western Montana in 1877, Charlo sent Adolph to Missoula to reassure the people that the Bitterroot Salish would keep the peace with the whites. While Adolph and the Salish delegates were camped along the Clarks Fork River, some young white citizens got on the bridge overlooking Adolph's camp and started shooting at the Salish tents. Adolph complained to the military and leading citizens in Missoula. The white leaders quickly stopped the harassment and tried to convince Adolph that no harm was intended. Due to the restraint of Adolph and the Salish, open conflict was avoided.[16]

By the summer of 1882, Adolph was apparently living on the Jocko Reservation and took part in the negotiations with Joseph K. McCammon over the right-of-way for the Northern Pacific Railroad through the reservation.[17] According to Agent Peter Ronan, Adolph died on the Jocko Reservation in 1887 at the age of 78.[18] Chief Adolph had led a remarkable life of adventure and service. He fought to protect the Bitterroot Salish community both in war and peace.

Chief Ambrose
Bitterroot Salish
ca. 1810–1871

Ambrose or Five Raven was born early in the second decade of the nineteenth century.[19] The Bitterroot Salish Indians were about to enter into a century of dramatic and wrenching change. As both a warrior and a diplomat, Ambrose was to help lead his tribe in its fight for survival.

In an 1839 battle against the Blackfeet Indians, Ambrose's bow broke. In the confusion of the battle, a Blackfeet warrior mistook the unarmed Ambrose for another Blackfeet and mounted the horse behind Ambrose. Ambrose declared he was Salish, wrestled the Blackfeet's gun away from him, and then killed the Blackfeet with the gun.[20]

A series of ledger drawings, in which Ambrose depicted some of his war honors, have survived. In one, Ambrose discovered and pursued a Blackfeet warrior near St. Mary's Mission in the Bitterroot Valley. Ambrose's gun misfired. Ambrose and the Blackfeet fought and the Blackfeet was shot and killed by another Salish. In another incident the Salish camp discovered five Blackfeet in a fortified position and killed four of them. Then Ambrose jumped into the fort and the last Blackfeet was killed. In one battle against the Bannack Indians, Ambrose was wounded by an arrow in his abdomen. In yet another battle with the Blackfeet, Ambrose counted two coups against the enemy.[21]

Ambrose became a loyal convert of the missionaries. Father Nicolas Point, S.J., drew a picture of Ambrose explaining the Catholic Ladder to a chief of the Little Robes Band of Blackfeet. The Catholic Ladder was a proselytizing device the missionaries used to explain Christian teachings. Another Point drawing showed Ambrose with his trademark Scottish tam hat and other Salish peacefully trading with the Little Robes.[22] In the early 1840s, Ambrose convinced several Pend d'Oreille families to join the Bitterroot community to prepare themselves for baptism.[23]

On the 1842 buffalo hunt, an old Salish widow was killed by a Blackfeet prowling around the camp. She left two orphaned children who were adopted by Ambrose.[24] In 1844, Ambrose and other mounted Salish warriors surprised a pedestrian party of thirty-seven Blackfeet. The Blackfeet surrendered to the Salish. The Blackfeet were uncomfortably invited into the Salish camp. Despite some hostility, the Salish were able to avoid conflict while the Blackfeet were visiting the Salish camp.[25]

When things got heated at the 1855 Hellgate Treaty negotiations between Chief Victor and Governor Isaac Stevens, Ambrose tried to smooth things over: "I say to the white chief, don't get angry, may be it will come all right. May be all the people have a great many minds, may be they will come all right. See my chiefs are now holding down their heads, thinking."[26] Ambrose signed the 1855 Hellgate Treaty ceding tribal land to the United States government and the Judith River Treaty in October 1855 which established intertribal peace and a common hunting ground for the Rocky Mountain tribes to hunt buffalo on the plains.[27]

In 1856 and 1857 while St. Mary's Mission was closed, Ambrose joined Victor in visiting St. Ignatius Mission in the Flathead Valley "to fulfill their religious duties." According to Father Adrian Hoecken, S.J., Ambrose had "convened several assemblies, in order to arrange and pay off old debts, to repair wrongs, etc." among the Bitterroot Salish.[28]

In the spring of 1860, Capt. John Mullan needed help moving construction supplies from Fort Benton to the Bitterroot Valley. Ambrose recruited 117 horses and twenty Salish men to assist Mullan. Mullan gratefully noted: "I never had a want but which, when made known to them they [the Salish] supplied and they always treated myself and my parties with a frank generosity and continuous friendship."[29]

Ambrose led a Salish party traveling between Hell Gate and Gold Creek in the spring of 1863. They met a white trader named Zeb B. Thibedeau who sold whiskey to some of the Salish. In retaliation Ambrose followed Thibedeau and seized and destroyed his stock of liquor.[30]

Ambrose was one of the Salish chiefs who signed a letter to the Montana Governor in April 1865 explaining Salish efforts to keep the peace, keep the young warriors from buying whiskey, and the need for a Salish reservation in the Bitterroot Valley.[31] In June 1867, at a council with the Flathead Indian Agent at Fort Owen, Ambrose complained that the treaty was not being kept. The Salish had not gotten most of the annuities promised and the Bitterroot Valley reservation had not been established.[32] At yet another meeting with a white government official at Fort Owen in August 1868, Ambrose complained that the promises made in the 1855 treaty had not been honored. Ambrose suggested: "We wish our Great Father would send us a list of the goods which he gives to us so that we may know if it all comes. We are afraid we do not get all the goods which are sent to us. . . . We want some farming tools, ploughs, axes, hoes &c."[33]

The Bitterroot question and government failures were still unsettled on July 1, 1871, when Ambrose died while leading a Salish camp gathering camas roots. Ambrose was about sixty years old.[34] Chief Ambrose was a brave warrior defending the Salish people in war, a fervent convert to the Christian teachings, and a responsible leader looking out for Salish interests in dealings with the United States government.

Chief Andre
Pend d'Oreille
born 1810

In 1878, Andre said he was 68 years old which would have meant he was born about 1810.[35] No references to Andre's younger years and war honors have survived in the written historical documents.

According to Michel Revais, Andre, the second chief of the Pend d'Oreille in the 1870s, declined election as head chief in 1868 when Chief Alexander died. Michelle was elected head chief instead.[36]

Andre was one of the reservation chiefs who signed the July 1, 1872, contract to hire James Fullerton, a Washington, D.C., attorney to represent the tribes. Fullerton was to "ask, demand and recover" money due the tribes from the Hellgate Treaty and other claims.[37]

According to Father Lawrence Palladino,. S.J., in the early 1870s the mission recruited Indian labor to dig an irrigation ditch. Andre was appointed foreman of the workers. Andre, however, began to doubt that the ditch would work as laid out. After some difficulty, the ditch was finished and Andre was invited to witness the first water flow. He was excited when the water ran successfully through the ditch to the crops. After this, several other Indian farmers dug their own irrigation ditches.[38]

On October 11, 1873, Flathead Agent, Daniel Shanahan reported that the Pend d'Oreille had forced some hostile Modoc, Paiute, Yakima, and Spokane Indians to leave the reservation. The Pend d'Oreille under Andre, the second Pend d'Oreille chief, left the reservation on their buffalo hunt. Andre carried with him an "American flag as an evidence of his friendship for the white man and the Government."[39]

Flathead Agent Peter Whaley complained on September 12, 1874, that Pend d'Oreille Chief Michelle was physically unable to accompany the hunters to the buffalo country, so Michelle's authority was "totally disregarded by the whole tribe." Whaley suggested that "I would in consequence recommend the promotion of Andre, second chief, to the position now occupied by Michelle." Whaley wrote that Andre "appears to have the confidence of his people and to influence them according to his will."[40]

On September 13, 1875, Flathead Agent Charles Medary wrote that Andre was "chief in all but drawing a salary from the Government."[41]

Bishop James O'Connor visited St. Ignatius Mission in June 1877. O'Connor said Andre had been converted in 1849 and in 1877 had "a rather sad expression of countenance." Andre told O'Connor that all seventeen of his children and his brothers were dead and buried in the St. Ignatius cemetery.[42]

Andre was one of the Flathead Reservation chiefs who assured the new Flathead Agent Peter Ronan and Captain C. C. Rawn, the Fort Missoula commander, that the Salish and Kootenai would remain neutral in July 1877 during the Nez Perce War.[43]

In his August 13, 1877, annual report, Agent Ronan noted that Pend d'Oreille Chief Michelle lived near the agency in the Jocko Valley while Andre, the second chief, lived in the Mission Valley with the bulk of the tribe. When problems arose, Andre decided a great many of the cases, but "Sometimes, when the adverse party is dissatisfied, an appeal to Michelle is taken, who generally reverses André's decisions to the vexation of all concerned."[44]

Andre organized "a very efficient force of Indian police" headquartered at St. Ignatius Mission in 1877. According to Ronan, "This force of police is composed of the very best men of the tribes, who perform any duty required of them by their chief without any payment."[45]

Ronan compiled an inventory of livestock on the reservation in March 1878. Andre was listed as having one cow and 17 head of horses.[46]

In an April 1878 interview with Agent Ronan, Andre denied reports of mistreatment of Indian prisoners in the jail he operated at St. Ignatius. Andre countered that prisoners were fed regularly with "everything that my people and my family have to eat themselves." Andre described the punishment dealt out to a wife who had deserted her husband for a young Indian of the Spokane tribe. Andre also denied whipping offenders since the government had recently forbidden that form of punishment. Andre concluded that he tried hard to police his people. His efforts were partially obstructed by white people in Missoula who sold Indians whiskey and refused to surrender offenders when he sent police to arrest them.[47]

Andre led a buffalo hunting party that left the reservation in the fall of 1878. When the Pend d'Oreille arrived in the buffalo country, the Blackfeet and Assiniboine Indians threatened them with war if they killed any buffalo. The Pend d'Oreille then retreated to the reservation without a supply of buffalo meat. Ronan requested authority to purchase beef and flour to subsist the frustrated hunters.[48]

In 1883, Andre complained that a party of Nez Perce Indians camped on the Jocko River were drinking and fighting with reservation Indians. Chief Michelle petitioned Ronan to have them removed, and soldiers from Fort Missoula arrested the intruders.[49]

Peter Ronan's wife, Mary, related an incident where Andre presented the agent with the gift of his favorite dog. Ronan gratefully accepted the gift and delivered his thanks in person on his next trip to St. Ignatius.[50]

Ronan described the 1878 Christmas eve celebration at St. Ignatius Mission. As part of the observance, Andre "stepped into the centre of the circle [after Mass], knelt down in the snow, made the sign of the cross, then, rising, addressed himself to the multitude. Of course, I was unable to understand his language, but from the deep pathos of his voice, which was loud and clear, and the elegant and graceful motions of this arms and body, I would judge that it was a masterpiece of Indian oratory."[51]

Chief Arlee
Salish/ Nez Perce
ca. 1815–1889

As a young man Arlee was an exceptionally brave warrior, and he became second chief of the Salish at the death of Chief Ambrose in 1871. He was part Nez Perce, but lived all his life with the Salish. After moving from the Bitterroot Valley to the Flathead Reservation in 1873, he was a frequent critic of the operation of the Flathead Agency and the St. Ignatius Mission. Despite his unhappiness, he cooperated with Flathead Agent Peter Ronan in keeping peace on the reservation and was a prominent speaker at church celebrations. Almost all we know about his views were recorded by his opponents, but he was obviously a capable, opinionated person who would not agree to let white men run tribal affairs.[52]

Arlee became well known as a warrior, but only a few examples of his bravery were recorded. In 1835 Arlee had a horse shot out from under him while leading the attack on a retreating party of Blackfeet who had just killed three Hawaiian Hudson's Bay Company employees at Evaro. According to Duncan McDonald, Arlee was "in many big battles which took place between the various western tribes."[53]

In addition to his war exploits, Arlee was a successful farmer and rancher in the Bitterroot Valley. In 1860 or 1861, Arlee traded 3¾ bushels of wheat to Thomas W. Harris, a white man living in the Bitterroot Valley, in exchange for $18.00 in merchandise at the local store. On February 20, 1864, Arlee sold Harris a two-year-old steer.[54]

Arlee was elected second chief of the Bitterroot Salish in 1871. According to Duncan McDonald, the younger Salish were worried that, since Charlo did not drink or gamble, they needed a second chief who would be less severe: "So the young gamblers elected Arlee as second Chief. But Arelee [sic] fooled the gamblers & wets. & reformed. change to a good sober temperate man he was more severe one than Charlo."[55]

Angus McDonald described the twenty-year-old Arlee as "a bold, well proportioned youth," but in later years Arlee was corpulent. In 1877 Bishop James O'Connor described Arlee: "He wore a white Kossuth hat and a blue blanket, and an eagle's wing hung at his girdle. Obesity had taken all grace from his figure, but I thought I had never seen a finer head or face than his. I could hardly take my eyes off him." Peter Ronan's wife, Mary, described Arlee as "a fat and pompous monarch." In 1887 he was five feet four inches tall and weighed over two hundred pounds.[56]

In 1872, when Congressman James Garfield came to the Bitterroot Valley to negotiate with the Salish, Arlee and Adolph agreed to leave, but Charlo refused. Arlee worried that the government would take the Jocko Valley from the Salish just as they had the Bitterroot Valley, but he finally signed.[57] Arlee and five related families moved from the Bitterroot Valley to the Jocko Valley on the Flathead Indian Reservation in 1873. Later that year, Flathead Agent Daniel Shanahan had the federal government recognize Arlee as head chief of all the Salish.[58] With the support of Agent Charles Medary, Arlee organized a police force among the Salish under Arlee's control in 1875.[59]

Between 1875 and 1877, Arlee was involved in a bitter fight with Flathead Indian Agent Charles S. Medary. Arlee's opposition to Medary had some support from Chief Michelle of the Pend d'Oreilles, and considerable financial and legal support from T. J. Demers, a white Frenchtown merchant who had married into the tribes. Arlee's complaints about Flathead Agency management under Medary were aired in Montana Territory newspapers and a federal grand jury. Arlee made so much trouble for Medary that the Commissioner of Indian Affairs asked for Medary's resignation. Basically Arlee and his allies were able to run the agent out of town.[60]

Arlee frequently criticized the Jesuit missionaries at St. Ignatius Mission, but also took a leading role in church festivals. In 1875, missionary Philip Rappagliosi, S.J., visited Arlee in the Jocko Valley and tried to mollify Arlee's anger at the mission. Rappagliosi never really explained Arlee's complaints and believed Arlee was motivated only by an irrational pique. Whatever the basis of Arlee's feelings, Rappagliosi claimed he won Arlee "back completely," and Arlee came to St. Ignatius for the next Easter feast.[61] In July 1883, Arlee complained to U.S. Indian Inspector S. S. Benedict about the management of the St. Ignatius Mission school and said "he wants his people to be taught something besides how to pray." [62] Ronan argued in two letters, November 24, 1883, and December 26, 1883, that Arlee was just a general complainer motivated by greed.[63]

That fall, Arlee repeated his complaints about the mission school to Senator G. G. Vest and his party who were visiting Flathead Agency. Vest concluded Arlee was upset because his son had been put to work on the harvest while a student at the school. Ronan made the same argument in his letter of November 24, 1883.[64] In 1887, Arlee wrote the "Supretenant of indian Afares" complaining about the Flathead Agency and St. Ignatius Mission: "we have a Cotholic Skool here 23 years and none of my children Can reade or write yet. we want a skoole here. we dont want any Priests they are no good."[65]

But, even as Arlee complained about the missionaries, he was an active speaker and participant in church celebrations. According to an oral tradition, on Christmas Day 1876 Arlee was on the buffalo plains and led a Christian religious service to celebrate the occasion.[66] A Helena newspaper story about the 1882 St. Ignatius Day celebration reported that after the school program was completed, Arlee spoke to the assembled crowd in Salish. He welcomed Archbishop Charles Seghers to the mission, condemned the young Indians for drinking and fighting, and led the crowd in the rosary. Arlee also spoke at the 1884 St. Ignatius Day celebration, but then his speech was that the school exhibition was "all very good but that he was very hungry, and that it was time to go and eat."[67]

Arlee's relations with Agent Peter Ronan could also be contradictory: including both support and complaints about how Ronan ran the agency. On July 11, 1877, Ronan reported that Arlee swore that he and his people would defend the white people against the hostile Nez Perces.[68] During the fall of 1881, Arlee was said to have told General John Gibbon that his opinion of Ronan was positive: "As the agent of the government we respect him; as a friend, an advisor and a neighbor, we love him, and I trust I may never live to see the appointment of his successor."[69] In 1882 a Col. Warrington visited the Flathead Reservation and Arlee's house. Warrington recollected that Arlee had a log cabin with a fenced yard which also enclosed a tepee and estimated that Arlee was worth some twenty thousand dollars. The cabin contained "a rusty stove, with an old tin coffee-pot on it, a deal table, a chair, a pile of blankets down in one corner, for a bed" and a picture of President James Garfield on the wall.[70]

Arlee could be very diplomatic in his personal relations. On one occasion he informed Ronan's young daughter, Mary, that she had been given the Indian name of "Red Hair," but little Mary objected. Arlee then declared that the girl's Indian name would be "Pretty Hair," which met with her approval.[71]

In August 1882 Arlee played a prominent role in the negotiations between the Flathead Reservation tribes and Joseph McCammon for the sale of the right-of-way for the Northern Pacific Railroad through the reservation. Arlee wanted the railroad to head down the Clark's Fork River and by-pass the reservation, but McCammon said he was not able to change the route. Arlee countered by asking for a million dollars for the right-of-way. A shocked McCammon argued that the whole reservation was not worth that much. McCammon finally conceded that the reservation might be worth a million dollars to the tribes, but refused to offer more than $16,000 plus reimbursement for the timber used by the railroad. The chiefs got McCammon to promise to use his influence to get the Upper Flathead Valley added to the reservation. With this concession, the chiefs finally agreed to let the railroad have use of the land — but not to outright sell the right-of-way land — and they signed the agreement. The written agreement, however, had language transferring full title to the right-of-way land to the railroad. McCammon did submit a request to the Department of Interior to enlarge the reservation, but by 1883 the tribes decided they could not risk any boundary changes and dropped the idea.[72]

On June 21, 1882, Koonsa Finley murdered Frank Marengo on the reservation during a drinking party. After sobering up, Koonsa went to Chief Michelle and confessed. Arlee and Michelle took Koonsa's horses and put him in the tribal jail as punishment for the murder. To Ronan's disgust, the U.S. District Court dismissed federal murder charges against Koonsa, because he had already been tried for the crime under tribal law and prosecution in federal court would be double jeopardy which was prohibited under the U.S. Constitution.[73]

This case was the opening volley in a long running battle between Arlee and Ronan over control of law and order on the reservation. Arlee's testimony in the federal case against Koonsa in late 1882 was published in a local newspaper. Arlee defended traditional Indian justice dispensed by the chiefs which did not allow for long terms in the territorial prison in Deer Lodge or hanging. Arlee also claimed that the white men who sold the liquor shared responsibility for the murder: "When an Indian is drunk and kills another Indian we don't consider that he did anything. The Indian never had whiskey before the white man came here, and we blame the white people who gave him the liquor."[74]

In December 1885, Arlee joined other tribal leaders and Agent Ronan to defuse a hazardous situation that developed from the killing of an intoxicated Indian by the white trader and the white postmaster at Arlee station. The crisis brought the Missoula County Sheriff and an armed white posse on the reservation. The sheriff wanted to arrest the surviving Indian involved in the altercation, Big Jim, and take him to Missoula. Some tribal members wanted to keep Big Jim on the reservation to try him under tribal law. Arlee supported allowing the sheriff to take Big Jim to Missoula to avoid conflict with the whites. The final decision by the assembled tribal members was to let the sheriff take Big Jim to be tried by the white justice system. In the end, the two white men were released by the court on the basis of self-defense and Big Jim was released for lack of evidence.[75]

In the final years of his life, Arlee opposed the Flathead Agency sponsored courts and police established in 1885, which undermined the authority of the traditional chiefs on the reservation. In an April 29, 1887, speech on the reservation before the Northwest Indian Commission, Arlee said, "We don't want any judges or policemen. We want the chiefs to rule the people." Arlee charged that the judges had a sick man and a pregnant woman whipped and the woman had a miscarriage.[76]

Ronan wrote on January 1, 1887, about his efforts to arrest a member of Arlee's household who had been accused of adultery. Arlee's refusal to acknowledge the authority of the agency court and police led to an impasse where Ronan would no longer deal with Arlee on tribal business. Ronan also charged that Arlee had received money from the government and grown personally rich and greedy.[77] The characterization of Arlee as personally greedy was also made by Agent Medary during their battles in the middle 1870s. Unfortunately, we do not have Chief Arlee's side of the argument to balance the charges against him.

Arlee did become well-to-do on the reservation. On March 19, 1878, Ronan reported that Arlee, his son, and his daughter together owned 2 hogs, 100 cattle, and 100 horses.[78] In his August 1885 annual report, Ronan credited Arlee as having 160 acres under fence and an 1884 crop of 800 bushels of wheat and oats.[79] In his August 17, 1885, testimony, Ronan listed Arlee as having 100 horses and 150 cattle.[80]

In early 1889, the conflict between Arlee and the agency sanctioned tribal court flared up again. Arlee made two trips to the offices of *The Weekly Missoulian* to complain about "merciless" whippings administered by the tribal judges to both men and women: "Recently, it is claimed, men and women have been beaten cruelly and out of all reason." During his second visit, Arlee's "right hand man" claimed "an Indian who had broke jail was hung up by his hands and kept there for forty-eight hours. An Indian woman who is supposed to have deserted her husband was given 120 lashes and is now lying in a precarious condition and her recovery is extremely doubtful." Arlee wanted offenders to be punished "just as white people are punished; no more and no less."[81] In letters to the Commissioner of Indian Affairs on May 1, 1889, and June 17, 1889, and a May 14, 1889, article in *The Helena Independent*, Ronan argued that Arlee's only supporters were murderers and rapists, particularly Larra Finley, who made "sensational and lying complaints against the cruelty of the Indian police."[82]

On August 8, 1889, Arlee died at his house in the Jocko Valley of dropsy at about 74 years of age. On his death bed Arlee was surrounded by his relatives, tribal leaders, and Agent Ronan and other agency employees. He had recently been visited by Bishop John Brondel and Father Jerome D'Aste, S.J., who gave him the last rites of the Roman Catholic Church. According to Mary Ronan, his funeral was "a grand occasion and Indians gathered from far and wide to attend." His funeral was at the Jocko Church and his burial in the Jocko Cemetery. One account said over a half a dozen fat steers were roasted for the funeral feast.[83]

Much of the surviving evidence about Chief Arlee's life is contradictory and incomplete. He was a dynamic but enigmatic figure in Flathead Reservation history.

Chief Charlo
Bitterroot Salish
1830–1910

Charlo succeeded his father, Victor, as chief of the Bitterroot Salish tribe in 1870. He continued Victor's policies of allying with the white men against the Blackfeet, Sioux, and other Plains tribes, and protecting the tribe's right to their homeland in the Bitterroot Valley. As the buffalo declined, he worked hard to expand the tribe's farms and stock herds to maintain its economic independence.

During the summer of 1872, the U.S. Congress passed a law providing for the removal of the Bitterroot Salish to the Jocko Reservation. Montana politicians had convinced President Ulysses Grant that it was in the tribe's interest for them to move to the reservation and free up land in the Bitterroot for white settlers. The Secretary of the Interior selected James A. Garfield, a congressman and Republican party leader who later became President, to negotiate arrangements for the removal. Garfield met Charlo and the other Salish chiefs in the Bitterroot and made generous promises of money and economic assistance to the Salish but passed over the failure of the government to carry out provisions of the 1855 treaty. Charlo responded that in 1855 Governor Isaac Stevens had agreed to the Salish remaining in the Bitterroot Valley. In addition, Charlo pointed out that the Great Father had neither visited western Montana nor had the Bitterroot Valley or the Jocko Valley been surveyed and examined to see which would be a better home for the Salish. Charlo refused to go to the Jocko Reservation: "We will not go, we will not accept the terms. I speak for my tribe."

At the conclusion of the final meeting at the Jocko Agency only sub-chiefs Arlee and Adolph signed the agreement. Charlo emphasized his desire for peace and wish to defuse the threat of violence from the whites: "I am not mad, but I must see what is done here [in the Jocko Valley] and see my people." Soon after Garfield's report was published, a bizarre controversy broke out about whether Charlo had signed the agreement. Garfield clearly stated in his official report that Arlee and Adolph had signed the contract, "but Charlo refused to sign." The published report, however, was printed with an "X" mark after Charlo's name. Charlo, of course, was deeply offended when told that his mark had been added to the published document, and the "forged" document quickly became a staple of Salish history. Garfield never tried to clear up the confusion over Charlo's X. Charlo and Adolph watched the government's failure to carry out the Garfield agreement, and they, with most of the Bitterroot Salish, remained in the Bitterroot Valley.[84]

In a July 11, 1877, letter, Flathead Indian Agent Peter Ronan reported that Charlo refused to join the Nez Perce in fighting the white settlers.[85] Charlo said he and his tribe would protect the Bitterroot whites if needed, but otherwise would not attack the Nez Perce. Charlo wanted peace with the white people, but insisted that a correct interpretation of the 1855 Hellgate Treaty entitled the Salish to a reservation in the Bitterroot Valley.[86]

Father Lawrence Palladino, S.J., characterized Charlo as

> a man of a quiet yet firm disposition, a true representative of his race and a thorough Indian. . . . His conduct during the Nez Percés outbreak gained him the admiration of all, and proved once more the loyal friendship for the whites on the part of the Flat Heads. . . . But while friendly toward the whites, he surely is not in love with their ways. . . .Charlot is a sincere and practical Christian.[87]

Between 1877, when Ronan began his term, and 1889, Charlo worked to develop his farm in the Bitterroot and encouraged other tribal members to do the same. In 1877 a newspaper reporter described his farm:

> Charlos, the Flathead chief, has a home in their midst. His dwelling is a two-story log house with four rooms, and his farm which covers over a pretty little park before his house, encloses seven or eight acres, upon which there is a good growing crop of wheat.[88]

In the Bitterroot Valley during the 1880s, Charlo and the other Salish maintained a delicate balance trying to protect their rights while also maintaining peace with their white neighbors. Ronan's November 1, 1881, letter described Charlo's efforts to get justice for the murder of Cayuse Pierre in a drunken brawl with two white men in Stevensville.[89]

Senator George G. Vest of Missouri and Montana Delegate Martin Maginnis arrived at Stevensville in September 1883 in another effort to convince Charlo to move to the Jocko Valley. The Salish had just returned from the Great Plains, and their buffalo hunt had been a failure. Vest made generous promises of improved ranches, wagons, homes, and horses if the Salish would move to Jocko. Vest also promised Charlo that the Salish could sell their improvements in the Bitterroot and keep the proceeds. Charlo was unimpressed with the new promises and "cooly [sic] refused" Vest's inducements: "You may carry me to Fort Missoula dead, but you will never carry me there alive. I heard before . . . that your great father had printed a book showing my name to the treaty, but I never signed nor told anybody else to sign it for me." On his return east, Vest went to the Secretary of the Interior to check the original copy of the 1872 Garfield agreement and verified that it did not have Charlo's mark or signature on it.[90]

Between January and March 1884, Charlo, four other Bitterroot Salish leaders, interpreter Michel Revais, and Ronan visited Washington, D.C. The government tried to induce the Salish to move to the Flathead Reservation, but Charlo insisted he only wanted to secure the tribe's right to remain in the Bitterroot Valley. Their time in Washington was well documented in Ronan's surviving writings and correspondence. While in Washington, Charlo had a successful operation to remove cataracts from his eyes.[91]

In the fall of 1889, the government sent Gen. Henry B. Carrington to the Bitterroot Valley in another attempt to induce Charlo to move to the Jocko Reservation. The Salish and other Bitterroot farmers had just suffered a record drought which destroyed their crops and pasture.[92] Carrington was able to treat Charlo with respect and avoid pressuring him during most of their dealings. Carrington's account describes Charlo as repeatedly and emphatically refusing to remove because he feared he would look weak if he changed his mind. According to Carrington, Charlo "declared 'he never would sign, but kill himself first.'" Following Mass on Sunday, November 3, 1889, Charlo arrived at Carrington's headquarters in Stevensville to make a dramatic speech lamenting the economic decline and breakdown of tribal discipline resulting from the wrenching economic and political crises of the past decade. After the speech, Charlo affixed his X to the agreement and then bargained for some additional benefits.[93]

After the removal in 1891, Ronan had trouble getting the government to fund the promises Carrington had made to Charlo and the other Salish. In March 10, 1892, Ronan described turning the agency farm over to Charlo in lieu of the late Chief Arlee's farm which Carrington had promised.[94] Ronan in November 30, 1892, related the difficulties the Salish had in getting the government to pay them for the Bitterroot allotments as they were sold.[95]

On the reservation, Charlo worked hard to preserve the tribal culture and ways and was worried about the negative impact schooling would have on Salish youth. An Ursuline Nun working at the Jocko Agency school during the early 1890s described dealing with Charlo:

> The chief was an Indian to the core. Although he had always been on good terms with the whites, he detested their

> ways. "Our children," he objected, "will learn English in school. When they know English, they will go to the white towns and buy whiskey. The white man would not understand them if they spoke in Indian. In the school the hair of our children will be cut. We do not wish to see them with short hair. Only the white man was made by God to wear his hair short. God made the Indian with long hair. Our children will become like whites in other ways in school and, when they grow up they will fly away like birds and leave their parents.". . . . The chief protested up to the very day we opened [the Jocko school]. Nevertheless, he sent his own son, little Victor.[96]

Charlo joined the other tribal leaders on the reservation in fighting to protect the reservation land base from white encroachment. During the early twentieth century he fought vigorously to prevent the reservation from being allotted and "surplus" land sold to white settlers. He died in the Jocko in 1910 just as the government was completing the forced allotment and opening of the reservation without tribal consent.[97]

Chief Eneas Big Knife
Kootenai/ Iroquois
1828–1900

Eneas, the chief of the Dayton Creek or Ksanka Kootenai for thirty-five years was born in 1828 to an Iroquois father, Big Knife, and a Kootenai mother, Suzette or Ahn-Akah.[98] The historical evidence suggested he was a remarkable man, and Flathead Indian Agent Peter Ronan obviously came to respect him highly over their years working together. During the 1880s and early 1890s, the reservation Kootenai faced white aggression in the Upper Flathead Valley, but somehow the Kootenai under Eneas' leadership were able to avoid war and continue the struggle to protect their interests and rights. The government often failed to fulfill its promises to protect Kootenai property and rights, but the small band avoided the destruction and death that could have resulted from open warfare.

As a young man, Eneas was a leading warrior and a war chief. He took part in repeated battles with the Blackfeet, Cree, and other tribes.[99] At six feet four inches tall, Eneas was an imposing figure.[100] According to Flathead Agent Charles Hutchins, Eneas became head chief on January 1, 1865, after his predecessor, Battiste, was killed by the Blackfeet while returning from the buffalo country. Eneas was only 37 years old then. In 1866, Flathead Agent Augustus Chapman requested funds to build a house for Eneas and his family.[101]

In his first annual report on August 13, 1877, Flathead Indian Agent Peter Ronan wrote that Eneas was "better respected and has more influence among his people than any other chief on the reservation." Ronan was especially impressed that Eneas used his salary as chief to purchase a mowing and reaping machine and a set of blacksmith's tools for the use of his tribe. Eneas was "a good man, kind and generous, and spends all the money he receives from Government in relieving the wants of his poor and struggling people."[102] In his August 12, 1879, report, Ronan commended Eneas for working to induce the Kootenai to turn to farming to replace the declining game and gathering resources in western Montana. By 1879, the Kootenai had enclosed several farms.[103]

By August 1885, Eneas and the Kootenai had 200 acres fenced and "about 1,000 bushels of wheat [were] raised in common, besides potatoes, turnips, cabbage, onions, carrots, parsnips, peas, &c."[104] But farming in common offended Ronan's Euro-American cultural values, and in August 15, 1886, Ronan proposed that a farmer be employed to show the Kootenai how to set up individual family farms like white people had.[105]

In 1883 when Joseph McCammon came to Montana to negotiate for the sale of the right-of-way for the Northern Pacific Railroad to cross the reservation, Eneas emphasized the importance of the reservation to the tribes. Eneas questioned selling part of the reservation because: "It is a small country; it is valuable to us; we support ourselves by it; there is no end to these lands supporting us; they will do it for generations."[106]

Due to their location on the northern boundary of the reservation, the Kootenai were particularly affected by problems with the survey of the reservation boundary. Eneas and the Kootenai thought the northern line followed a ridge of hills which provided a well-defined natural boundary. The official survey placed the line several miles south of the natural boundary. In the twentieth century the U.S. Court of Claims decided the official boundary had been in error but still placed the line south of the boundary preferred by the Kootenai. This change in the northern boundary made it harder to keep white owned cattle off the reservation and also cut off hay and pasture land used for years by the Kootenai. Some of the white cattle owners paid Eneas for grazing, but trespassing cattle and loss of land caused problems for Eneas and his tribe for the rest of the nineteenth century.[107]

During the late 1880s and early 1890s, the Kootenai continued to exercise their right to seasonally hunt, fish, and gather plants in the Upper Flathead Valley. Most of the Kootenai-white interactions were peaceful but some were complicated by language and cultural differences, alcohol, and white aggression. In 1888, two reservation Kootenai were lynched for murdering two white men at the head of Flathead Lake in 1887. After the lynching, an armed mob of white men invaded the reservation and confronted Eneas and the Kootenai. Eneas kept calm and was able to defuse the crisis and no further violence broke out. Eneas did not object to the punishment of Kootenai murderers, but he felt they should at least receive a fair trial.[108]

In 1889, Eneas kept up his efforts to get justice while avoiding open warfare. Two white men killed a Kootenai Indian in an altercation that probably involved alcohol. Eneas threatened to kill the two guilty whites but made clear that other white people would not be harmed.[109]

In a June 8, 1889, council with Ronan and a special agent of the U.S. Justice Department about the whiskey problem, Eneas emphasized his work to punish Kootenai guilty of violence resulting from alcohol use. Traditional Kootenai practice had the chief use the whip to punish lawbreakers, but white officials opposed whipping because it offended nineteenth century white sensibilities. Eneas complained that without the whip, he could not control tribal members who got drunk and committed adultery or other crimes. He pointed out that the Kootenai did not have good jails, so he had no alternative punishment available. One account quotes Delima Demers Clifford, a tribal member, as seeing Eneas drinking alcohol on New Years Eve 1887. But, even if Eneas was not a teetotaler, he vigorously opposed the violence and other crimes that sometimes resulted from drinking.[110]

Eneas' struggle to get justice for the Kootenai while keeping the peace struck a personal note in August 1889 when his son, Samuel, was murdered by white people in Demersville. Eneas traveled to Demersville to find out what happened. The white people fed the Kootenai but refused to help bring the murderer to justice. The Demersville whites fumed and ranted that Eneas' visit had been an invasion. Ronan put Eneas' side of the story in writing, sent it to Washington, D.C., and had it published in a Helena newspaper and the Commissioner of Indian Affairs' annual report.[111] In December, Ronan tried to get the case before a grand jury, but the jury adjourned before he was able to get Eneas and the Indian witnesses to the courthouse. No one was ever punished for the murder.[112]

In July 1890, U.S. Army troops and a posse of white men surrounded the Kootenai camp and demanded that Eneas surrender Kootenai Indians accused of murdering white men. Eneas offered to cooperate, but he asked why white men who killed Kootenai were not also punished. According to newspaper reports, Missoula County Sheriff William Houston held Eneas hostage until the accused Indian murderers were surrendered, but Ronan's letters suggested

Eneas decided himself to help the sheriff. Ronan wrote that Eneas did not object to Indians murderers being punished but wanted equal justice for white people who murdered Indians.[113] Father Jerome D'Aste, S.J., recorded the hostage version of Eneas' role in his diary.[114] One newspaper account noted that "it is largely due to his [Eneas'] aid that Pascale and other Indian criminals have been apprehended."[115] Two Kootenai Indians were convicted in a Montana court of murder and hung in Missoula in December 1890.

In January 1891, Robert H. Irvine, a mixed blood tribal member chosen by Eneas, was finally appointed as Kootenai farmer and moved to Dayton Creek to begin work. That October Eneas and the Kootenai brought several wagon-loads of wheat to the agency to be ground into flour. The trip of 60 miles to the agency took six days and a ferry crossing the Flathead River at the Foot of Flathead Lake. According to Ronan, Eneas was "much elated at the acchievement [sic]."[116] That summer Eneas and the reservation Kootenai extended an invitation to the Bonners Ferry Kootenai to settle with them at Dayton Creek.[117]

In August 1891 Ronan traveled to the Kootenai camp and laid out off-reservation allotments for land just north of the official reservation boundary. The land had been used by the Kootenai for years believing it was on the reservation. Unfortunately, by December of that year, white homesteaders were already jumping the Kootenai allotments. Ronan was able to get the government to remove the first white trespassers, but others persisted in harassing the Kootenai farmers.[118]

In one particularly egregious example of white belligerence, Clarence Proctor actually built a fence around the improvements of a Kootenai farmer and claimed the right to the land in the enclosure, including the Kootenai farm.[119] In another case, Eugene McCarthy, a white settler who had worked on the erroneous boundary survey, claimed the land of a Kootenai farmer, Jean Jan Graw (Gingras), which contained a house, barn, and enclosed field that the Kootenai had occupied for twelve years. Eneas was crippled by rheumatism and hindered by language problems, but he tried to explain to McCarthy that the land belonged to the Kootenai farmer as a result of years of occupancy and a government allotment. McCarthy then proceeded to Demersville and filed charges against Eneas claiming that Eneas had personally threatened him. Ronan put up a bond for Eneas to appear in court on the charge since Eneas was too sick to travel just then. Apparently, the charges were later dropped as the case dragged on in the courts.[120] The restraint shown by Eneas and the aggrieved Kootenai farmers was remarkable. No open conflict flared, but white trespassers continued over the years to encroach on the Kootenai claims, and, after Ronan died in 1893, no one else seemed to pressure the government to act. Finally, in the early twentieth century the Kootenai had lost possession of almost all of the allotments and the government pressured the Kootenai allottees to relinquish their claims in return for small payments from the white trespassers.

On February 1, 1894, Eneas, most reservation tribal leaders, and many tribal members signed a petition asking for a resurvey of the northern boundary of the reservation, but then agent Joseph Carter panned it as a "matter worthy of little attention." The Commissioner of Indian Affairs refused to consider a resurvey.[121] In 1895 Eneas returned Goosta, a Kootenai Indian accused of horse stealing, to jail after he escaped.[122] Eneas was again called upon to defend the tribe in 1898 when Missoula County tried to tax most of the mixed bloods and adopted tribal members on the reservation. When Eneas claimed jurisdiction over the reservation and tribal members, the Missoula Deputy County Treasurer replied: "What I want to tell that old Indian is that he may go to h---. . . . Tell him that this is not his country, but that it belongs to the government at Washington." Fortunately, despite the racist hostility of the county officials, the government won most of the court cases against the taxes.[123]

In much of the late 1890s, Eneas was confined to his bed and not able to exercise his authority as chief. Father Augustine Dimier, S.J., complained that Eneas' disability permitted gambling and other sins to re-infect Kootenai life.[124] Eneas died in 1900.[125]

Chief Michelle
Pend d'Oreille
1805–1897

Chief Michelle of the Upper Pend d'Oreille Indians worked to maintain peace with the white settlers and supported the missionaries at St. Ignatius Mission. Most accounts suggest he was less active and influential in tribal affairs than his predecessor Alexander. He was spokesman for decisions reached by the tribal community, often after long hours of collective deliberation.[126]

According to information that probably came from Michel Revais, the Pend d'Oreille Flathead Agency Interpreter, Michelle was elected Pend d'Oreille chief in 1868. Michelle had previously been only a minor chief, but two more senior sub-chiefs, Andre and Pierre, declined the office. Little has been recorded about his life before 1868.[127]

The one event before 1868 that has been documented was the 1864 lynching of Michelle's son by white miners at Hell Gate, near present day Missoula. A white miner named Ward had been killed near Hell Gate by an Indian in the fall of 1863. Michelle's son was accused of the murder but maintained his innocence. According to an account given by Michelle in the early 1880s, Michelle asked his son to "sacrifice his life for the good of his people" and "go bravely to death" to avoid war with the whites. His son was lynched and later evidence indicted the murder had been committed by an Indian from another tribe.[128]

Michelle was known for his Christian piety and loyalty to the missionaries. In 1882 he delivered a speech at the St. Ignatius Day celebrations, but the topic was not recorded. According to Duncan McDonald, Michelle "punishes severely to this day any member of his tribe who refuses to believe in his creed." McDonald also reported that sometime around 1870, Chief Michelle used traditional Indian medicine to attract buffalo to a Pend d'Oreille hunting camp on the Plains. He may have valued the power of both Christianity and traditional Pend d'Oreille religious beliefs.[129]

Michelle suffered a tragic accident in late April 1872 when he was thrown from his horse and dislocated his hip. The agency doctor and Father Anthony Ravalli were not able to reset the joint, and Michelle was crippled for the rest of his life.[130]

In December 1873, Michelle recounted the recent history of conflict between the Pend d'Oreille and the Crow Indians. The Crows had killed four Pend d'Oreille during the summer of 1873, including Michelle's father-in-law Cow-ackan. During spring 1873, the Crows killed two more Pend d'Oreille and wounded three women and a boy. One of the women was not expected to survive. The Crows stole 31 Pend d'Oreille horses and a mule from a hunting camp in the Little Blackfoot in the fall of 1872. Ten years before, in 1863, the Crows stole 80 Pend d'Oreille horses and blamed it on the Snakes, igniting a war between the Pend d'Oreille and the Snakes. Michelle complained: "When we go to the Crow country we always go in peace but the Crows always attack us first."[131]

Michelle swore out a statement on May 2, 1874, before a justice of the peace complaining about Flathead Agent Daniel Shanahan. The statement was forwarded to Washington, D.C., by T. J. Demers, a white Frenchtown merchant who had married into the tribes. Michelle accused Shanahan of stealing tribal annuities and of trying to force off the reservation five white men who had tribal member wives and had mixed blood children. Michelle also complained that Shanahan had stopped the treaty payments to the St. Ignatius Mission schools. Other treaty promises of services to the tribes had never been fulfilled. Michelle wanted Shanahan removed as agent and asked that "the choice of an agent for them [the Flathead Reservation tribes] be left to the Indians themselves and that they by Election or otherwise with the approval of the reverend fathers of the mission — shall name who shall be agent for them."[132]

During 1874, Chiefs Michelle and Arlee demanded that the agency employees cut their hay and grain. Agent Peter Whaley asked the Commissioner of Indian Affairs for instructions because, while Michelle was poor and crippled, Arlee was well-to-do and, according to Whaley, did not need the help.[133] In his September 12, 1874, annual report, Whaley reported that, while on the annual buffalo hunt, the Pend d'Oreille stole horses from other tribes and refused to return them. Since Michelle was crippled, he could no longer accompany the buffalo hunters and was unable to stop the raids. Michelle was "powerless to exact obedience to his commands." Whaley wanted the government to promote the second chief, Andre, to head the Pend d'Oreille, because Andre "appears to have the confidence of his people and to influence them according to his will."[134]

Michelle's dealings with Flathead Agent Charles S. Medary between 1875 and 1877 were also stormy. Michelle supported Chief Arlee's complaints against Medary about the operation of the agency. In December, Michelle, Arlee, and Duncan McDonald, a mixed blood trader on the reservation, traveled to Deer Lodge to present their complaints to the United States grand jury. Most of the indictments referred to the failure of the government to fulfill promises made in the 1855 Hellgate Treaty and 1872 agreement between Congressman James Garfield and the Bitterroot Salish. During the 1870s, Michelle lived on a farm near the agency in the Jocko Valley while most of the Pend d'Oreille lived near the St. Ignatius Mission in the Lower Flathead Valley. Since Michelle did not live among his tribe and could not accompany them on the buffalo hunts, in 1875 Medary wrote that Andre was "chief in all but drawing a salary from the Government." Medary did claim in September 1876 that he had convinced Michelle to give up the practice of whipping women who were guilty of adultery.[135]

Michelle's relations with Flathead Agent Peter Ronan, 1877-1893, were much more cordial. In his July 11, 1877, letter during the Nez Perce War crisis, Ronan wrote that Michelle joined the other reservation chiefs in promising to maintain peace with the whites. Michelle personally assured the Ronan family of protection during the scare and offered to guard the agency.[136]

In his August 13, 1877, annual report, Ronan wrote that Michelle had lost influence among the Pend d'Oreille because he lived at the agency, some twenty miles from most of the tribe, and could no longer travel on the buffalo hunts. Ronan concluded that Michelle "has in a great measure lost control, a fact which he is well aware of himself, as he came to consult in regard to removing from the agency and going back among his people, with a view of regaining his lost influence."[137] On March 19, 1878, Michelle lived in the Jocko Valley and had 26 cattle and 19 horses.[138]

Ronan forwarded a report to the Commissioner of Indian Affairs on July 29, 1878, about a July 14, 1878, council with Chief Michelle about recent violence committed by some Nez Perce refugees returning from exile in Canada. Michelle informed Ronan of a message he had received from Sitting Bull threatening the Pend d'Oreille if they did not join the fight against the whites. Michelle replied that the Pend d'Oreille were friends of the whites and traditional enemies of the Sioux. He assured Sitting Bull that: "We are not well armed, and have nearly forgotten the modes of war; but a mouse though small, if trodden upon will turn and bite. Tell your chief if he comes we will give him battle, and die by our homes." When asked to provide scouts to watch for possible war parties coming west across the mountains, Michelle agreed, but only if the scouts were given supplies, arms, and pay and were under his and Ronan's control.[139]

In November 1878, Michelle demonstrated his personal diplomatic skills when he bestowed his Indian name, Plenty Grizzly Bear, on the Ronans' newborn son. Michelle then had no Indian name until the Lower Kalispel granted him permission to take the Indian name of their recently deceased chief, Man Who Regrets His Country. The name transfers were formally announced at the 1878 Christmas celebrations at St. Ignatius Mission.[140]

Koonsa Finley committed murder on June 21, 1882, but, after sobering up, he went to Chief Michelle and confessed. Michelle and Arlee took Finley's horses and put him in the tribal jail for a short term. When Ronan came to arrest Finley and transport him to Missoula, Michelle argued that he was chief and had already decided the case. Ronan countered that Finley had committed an offense against the United States government and so fell under the jurisdiction of the agent and the federal courts. Finley was tried for murder in the United States court in Deer Lodge but was released because he had already been tried and punished under tribal law. This frustrated Ronan's efforts to try Finley in a white court where he could have been sentenced to the penitentiary at Deer Lodge or hung.[141]

During the September 1882 negotiations between Joseph McCammon of the U.S. Interior Department and the Flathead Reservation tribes for the Northern Pacific Railroad right-of-way, Michelle supported selling the right-of-way. When McCammon replied to Chief Arlee's request for $1,000,000 for the right-of-way by stating that the whole reservation was not worth that much, Michelle was offended: "Now I do not agree with you." McCammon explained that he did not mean the reservation was not worth a million dollars to the Indians. Michelle countered that the government's offer of $15,000 was too low, as after the railroad was completed, it would make that much in a day. Michelle offered to exchange the right-of-way for an extension of the reservation boundary to include the Upper Flathead Valley. During the negotiations Michelle emphasized that the tribes were not selling the land, just the use of the right-of-way:

> Michelle. . . . it is borrowing this strip of land.
>
> Commissioner. It is the use of it.
>
> Michelle. I don't want you, after you get away, to let the white people suppose you have bought the reservation, and let the white people squat on it. That is the way I think. It is like the railroad borrowing the strip of land.
>
> Commissioner. It is just buying the use of the strip of land.

The written agreement, however, said the tribes "do hereby surrender and relinquish to the United States, all the right, title, and interest which they now have" to the right-of-way land.[142]

When Senator G. G. Vest of Missouri and Montana Delegate Martin Maginnis visited the reservation in September 1883, tribal members met for two days ahead of time to discuss the issues and select Michelle to be their spokesman for the collective decisions. Tribal members decided they did not want to run the risk of being cheated in moving the boundary of the reservation north to the Canadian border, so they opposed any boundary changes. The Bitterroot Salish were welcome to move to the reservation, but the tribes categorically rejected allotment:

> Senator Vest. Don't you think it would be better to have more money and cattle and less land?
>
> Michelle. If I had good and plenty land and few cattle and a little money I would be glad. The reverse would not please me, because my children are cultivating the land more and so get money.

When asked if the St. Ignatius school children were happy, Michelle replied: "Yes; because their fathers send the children to learn, and therefore they will be happy if they are taught to read and write." Michelle also wanted the white people to stop selling liquor and playing cards to the Indians.[143]

The Northwest Indian Commission negotiated with the Flathead Reservation tribes in April 1887, and Michelle declared that the Lower Pend d'Oreille or Kalispel Indians and Spokane Indians would be welcome on the reservation. The proposed agreement also "set apart" two sections of land for the use of the Jesuits and Sisters at the St. Ignatius schools "for educational and religious purposes, as long as they are used for said purposes and no longer."

Michelle made sure during the negotiations that the land was being lent and not sold to the missionaries.[144]

By the middle of the 1880s, Michelle had moved to a ranch on Mud Creek, 16 miles north of the Mission. In 1885 he had 160 acres under fence and in 1884 he raised 250 bushels of wheat and oats. In 1885 he had 20 horses and 15 cattle. In 1887 he purchased $31.00 worth of fruit trees for his ranch.[145]

Some time during the summer or autumn of 1888 Chief Michelle's nephew and family were murdered while hunting in the Sun River area. Evidence found at the scene suggested that the murderers were either white men or Cree mixed bloods. Despite Ronan's efforts to publicize the case and get the local white authorities to investigate, no one was ever charged with the crime.[146]

The white Montana justice authorities showed much more interest in pursuing Indian people who were accused of murdering white people. During August 1890, Missoula County Sheriff William Houston arrested Chief Eneas of the Kootenai and Chief Michelle and held them hostage until local Indian people and the Indian police delivered up tribal members wanted for murdering white men. Baptiste Kakashe and a party of armed Pend d'Oreille tried to force the white posse to release Michelle, but, in order to avoid conflict, Michelle refused to go. Michelle was released after Pierre Paul was captured by the Indian police and a white posse. Ronan gave most of the credit to the Indian police, but the Montana newspapers played up the role of the sheriff and posse.[147]

On May 11, 1897, Chief Michelle died at his home on Mud Creek at the age of 92. He was buried at St. Ignatius Mission.[148]

Chief Victor
Bitterroot Salish
ca. 1795–1870

Chief Victor led the Bitterroot Salish Indians in their nineteenth century conflict with the Blackfeet and other Plains tribes over buffalo hunting on the Great Plains. He embraced the Salish alliance with the white trappers and, later, the Christian missionaries despite occasional cultural misunderstandings and tensions within the tribe. He argued strenuously in the 1855 Hellgate Treaty council to keep the Bitterroot Valley as the tribal homeland.

Victor was born in the middle 1790s and was still a boy in 1805 when the Bitterroot Salish met the Lewis and Clark Expedition.[149] As a young man, Victor obtained rabbit power when he protected a rabbit that was being chased by a hawk.[150]

On a solitary raid on a Blackfeet camp, Victor stole a prize horse picketed outside the lodge of Blackfeet warrior. Instead of sneaking off, he shook the lodge pole to which it was tied, to awaken the Blackfeet camp, and then he rode off with the prize horse. But the stolen horse fell as Victor was being chased by the pursuing Blackfeet. Victor fled to a stand of thick brush for cover. The Blackfeet riddled the brush with arrows. They then went back to their camp, intending to collect Victor's body and scalp the next morning. But Victor's rabbit power had protected him from the arrows, and he slipped away into the night. The audacious escape earned Victor his first adult name: Lodge Pole.[151]

Father Nicholas Point made a series of drawings of Salish battles against the Plains tribes with captions giving brief glimpses into Victor's war honors. In one drawing Victor (with his trademark stovepipe hat and two attached feathers) led a Salish charge against the Blackfeet. In another drawing, Victor saved himself after the Blackfeet surrounded him and his bow was broken. A single arrow was his only armament. In yet another incident, Victor put to flight a large enemy party that attacked him while he was hunting mountain goats.[152]

In 1840 Victor had matured into a handsome adult with coal black hair.[153] He became a loyal follower of the missionaries, and, according to Father Pierre DeSmet, S.J., expressed "joy and happiness" on his baptism.[154] In December 1846 the priests gave him his baptismal name, Victor, in honor of his military abilities. He was elected president of the new Christian men's society and his wife, Agnes, became president of the women's society. Victor's children were selected to lead the new youth societies.[155] DeSmet wrote that Victor and his family were selected for these honors "not through any deference to their dignity or birth, but solely on account of their great personal merits."[156]

When Victor heard that the Pope in Rome was in danger from enemies, Victor asked DeSmet to invite the Pope to take refuge in the Salish country and the Salish would protect him and provide him with meat and other provisions.[157] In 1842 Victor was chosen as the new head chief of the tribe. The priests were pleased to see such a loyal convert selected as the new head chief. Victor continued his predecessor's practice of delivering morning and evening harangues or exhortations to the camp to encourage pro-social behavior.[158] Victor also took to wearing a stovepipe hat with two feathers attached as his personal status symbol.[159] It may have been at this point that Victor's Indian name was changed from Lodge Pole to Many Horses to reflect his new status as a wealthy elder.[160]

Victor was closely allied with the missionaries, but sometimes the priests imposed their views on the Salish battle for survival on the plains. In 1843, a Blood Indian horse thief was wounded near St. Mary's and Father Gregory

Mengarini insisted the Blood be welcomed into the Salish camp to recover and head home.[161] But later in 1844, the same Blood was captured again by the Salish as he was attempting to steal Salish horses. Father Mengarini again intervened to spare the Blood's life. While the Salish debated the fate of the Blood and his war party companions, Victor repaired to a nearby hill "to see how things would develop." While Victor was away, the Salish reluctantly agreed to grant the captured war party mercy and they were released. After being twice-pardoned by the Salish, a few weeks later the same Blood Indian stole twenty Salish horses from St. Mary's.[162]

Relations with the missionaries reached a crisis in 1846 as the priests moved to share their teaching and powers with the Piegan Blackfeet. In return the Blackfeet stole 100 Salish horses as they returned from the buffalo hunt.[163]

Another irritant was Victor's friction with Father Gregory Mengarini, S.J., the resident missionary at St. Mary's in the late 1840s. In 1847, Mengarini blamed Victor when some tribal members complained about a change in how the potato crop from the mission garden was distributed among tribal households. Mengarini humiliated Victor by publicly blaming Victor for failing to calm the discontent.[164]

Later in 1847, a Salish man usually referred to as Little Faro led a rebellion in the camp against the missionaries and Victor's authority. The missionaries pressured Victor into accepting Moiese as the second chief to try and put down the discontent.[165] The historical sources give little detail of the following events, but at one point Moiese publicly struck Victor in the face. Victor was humiliated but declined to retaliate.[166]

In 1850, the Jesuits closed St. Mary's Mission, but Victor continued his policy of allying with the missionaries and the whites. For example, in 1853, Victor insisted the Pend d'Oreille return horses they had stolen from the white traders at Fort Benton.[167]

Maintaining the alliance with the white men could be complicated. In July 1855, Victor led the Salish delegation at the Hellgate Treaty council convened by Gov. Isaac Stevens near present-day Missoula. The Indian leaders expected that the council would discuss establishing peace between the Salish and Kootenai and the Plains Indian tribes. But Stevens wanted to discuss land cessions to the whites and consolidation of the Salish and Kootenai on a single reservation. Victor wanted to keep their home in the Bitterroot Valley. Stevens was condescending and in a hurry to make an agreement. Exchanges got heated and Victor complained: "I was talking to you, and I told you no." Stevens' temper got the best of him and he attacked Victor in an angry outburst:

> Does Victor want to treat? Why did he not say to Alexander yesterday, come to my place? or is not Victor a chief? Is he as

> one of his people has called him an old woman: dumb as a dog?
> If Victor is a chief let him speak now.

Victor walked out of the council.[168] Victor finally signed the treaty after a provision was added for the President to consider a second reservation in the Bitterroot Valley.[169] Victor also signed the Judith River Treaty in October 1855 which established intertribal peace and a common hunting ground for the Rocky Mountain tribes to hunt buffalo on the plains.[170]

In 1856 and 1857, Victor was among the Salish chiefs who visited St. Ignatius Mission in the Flathead valley "to fulfill their religious duties."[171]

The 1855 Hellgate Treaty was not ratified by the U.S. Senate until 1859. In the 1850s Victor and the Bitterroot Salish welcomed white settlers in the valley as allies against Blackfeet war parties.[172] By the 1860s, Victor and the Salish were becoming anxious about being overwhelmed by the incoming whites. In an 1865 letter to the Montana Governor and an 1869 letter to the President, Victor pointed out Salish farming efforts and the need for a Bitterroot reservation.[173]

The status of the Bitterroot Salish was still in limbo in June 1870 when Victor died while returning from a buffalo hunt on the Yellowstone. A funeral feast was held for him in the Bitterroot Valley in July 1870. That fall Victor's widow, Agnes, followed Victor's dying instructions and presented his old war horse to Angus McDonald, the retired Hudson's Bay Company trader.[174]

Sam Resurrection
Bitterroot Salish
1857–1941

Resurrection was born in the Bitterroot Valley in 1857.[175] As a young child, Resurrection came back to life after he apparently died and was being prepared for burial. Salish elder Agnes Vanderburg described the events that led to his name:

> he died when he was about three or four years old. His little legging was all wore. His moccasins was poor. So, his mother and another woman was making a new pair for him while he was laying there dead. After they was just about done with everything, this other old lady said, "Look at your boy." She looks, and, "My boy ghosted me?" She went over there and picked him up. "Why, you are alive?" He says, "No, I was

sleeping.". . . That was still in Stevensville when it happened.
So, that's how they called him Resurrection.[176]

According to the story Resurrection related to anthropologist Harry Holbert Turney-High, as a teenager Resurrection took part in a buffalo hunt near the present-day town of Browning. One night, a Blackfeet war party stole many of the Salish horses. Resurrection and his friends pursued the thieves and the Salish retrieved the horses and captured one of the Blackfeet. The Salish, including Resurrection, counted coup on the captive. Then the Blackfeet was stripped and left in the winter weather to either freeze or find his way home.[177]

In 1877 he served as an Indian scout for the U.S. Army when Chief Joseph and the Nez Perce passed through the Bitterroot Valley. Resurrection moved to the Jocko Valley in 1891 with Chief Charlo's band of Bitterroot Salish.[178]

In the early twentieth century, Resurrection was the most prolific opponent campaigning against the allotment and opening of the Flathead Reservation. He signed many letters to officials in Washington, D.C., complaining that the opening was a violation of the 1855 Hellgate Treaty. Montana newspapers treated his campaign against allotment as a joke and emphasized Resurrection's problems with alcohol. The oral history being compiled by the Salish–Pend d'Oreille Culture Committee should help balance the biased written sources.

According to some 1910 correspondence in the Commissioner of Indian Affairs records at the National Archives, Resurrection was approached by a Baltimore, Maryland, attorney, Robert F. Leach, Jr., and told that Leach could prevent the opening of the reservation if the tribal members would raise $5,000 to pay for his legal work. Leach (1873-1946) was a graduate of the University of Virginia and later in life was State's attorney for Baltimore City. No record has been found to show how the Leach affair worked out, but the episode did indicate the desperation of tribal leaders as the reservation was opened to white homesteaders in 1910.

After 1910, Resurrection and most tribal members were upset when the state of Montana moved to control the hunting and fishing on the reservation. They were even more upset when they learned that the construction of the irrigation project on the reservation was to be paid for with tribal money. They had not asked for the project and were especially insulted when it turned out their tribal funds were being used to pay the expenses of the opening of the reservation, the operation of the Flathead Agency, and to fund the irrigation construction. Most of the benefits of the irrigation system went to the white homesteaders.

For over twenty years, Resurrection pursued his campaign to demand that tribal members decide about the government policy on the Flathead Reservation. The climax was in 1919 when he was able to personally deliver a petition to President Woodrow Wilson when Wilson was in Helena to deliver a speech.[179]

In his later years, Resurrection was an informant for Turney-High while the anthropologist was compiling his ethnography of "The Flathead Indians of Montana."[180] Resurrection died on the reservation in 1941. He was not a chief, but he dedicated his life to fighting for the rights and land of the Flathead Reservation people.[181]

Michel Revais
French/ Pend d'Oreille Interpreter
1837–1911

Michel Revais was a longtime interpreter at the Flathead Indian Agency in Jocko. He was born in 1837 to Antoine Revais, of French, Pend d'Oreille, and Salish heritage, and Emelie, a Pend d'Oreille Indian.[182] As a young man, Michel and his father panned for gold in the Thompson River country in British Columbia.[183] In 1860 he married a Kalispel woman named Susan, and they had four children.[184]

In 1877, Revais was appointed agency interpreter at the Flathead Agency, and in the early 1880s he became totally blind. In addition to English, Revais spoke French and several Indian languages. Mary Ronan, the wife of Agent Peter Ronan, described Revais as

> about medium height, slender, with the fine features of his French father and the bronze color of his Indian mother. His straight black hair he wore in the long bob we associate with a page or herald of medieval times. His costume was quaint and all his own. It was neither the dress of the white man nor that of the Indian, but a nondescript assortment of the two modes.

He had learned to play the violin and also led the congregational singing at the Jocko Catholic church.[185] He led the church service at Jocko in June 1890 when no priest was available.[186]

Revais was interpreter for many meetings and trials involving Flathead Reservation Indians. In 1884, he accompanied Chief Charlo, Agent Peter Ronan, and a delegation of Bitterroot Salish Indians who traveled to Washington, D.C., for negotiations over the Bitterroot Valley. While in Washington, Revais' and Charlo's eyes were operated on by Dr. William V. Marmion. The surgery was successful in restoring Charlo's eyesight, but did not return Revais' vision.[187]

Michel Revais
Source" Missoula Publishing Co., *Flathead Facts: Descriptive of the Resouces of Missoula County* (Missoula, Mont.: Missoula Publishing Co., 1890), p. 22.

He was also interpreter for Gen. Henry B. Carrington in 1889 and 1891 when Carrington negotiated with Chief Charlo and arranged the removal of the Bitterroot Salish to the Jocko Valley. In 1889, Carrington and Revais were riding in a wagon in the Bitterroot when Revais started humming a Christian hymn. Carrington joined Revais and they sang the song together.[188]

Revais was interviewed by a reporter for the *Helena Journal* in November 1890 and complained about discrimination in law enforcement:

> He says the Indians cannot understand why if an Indian kills a white man he should be hunted down for years, while if a white man kills an Indian that is the last of it. He says in his recollection thirty Indians have been killed on the reservation by white men, and not one of these was ever punished.[189]

In 1885, Revais had 5 cattle and 25 horses.[190] Revais also did some farming. In September 1894 he sent "some very fine potatoes, two large cabbages, some sweet corn and some excellent cucumbers" to be displayed in the window of the *Anaconda Standard* office in Missoula.[191]

His children preceded him in death, and in 1897 novelist Hamlin Garland described the parents' mourning: "His son went wild and was gone along time. He came back stricken with consumption and the old people nursed him until he died. They mourned inconsolably. Then their daughter died and since then the mother mourns unceasingly."[192]

Revais was the principle source for James A. Teit's ethnography of the Salish Indians of the Flathead Reservation. Revais was interviewed during the summer of 1909. Teit's research was published by the U.S. Bureau of American Ethnology in 1930 as part of "The Salishan Tribes of the Western Plateaus."[193]

In January 1910, Revais interpreted for the white men from Missoula who came to Jocko for Chief Charlo's funeral.[194] A year later in January 1911, Revais died and was buried at the Jocko Agency church cemetery.[195]

Francois Saxa
Iroquois/ Pend d'Oreille Interpreter
ca. 1825–1918

Francois Saxa, of mixed Iroquois–Pend d'Oreille descent, served as interpreter for many of the missionaries and traders in the nineteenth century. He was also known as Francois Eneas. According to Henry R. Crosby, who was secretary at the Hellgate Treaty council, Francois was "a farmer, speaks English tolerably well, French and several Indian languages. He is considered very reliable and trustworthy."[196]

Francois Saxa, 1859
Source: Detail from photogaph 802.21a, Oregon Province Archives, Jesuit Archives and Research Center, St. Louis, Missouri.

Francois was born to Ignace Lamoose, an Iroquois trapper and fur trader, and Sinshe, a Pend d'Oreille woman about 1825.[197] In 1835, Francois accompanied his father and brother to St. Louis, Missouri, where Francois and his brother were baptized.[198] Lamoose left his sons in Missouri to attend school. In the summer of 1837, Lamoose accompanied a Protestant missionary, William Gray, on a return trip to St. Louis to pick up his sons from school. But on this trip, Lamoose was killed by the Sioux Indians. After her husband's death, Sinshe travelled to St. Louis herself to retrieve her sons from school.[199]

At about the age of 15, Francois was on a buffalo hunt east of the Rocky Mountains. The Pend d'Oreille hunters were surrounded and attacked by Piegan warriors. Francois knelt down and recited Christian prayers while a Pend d'Oreille medicine man conducted his traditional rituals. Between the two of them a violent thunderstorm was called up which scattered the Piegan attackers and saved the Pend d'Oreille hunters.[200]

Francois was loyal to the Christian teachings which were brought to the Salish by his father and the missionaries. He served the missionaries as interpreter in the 1840s. Father Gregory Mengarini, S.J., wrote that Francois "for many years served as interpreter for the missionaries, walks in his father's footsteps, always loyal to the faith and most attached to the missionaries, a hardworking man and an example" to the Indians.[201] In 1847, when conflict broke out between the missionaries and the Bitterroot Salish, Francois was the only one to speak up in defense of the missionaries.[202]

In the later 1850s, Francois worked for trader John Owen as interpreter, laborer, and traveling companion. On May 9, 1856, Owen noted Francois had finished repairing the fence around Owen's wheat field. On May 7, 1858, Owen hired Francois as a horse guard for $20 a month.[203]

Francois accompanied Father Pierre DeSmet, Pend d'Oreille Chief Alexander, Salish Chief Adolph, and four other interior Salish chiefs to Fort Vancouver in the spring of 1859. The chiefs met with U.S. Army General W. S. Harney to assure him that the interior Salish tribes meant to keep the peace and not join the fighting on the lower Columbia between the Indians and the U.S. Army.[204] In 1872, Francois was interpreter for Congressman James A. Garfield during Garfield's fraught negotiations with Chief Charlo and the Bitterroot Salish.[205]

Francois joined Alexander Matt's militia company to protect the whites and Indians in the Bitterroot Valley in 1877, when Chief Joseph and the hostile Nez Perce Indians passed through the valley.[206] Will Sutherlin, a newspaperman, described Francois' farm in the Bitterroot Valley in July 1877: "He lives in a two story log house, has a good barn and stables, and about 15 acres of land under fence, but not in cultivation. He is represented to be very wealthy, his wealth being in cattle and Indian horses. He speaks English and is said to be a good financier."[207] At about the same time, Peter Matt and some white compatriots stole 27 horses belonging to Francois. Some Salish camped on the Big Blackfoot recognized the horses Matt was driving east as belonging to Francois. Francois' friends took the horses from Matt and returned them to their rightful owner.[208]

In 1889, Francois served as interpreter for Gen. Henry B. Carrington as Carrington negotiated with Chief and the Bitterroot Salish. He and Michel Rivais also interpreted for Carrington in 1891, when Carrington returned to escort the Salish to the Jocko Valley.[209]

In 1890, Palmer Henderson, a journalist, visited the Jocko Valley and met Francois. Henderson noted Francois had "a well cultivated farm." He also had a sweat lodge and a tepee near his house.[210]

On his death in 1918, Francois was eulogized by one of the St. Ignatius Missionaries, Ambrose Sullivan, S.J.:

> Francois Saxa was a man of remarkable intelligence. His honesty and upright conduct won the admiration of the Indian and the white man. His eyesight failed him some years ago. He was a devout Catholic. . . . Francois was an industrious Indian and provided well for his family.[211]

Endnotes

1. Peter Ronan, *History of the Flathead Indians* (Minneapolis, Minn.: Ross & Haines, Inc., 1965 [1890]), pp. 80-81.

2. Robert Bigart and Joseph McDonald, eds., "*Sometimes My People Get Mad When the Blackfeet Kill Us": A Documentary History of the Salish and Pend d'Oreille Indians, 1845-1874* (Pablo, Mont.: Salish Kootenai College Press, 2019), p. 18.

3. James D. Keyser, *The Five Crows Ledger: Biographic Warrior Art of the Flathead Indians* (Salt Lake City, Utah: Utah, 2000), pp. 56-60.

4. Ronan, *History of the Flathead Indians*, pp. 80-81; Rich Aarstad, et. al., *Montana Place Names from Alzada to Zortman* (Helena, Mont.: Montana Historical Society Press, 2009), p. 79.

5. Robert Bigart and Joseph McDonald, eds., "*You Seem to Like Your Money, and We Like Our Country": A Documentary History of the Salish, Pend d'Oreille, and Kootenai Indians, 1875-1889* (Pablo, Mont.: Salish Kootenai College Press, 2019), p. 69.

6. Bigart and McDonald, eds., *Sometimes My People Get Mad*, p. 166.

7. John C. Ewers, *Gustavus Sohon's Portraits of Flathead and Pend d'Oreille Indians, 1854*, Smithsonian Miscellaneous Collections, vol. 110, no. 7 (1948), p. 37

8. Bigart and McDonald, eds., *Sometimes My People Get Mad*, pp. 132, 150.

9. Ibid, pp. 192-200.

10. Ibid, pp. 247-248.

11. Ibid, pp. 261-265.

12. Ibid, pp. 266-274.

13. Ibidd, pp. 311-313.

14. Ibid, pp. 338-340; July 1, 1872, in this volume.

15. Ibid, pp. 347-357.

16. Bigart and McDonald, eds., *You Seem to Like Your Money*, pp. 69-72.

17. Ibid, pp. 182-202.

18, Ronan, *History of the Flathead Indians*, pp. 80-81.

19. Robert J. Bigart, ed., *Life and Death at St. Mary's Mission, Montana: Births, Marriages, Deaths, and Survival Among the Bitterroot Salish Indians, 1866-1891* (Pablo, Mont.: Salish Kootenai College Press, 2005), p. 128.

20. George Capps, "Leadership in Eastern Salish Communities, 1781-1850," unpublished manuscript in possession of the author, June 2019, p. 118; Pierre DeSmet, S.J., *Letters and Sketches with A Narrative of a Year's Residence among the Indian Tribes of the Rocky Mountains,* in Reuben Gold Thwaites, ed., Early Western Travels, 1748-1846 (New York: AMS Press, Inc., 1966 [1843], vol. 27, p. 286.

21. Keyser, *The Five Crows Ledger*, pp. 33, 37-39, 49-50.

22. Bigart and McDonald, eds., *Sometimes My People Get Mad*, pp. 13-14.

23. George Capps, Leadership in Eastern Salish Communities, p. 118.

24. Nicolas Point, S.J., *Wilderness Kingdom: Indian Life in the Rocky Mountains, 1840-1847,* trans. and ed. by Joseph P. Donnelly, S.J. (New York: Holt, Rinehart and Winston, 1967), p. 170; P. J. De Smet, S.J., *Oregon Missions and Travels Over the Rocky Mountains in 1845-46* (New York: Edward Dunigan, 1847), p. 381.

25. De Smet, *Oregon Missions*, pp. 400-405; Point, *Wilderness Kingdom*, pp. 184-185.

26. Robert Bigart and Clarence Woodcock, eds., *In the Name of the Salish & Kootenai Nation: The 1855 Hell Gate Treaty and the Origin of the Flathead Indian Reservation* (Pablo, Mont.: Salish Kootenai College Press, 1996), p. 52.

27. Ibid, p. 16; Bigart and McDonald, eds., *Sometimes My People Get Mad*, p. 150.

28. Bigart and McDonald, eds., *Sometimes My People Get Mad*, pp. 166, 173.

29. John Mullan, *Report on the Construction of a Military Road from Fort Walla-Walla to Fort Benton* (Fairfield, Wash.: Ye Galleon Pr., 1994), p. 21.

30. Bigart and McDonald, eds., *Sometimes My People Get Mad*, pp. 231-232.

31. Ibid, pp. 247-248.

32. Ibid, pp. 263-265.

33. Ibid, pp. 273-274; Aug. 22, 1868, in this volume.

34. Bigart, ed., *Life and Death at St. Mary's Mission*, p. 128.

35. "The Indian Side of the Question," *The Weekly Missoulian*, Apr. 12, 1878, p. 3, c. 3-4.

36. James A. Teit, "The Salishan Tribes of the Western Plateaus", ed. by Franz Boas, *Forty-fifth Annual Report of the Bureau of American Ethnology, 1927-1928*, p. 377.

37. Bigart and McDonald, eds., *Sometimes My People Get Mad*, pp. 338-340; July 1, 1872, in this volume.

38. L. B. Palladino, S.J., *Indian and White in the Northwest: A History of Catholicity in Montana, 1831 to 1891*. Second edition. (Lancaster, Penna.: Wickersham Publishing Company, 1922), p. 163.

39. Daniel Shanahan to Commissioner of Indian Affairs [hereafter CIA], Oct. 11, 1873, U.S. Office of Indian Affairs, "Letters Received by the Office of Indian Affairs, 1824-1880," National Archives Microfilm Publication M234 (hereafter NAmf 234), reel 496, fr. 117-119.

40. Peter Whaley to CIA, Sept. 12, 1874, U.S. Commissioner of Indian Affairs, *Annual Report of the Commissioner of Indian Affairs* (hereafter ARCIA) (1874), p. 263.

41. Bigart and McDonald, eds., *You Seem to Like Your Money*, p. 21.

42. Ibid, p. 61.

43. Peter Ronan to CIA, July 11, 1877, Peter Ronan, *"A Great Many of Us Have Good Farms": Agent Peter Ronan Reports on the Flathead Indian Reservation, Montana, 1877-1887*, ed. Robert J. Bigart (Pablo, Mont.: Salish Kootenai College Press, 2014), p. 17.

44. Peter Ronan to CIA, Aug. 13, 1877, Ibid, p. 22.

45. Ibid, p. 23.

46. Peter Ronan to CIA, Mar. 19, 1878, Ibid, p. 53.

47. "The Indian Side of the Question," *The Weekly Missoulian*, Apr. 12, 1878, p. 3, c. 3-4.

48. Peter Ronan to CIA, Nov. 27, 1878, Ronan, *A Great Many of Us Have Good Farms*, pp. 86-87.

49. Peter Ronan to CIA, Oct. 9, 1883, Ibid, pp. 227-229.

50. Margaret Ronan, "Memoirs of A Frontiers Woman: Mary C. Ronan," masters thesis, State University of Montana, 1932, pp. 298-300.

51. "The Holidays Among the Catholic Indians," *The Pilot* (Boston, Mass.), Feb. 8, 1879, p. 6, c. 5-6.

52. Bigart, ed., *Life and Death at St. Mary's Mission*, pp. 238-40; *Challenge to Survive: History of the Salish Tribes of the Flathead Indian Reservation: Unit IV: Charlo and Michel Period, 1870-1910* (Pablo, Mont.: Salish Kootenai College Tribal History Project, 2011), pp. 64-69.

53. "Historical," *The Weekly Missoulian*, Feb. 3, 1882, p. 3, col. 4; "When the Indians Owned the Land," *The Anaconda Standard*, Mar. 25, 1906, p. 13, col. 3-4; Bigart, ed., *Life and Death at St. Mary's Mission*, pp. 322-23.

54. Thomas W. Harris Diaries, SC 231, Montana Historical Society Archives, Helena, folders 2 and 3.

55. Duncan McDonald to L. V. McWhorter, May 30, 1930, Lucullus Virgil McWhorter Manuscripts, Archives and Special Collections, Holland Library, Washington State University, Pullman, file 184.

56. "Historical," *The Weekly Missoulian,* Feb. 3, 1882, p. 3, c. 4; Rev. James O'Connor, "The Flathead Indians," *Records of the American Catholic Historical Society of Philadelphia,* vol. 3 (1888-1891), p. 104; Mary Ronan, *Girl from the Gulches: The Story of Mary Ronan,* as told to Margaret Ronan, ed. by Ellen Baumler (Helena: Montana Historical Society Press, 2003), p. 182; "Missoula Mentionings," *Butte Semi-Weekly Miner,* Jan. 15, 1887, p. 1, c. 8.

57. James A. Garfield, "Conference of Hon. James A. Garfield, Special Commissioner, with the Indians of the Bitter Root Valley, Montana," *Fourth Annual Report of the Board of Indian Commissioners* (1872), pp. 171-74; J. U. Sanders, "When Garfield Visited Montana," *The Anaconda Standard,* May 24, 1908, part 2, p. 7, c. 1-4.

58. Peter Whaley to CIA, Sept. 12, 1874, ARCIA (1874), p. 263; Daniel Shanahan to CIA, Dec. 12, 1873, NAmf M234, reel 496, fr. 153.

59. Chas. S. Medary to CIA, Sept. 13, 1875, ARCIA (1875), p. 306.

60. Robert Bigart, "The Travails of Flathead Indian Agent Charles S. Medary, 1875-1877," *Montana: The Magazine of Western History,* vol. 62, no. 3 (Autumn 2012), pp. 27-41.

61. Philip Rappagliosi, *Letters from the Rocky Mountain Indian Missions,* ed. Robert Bigart (Lincoln: University of Nebraska Press, 2003), pp. 55-58.

62. S. S. Benedict to Secretary of Interior, July 10, 1883, U.S. Department of the Interior, "Reports of Inspection of the Field Jurisdictions of the Office of Indian Affairs, 1873-1900," National Archives Microfilm Publication M1070 [hereafter NAmf M1070], reel 11, Flathead Agency, 3093/1883.

63. Ronan, *A Great Many of Us Have Good Farms,* pp. 232-236.

64. G. G. Vest and Martin Maginnis, "Report of the Subcommittee of the Special Committee of the United States Senate, Appointed to Visit the Indian Tribes in Northern Montana," Senate Report No. 283, 48th Congress, 1st Session (1884), serial 2174, p. xiv; Ronan, *A Great Many of Us Have Good Farms,* pp. 232-234.

65. Arlee Antwine Skulep Squalshey to Supretenant of indian Afares, Feb. 17, 1887, 5,858/1887, Letters Received, RG 75, Records of the Commissioner of Indian Affairs, National Archives, Washington, D.C.

66. "Indians in State Celebrate Yule Fifty-First Time," *The Daily Missoulian,* Dec. 23, 1937, p. 1, c. 5; p. 6, c. 3.

67. Robert J. Bigart, ed., *A Pretty Village: Documents of Worship and Culture Change, St. Ignatius Mission, Montana, 1880-1889* (Pablo, Mont.: Salish Kootenai College Press, 2007), pp. 76-82, 149-53.

68. Ronan, *A Great Many of Us Have Good Farms,* pp. 15-19.

69. *The Weekly Missoulian,* Jan. 27, 1882, p. 3, c. 2.

70. Lucy S. White, "Garfield!: An Incident," *The Christian Union* (New York), vol. 32, no. 21 (Nov. 19, 1885), pp. 10-11.

71. Mary Ronan, *Girl from the Gulches,* p. 155.

72. U.S. President, "Message from the President of the United States, Transmitting a Letter from the Secretary of the Interior Respecting the Ratification of an Agreement with the Confederated Tribes of Flathead, Kootenay, and Upper Pend d'Oreilles Indians, for the Sale of a Portion of Their Reservation in Montana Territory," Senate Executive Document No. 44, 47th Congress, 2d Session (1883), serial 2076, pp. 8-18.

73. Ronan, *A Great Many of Us Have Good Farms,* pp. 198-199; E. D. Bannister to Secretary of Interior, Oct. 20, 1888, NAmf M1070, 5,261/1888.

74. "The Kuntza-Marengo Murder Trial," *The New North-West* (Deer Lodge, Mont.), Jan. 12, 1883, p. 3, c. 4.

75. Mary Ronan, *Girl from the Gulches*, pp. 205-207; Ronan, *A Great Many of Us Have Good Farms*, pp. 343-346.

76. "Reduction of Indian Reservations," House of Representatives Executive Document No. 63, 50th Congress, 1st Session (1888), serial 2557, p. 71.

77. Ronan, *A Great Many of Us Have Good Farms*, pp. 381-383.

78. Ibid, pp. 50-58.

79. Ibid, pp. 316-321.

80. Ibid, pp. 322-326.

81. Bigart and McDonald, eds., *You Seem to Like Your Money*, pp. 335-337.

82. "A Red Desperado," *Helena Independent*, May 14, 1889, p. 1, c. 7; Peter Ronan, *Justice to Be Accorded to the Indians: Agent Peter Ronan Reports on the Flathead Indian Reservation, Montana, 1888-1893*, ed. Robert J. Bigart (Pablo, Mont.: Salish Kootenai College Press, 2014), pp. 34-35, 45-48.

83. "To the Happy Hunting Grounds," *Helena Journal*, Aug. 13, 1889, p. 1, c. 5; "Death of an Indian Brave," *Butte Semi-Weekly Miner*, Aug. 21, 1889, p. 3, c. 2; Mary Ronan, *Girl from the Gulches*, p. 212; Missoula Publishing Company, *Flathead Facts: Descriptive of the Resources of Missoula County* (Missoula, Mont.: Missoula Publishing Company, 1890), p. 15; Hubert A. Post, S.J., "Sweet Revenge," *The Indian Sentinel*, vol. 2, no. 1 (Jan. 1920), pp. 15-16.

84. Robert J. Bigart, *Getting Good Crops: Economic and Diplomatic Survival Strategies of the Montana Bitterroot Salish Indians, 1870-1891* (Norman: University of Oklahoma Press, 2010), pp. 119-128.

85. Ronan, *A Great Many of Us Have Good Farms*, pp. 15-19.

86. See Ibid, pp. 135-137.

87. Palladino, *Indian and White in the Northwest*, pp. 85-86.

88. Bigart and McDonald, eds., *You Seem to Like Your Money*, pp. 73-74.

89. Ronan, *A Great Many of Us Have Good Farms*, pp. 170-172.

90. Bigart, *Getting Good Crops*, pp. 129-130.

91. Ronan, *A Great Many of Us Have Good Farms*, pp. 243-254.

92. Bigart, *Getting Good Crops*, pp. 190-192.

93. Ibid, pp. 198-203.

94. Ronan, *Justice to be Accorded to the Indians*, p. 288.

95. Ibid, pp. 342-343.

96. Gabriel M. Menager, S.J., "Reminiscences of a Missionary Sister," *The Indian Sentinel*, vol. 22, no. 4 (Apr. 1942), pp. 59-61.

97. Bigart, ed., *Life and Death at St. Mary's Mission*, pp. 252-54; Bigart, *Getting Good Crops*; *Challenge to Survive: History of the Salish Tribes of the Flathead Indian Reservation: Unit IV: Charlo and Michel Period, 1870-1910* (Pablo, Mont.: Salish Kootenai College Tribal History Project, 2011), pp. 12-15, 61-64, 82-86; Rappagliosi, *Letters from the Rocky Mountain Indian Missions*, pp. 108-109.

98. "Kootenai Chiefs Memorial Draws Hundreds," *Char-Koosta* (Dixon, Mont.), vol. 2, no. 14 (Nov. 15, 1972), pp. 11-12; Chas. Hutchins to Montana Superintendent of Indian Affairs, June 30, 1865, ARCIA (1865), p. 246; Harry Holbert Turney-High, *Ethnography of the Kutenai*, Memoir of the American Anthropological Association, No. 56 (1941), pp. 134-39; Carling Malouf and Thain White, "Kutenai Calendar Records," *Montana: Magazine of History*, vol. 3, no. 2 (Spring 1953), pp. 34-39.

99. Ronan, *Justice to Be Accorded to the Indian*, pp. 42-45; Mary Ronan, *Frontier Woman: The Story of Mary Ronan as Told to Margaret Ronan*, ed. H. G. Merriam (Missoula: University of Montana Publications in History, 1973), pp. 124-125.

100. Rev. James O'Connor, "The Flathead Indians," *Records of the American Catholic Historical Society of Philadelphia*, vol. 3 (1888-1891), p. 104.

101. Chas. Hutchins to Montana Superintendent of Indian Affairs, June 30, 1865, ARCIA (1865), p. 246; Augustus Chapman to CIA, Apr. 20,1866, NAmf M234, reel 488, fr. 178.

102. Ronan, *A Great Many of Us Have Good Farms*, pp. 20-24.

103. Ibid, pp. 111-114.

104. Ibid, pp. 316-321.

105. Ibid, pp. 360-364.

106. U.S. President, "Message from the President of the United States Transmitting a Letter from the Secretary of the Interior Respecting the Ratification of an Agreement with the Confederated Tribes of Flathead, Kootenay, and Upper Pend d'Oreilles Indians, for the Sale of a Portion of Their Reservation in Montana Territory," Senate Executive Document No. 44, 47th Congress, 2d Session (1883), serial 2076, p. 11.

107. Ronan, *A Great Many of Us Have Good Farms*, pp. 219-222, 391-393.

108. Ronan, *Justice to Be Accorded to the Indians,* pp. 4-7.

109. Ibid, pp. 32-33.

110. Ibid, pp. 42-45; E. D. Bannister to Secretary of Interior, Oct. 20, 1888, NAmf M1070, 5261/1888, p. 6.

111. "The Red Man's Story," *Helena Journal* (daily), Oct. 25, 1889, p. 5, c. 1-2; Ronan, *Justice to Be Accorded to the Indians*, pp. 148-157.

112. Ibid, pp. 75-83, 142-145.

113. Ibid, pp. 142-145, 157-160, 170-172; and newspaper reports in the footnotes to these letters.

114. Robert J. Bigart, ed., *Zealous in All Virtues: Documents of Worship and Culture Change, St. Ignatius Mission, Montana, 1890-1894* (Pablo, Mont.: Salish Kootenai College Press, 2007), p. 54.

115. "Four of a Kind," *Missoula Weekly Gazette*, Nov. 12, 1890, p. 3, c. 1-3.

116. Ronan, *Justice to Be Accorded to the Indians*, pp. 186-188, 253-254.

117. Ibid, pp. 219-222.

118. Ibid, pp. 225-228, 262-263.

119. Ibid, pp. 330-333.

120. Ibid, pp. 312-316, 330-333.

121. Joseph Carter to CIA, Feb. 6, 1894, 6,591/1894, Letters Received, RG 75, Records of the Commissioner of Indian Affairs, National Archives, Washington, D.C.; CIA to Carter, Feb. 21, 1894, land, letterbook 274, pp. 394-96, Letters Sent, RG 75, Records of the Commissioner of Indian Affairs, National Archives, Washington, D.C.

122. "Very Near a Good Indian," *The Kalispell Graphic*, Mar. 13, 1895, p. 3, c. 1.

123. "All Same M'Kinley," *The Anaconda Standard*, Aug. 24, 1898, p. 10, c. 2.

124. Augustine Dimier to Rev. Father Provincial, Apr. 1901, Robert Bigart and Clarence Woodcock, eds., "St. Ignatius Mission, Montana: Reports from Two Jesuit Missionaries, 1885 & 1900-1901 (Part II)," *Arizona and the West*, vol. 23, no. 3 (Autumn 1981), pp. 275-276.

125. "Noted Chief Dead," *The Kalispell Bee*, July 27, 1900, p. 1, c. 5.

126. Ewers, *Gustavus Sohon's Portraits*, pp. 50-52.

127. Teit, The Salishan Tribes of the Western Plateaus, p. 377.

128. W. P. Clark, *The Indian Sign Language* (Philadelphia: L. R. Hamersly, 1885), p. 301; Frank H. Woody, "Historical Sketch of Missoula County," *The Weekly Missoulian*, July 19, 1876, p. 2, c. 3-7 and p. 3, c. 1-4; Arthur L. Stone, *Following Old Trails* (Missoula, Mont.: Morton John Elrod, 1913), p. 134.

129. Bigart, ed., *A Pretty Village*, p. 78; Duncan McDonald, "More About Indian 'Medicine,'" *The New North-West*, Feb. 21, 1879, p. 3, c. 3.

130. "Accident," *The Pioneer* (Missoula, Mont.), May 4, 1872, p. 3, c. 1.

131. Daniel Shanahan to CIA, Jan. 21, 1874, NAmf M234, reel 500, fr. 262.

132. T. J. Demers to Martin Maginnis, May 2, 1874, Martin Maginnis Papers, MC 50, Montana Historical Society Archives, Helena, box 1, folder 22.

133. Peter Whaley to CIA, Aug. 14, 1874, NAmf M234, reel 500, fr. 1124; President to Secretary of Interior, Nov. 18, 1874, NAmf M234, reel 500, fr. 190.

134. Peter Whaley to CIA, Sept. 12, 1874, ARCIA (1874), pp. 262-263

135. Attorney General to Secretary of Interior, Jan. 8, 1876 [1877], NAmf M234, reel 508, fr. 382; Chas. S. Medary to CIA, Sept. 13, 1875, ARCIA (1875), p. 304; Chas. S. Medary to CIA, Sept. 1, 1876, ARCIA (1876), p. 493.

136. Mary Ronan, *Girl from the Gulches*, pp. 158-59; Ronan, *A Great Many of Us Have Good Farms*, pp. 15-19.

137. Ronan, *A Great Many of Us Have Good Farms*, pp. 20-24.

138. Ibid, pp. 50-58.

139. Ibid, pp. 69-74; "Indian Matters," *Helena Independent*, July 21, 1878, p. 3, col. 3.

140. Mary Ronan, *Girl from the Gulches*, pp. 184-86; "Wayside Notes, "*Helena Independent*, Nov. 22, 1878, p. 3, c. 3.

141. Ronan, *A Great Many of Us Have Good Farms*, pp. 198-199; *The Weekly Missoulian*, June 30, 1882, p. 3, col. 3.

142. U.S. President, "Message from the President of the United States, Transmitting a Letter from the Secretary of the Interior Respecting the Ratification of an Agreement with the Confederated Tribes of Flathead, Kootenay, and Upper Pend d'Oreilles Indians, for the Sale of a Portion of Their Reservation in Montana Territory," Senate Executive Document No. 44, 47th Congress, 2d Session (1883), serial 2076, pp. 11-19.

143. G. G. Vest and Martin Maginnis, "Report of the Subcommittee of the Special Committee of the United States Senate, Appointed to Visit the Indian Tribes in Northern Montana," Senate Report No. 283, 48th Congress, 1st Session (1884), serial 2174, pp. xxv-xxvii.

144. "Reduction of Indian Reservations," House of Representatives Executive Document No. 63, 50th Congress, 1st Session (1888), serial 2557, pp. 58-60, 69-72.

145. Ronan, *A Great Many of Us Have Good Farms*, pp. 316-326, 401-408.

146. Ronan, *Justice to Be Accorded to the Indians*, pp. 58-60, 68-74.

147. "Cleverly Caught," *Missoula Gazette* (daily), Aug. 5, 1890, p. 1, c. 3-4; "One of Them Caught," *Missoula Gazette* (daily), Aug. 7, 1890, p. 1, c. 5; Bigart, *Zealous in All Virtues*, p. 54.

148. "Old Cheif [sic] Michel," *The Daily Missoulia*n, May 14, 1897, p. 1, c. 3; "Chief Michael Dead," *The Anaconda Standard*, May 14, 1897, p. 10, c. 2.

149. Bigart and McDonald, eds., *Sometimes My People Get Mad*, pp. 255-258.

150. Ewers, *Gustavus Sohon's Portraits*, p. 28.

151. Capps, Leadership in Eastern Salish Communities, p. 46.

152. Bigart and McDonald, eds., *Sometimes My People Get Mad*, pp. 15-17.

153. John Owen, *The Journals and Letters of Major John Owen, 1850-1871*, ed. Seymour Dunbar and Paul C. Phillips. (New York: Edward Eberstadt, 1927), v. 2, pp. 42.

154. Pierre-Jean DeSmet, S.J., *Life, Letters and Travels of Father Pierre-Jean De Smet, S.J., 1801-1873*, ed. Hiram Martin Chittenden and Alfred Talbot Richardson (New York: Francis P. Harper, 1905), v. 4, p. 1337.

155. Point, *Wilderness Kingdom*, p. 46.

156. DeSmet, *Letters and Sketches*, p. 355.

157. DeSmet, *Life, Letters and Travels*, v. 4, pp. 1340-1341.

158. DeSmet, *Letters and Sketches*, p. 356.

159. Cornelius M. Buckley, S.J., *Nicholas Point, S.J.: His Life & Northwest Indian Chronicles* (Chicago: Loyola University Press, 1989), p. 284; Ewers, *Gustavus Sohon's Portraits*, plate 8.

160. Teit, The Salishan Tribes of the Western Plateaus, p. 377.

161. Buckley, *Nicholas Point*, p. 256.

162. Capps, Leadership in Eastern Salish Communities, pp. 47-48; Buckley, *Nicholas Point*, p. 256-259; Point, *Wilderness Kingdom*, p. 185.

163. Capps. Leadership in Eastern Salish Communities, p. 49.

164. Ibid, p. 50.

165. Ibid, p. 51; Bigart and McDonald, eds., *Sometimes My People Get Mad*, pp. 49-52.

166. Gilbert J. Garraghan, S.J., *The Jesuits of the Middle United States* (New York: America Press, 1938), v. 2, p. 386.

167. Bigart and McDonald, eds., *Sometimes My People Get Mad*, p. 89.

168. Bigart and Woodcock, eds., *In the Name of the Salish & Kootenai*, pp. 50-55.

169. Ibid, pp. 15-16.

170. Bigart and McDonald, eds., *Sometimes My People Get Mad*, p. 150.

171. Ibid, pp. 166, 173.

172. Ibid, pp. 109-110.

173. Apr. 25, 1865 and May 3, 1869, in this volume.

174. Bigart and McDonald, eds., *Sometimes My People Get Mad*, pp. 293-296.

175. Salish–Pend d'Oreille Culture Committee and Elders Cultural Advisory Council, Confederated Salish and Kootenai Tribes, *The Salish People and the Lewis and Clark Expedition* (Lincoln: University of Nebraska Press, 2005), pp. 126-127.

176. Agnes Vanderburg, *"What I Know About the Old Ways": The Life and Wisdom of a Flathead Indian Reservation Elder* (Pablo, Mont.: Salish Kootenai College Press, 2022), p. 49.

177. Harry Holbert Turney-High, *The Flathead Indians of Montana*, Memoir of the American Anthropological Association No. 48 (1937), p. 64.

178. Salish–Pend d'Oreille Culture Committee, *The Salish People and the Lewis and Clark Expedition*, p. 126.

179. Robert Bigart and Joseph McDonald, eds., *"Us Indians Don't Want Our Reservation Opened": Documents of Salish, Pend d'Oreille, and Kootenai Indian History, 1907–1911* (Pablo, Mont.: Salish Kootenai College Press, 2021), pp. 11-52.

180. Turney-High, *The Flathead Indians of Montana*, p. 64.

181. Salish–Pend d'Oreille Culture Committee, *The Salish People and the Lewis and Clark Expedition*, pp. 126-127.

182. Bigart, ed., *Life and Death at St. Mary's Mission*, p. 320.

183. "A Canadian Traveler in Montana," *The Northwest* (New York), vol. 2, no. 5 (May 1884), p. 4.

184. Bigart, ed., *Life and Death at St. Mary's Mission*, p. 320.

185. Mary Ronan, *Girl from the Gulches,* pp. 188-189.

186. Robert Bigart and Joseph McDonald, eds., *To Keep the Land for My Children's Children: Documents of Salish, Pend d'Oreille, and Kootenai Indian History, 1890-1899* (Pablo, Mont.: Salish Kootenai College Press, 2020), p. 118.

187. Ronan, *A Great Many of Us Have Good Farms,* pp. 247, 250-254, 260.

188. Bigart and McDonald, eds., *You Seem to Like Your Money*, pp. 380-382; Bigart and McDonald, eds., *To Keep the Land for My Children's Children*, pp. 75, 84, 90.

189. Ronan, *Justice to Be Accorded to the Indians*, p. 176.

190. Ronan, *A Great Many of Us Have Good Farms,* p. 326.

191. "Raised by the Indians," *The Anaconda Standard*, Sept. 28, 1894, p. 6, c. 1.

192. Hamlin Garland, Notes on the Flathead Reservation (1897), Hamlin Garland Collection, Special Collections, University of Southern California Library. Los Angeles, Cal., item 49-2, page 140.

193. Teit, The Salishan Tribes of the Western Plateaus; James Teit to Franz Boas, July 4, 1909, Manuscripts Relating to the American Indian, American Philosophical Society, Philadelphia, Penna., entry 2484.

194. Bigart and McDonald, eds., *Us Indians Don't Want Our Reservation Opened*, pp. 219-220.

195. "Michel Revais' Life Ends After Many Useful Years in Service of Government," *The Daily Missoulian*, Jan. 15, 1911, p. 1, c. 3-5.

196. Bigart and McDonald, eds., *Sometimes My People Get Mad*, p. 111.

197. Bigart, ed., *Life and Death at St. Mary's Mission,* p. 284-287.

198. Garraghan, *The Jesuits of the Middle United States*, vol. 2, pp. 246-247.

199. Capps, Leadership in Eastern Salish Communities, pp. 146-147.

200. Bon I. Whealdon and others, *"I Will Be Meat for My Salish": The Buffalo and the Montana Writers Project Interviews on the Flathead Indian Reservation*, ed. Robert Bigart (Pablo and Helena, Mont.: Salish Kootenai College Press and Montana Historical Society Press, 2001), pp. 41-42.

201. Gregory Mengarini, S.J., *Recollections of the Flathead Mission*, ed. and trans. by Gloria Ricci Lothrop (Glendale, Cal.: Arthur H. Clark Company, 1977), pp. 178-179.

202. Bigart and McDonald, eds., *Sometimes My People Get Mad*, p. 50.

203. Owen, *The Journals and Letters of Major John Owen*, vol. 1, pp. 125, 199.

204. Bigart and McDonald, eds., *Sometimes My People Get Mad*, pp. 192-200.

205. Ibid, p. 347.

206. Bigart and McDonald, eds., *You Seem to Like Your Money*, p. 84.

207. Will Sutherlin, "Up the Bitter Root Valley," *Rocky Mountain Husbandman* (Diamond City, Mont.), July 26, 1877, p. 2, c. 2-3.

208. Bigart and McDonald, eds., *You Seem to Like Your Money*, p. 102.

209. Ibid p. 380; Bigart and McDonald, eds., *To Keep the Land*, pp. 75, 90.

210. Ibid, pp. 120-121.

211. A. Sullivan, S.J., "Francois Saxa," *Indian Sentinel*, vol. 1, no. 9 (July 1918), pp. 41-42.

Index